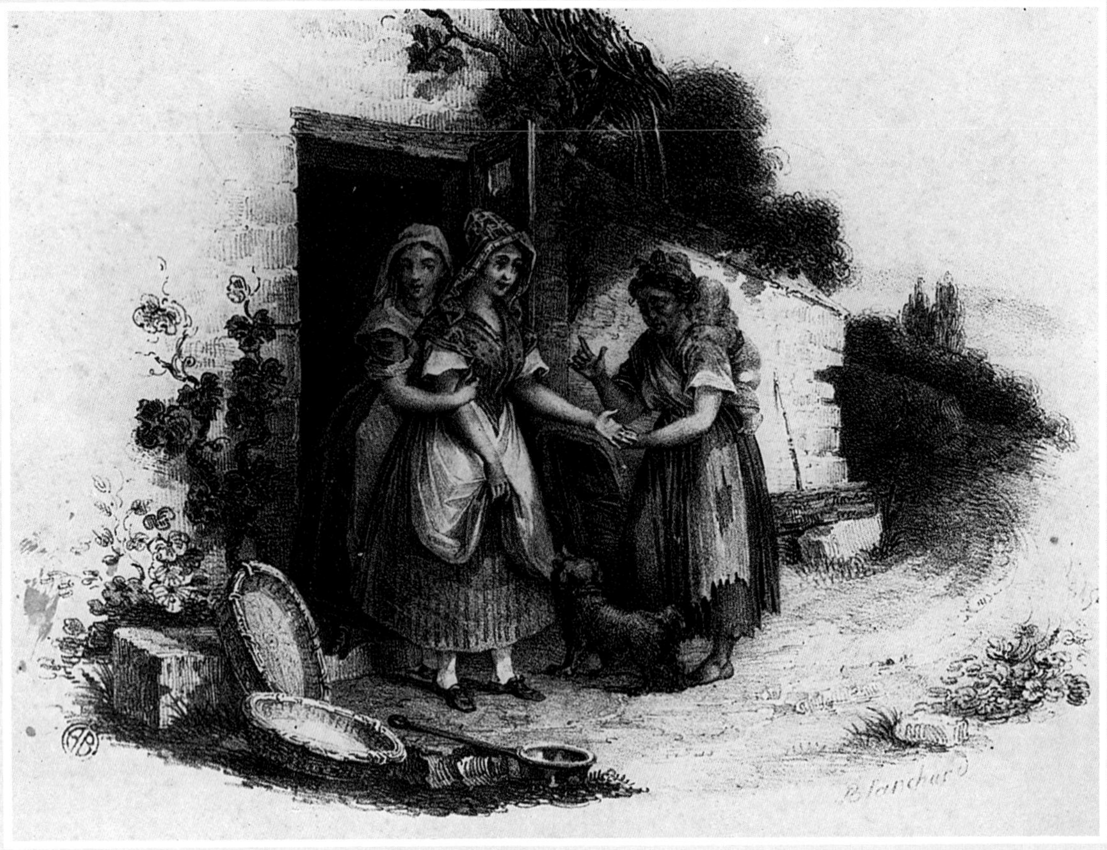

Maria Gardini

The Secrets of the Hand

Divine Your Personality and Destiny
through the Ancient Art of Palmistry

Collier Books
Macmillan Publishing Company
New York

p. 2, A hand being read in a nineteenth-century lithograph entitled *Bohémienne* (Civica Raccolta di Stampe "Bertarelli," Milano)

Macmillan books are available at special discounts for bulk purchases for sales promotions, premiums, fund-raising, or educational use. For details, contact:

Special Sales Director
Macmillan Publishing Company
866 Third Avenue
New York, N.Y. 10022

Drawings by Maria Pozzi

Photographs by Lionel Pasquon

Translated by Judith Spencer

Copyright © 1984 by Arnoldo Mondadori Editore S.p.A., Milano
English translation copyright © 1985 by Arnoldo Mondadori Editore S.p.A., Milano

All rights reserved. No part of this book may be reproduced or transmitted in any form or by any means, electronic or mechanical, including photocopying, recording or by any information storage and retrieval system, without permission in writing from the Publisher.

First published in the United States of America by Macmillan Publishing Company
866 Third Avenue, New York, N.Y. 10022
Collier Macmillan Canada, Inc.

Library of Congress Cataloging in Publication Data

Gardini, Maria,
　The secrets of the hand.

　Translation of: Il libro della mano.
　Includes index.
　1. Palmistry.　I. Title.
BF921.G3713　1985　133.6　85-12793
ISBN 0-02-011450-8 (pbk.)

10 9 8 7 6 5 4 3 2 1

Printed in Spain by Artes Graficas Toledo S.A.
D. L. TO: 1031 -1985

Contents

7	*Introduction*
9	**The study of the hand and its history**
11	*Chiromancy, Chirognomy, and Chirology*
13	*A brief history of palmistry*
21	**The shape of the hand**
23	*The hand and its different types*
24	Basic types of hands
28	Other types
30	The curve of creativity
30	The arc
31	**The fingers**
33	*The fingers and the world of reason*
40	Knots
40	The fingertips
42	The drop of water
45	*The thumb*
51	*The other four fingers*
51	The index finger
51	The middle finger
52	The fourth finger
53	The little finger
54	*The nails*
59	**The palm and the mounts**
61	*The palm*
61	The dating system
64	*The mounts*
66	The mount of Jupiter
66	The mount of Saturn
66	The mount of Apollo
69	The mount of Mercury
69	The mount of Mars
69	The mount of Venus
70	The mount of the Moon
72	The plains of Mars
72	The plain of Neptune
73	**The lines and signs of the hand**
75	*The four principal lines*
75	The life line
82	The heart line
87	The head line
99	The fate line
104	*Secondary lines*
104	The sun line
105	The line of Mercury
110	The line of marriage
112	The line(s) indicating children
114	The line of widow(er)hood
114	Wrist wrinkles
115	Rings
117	Capillary lines
119	The "other" rings
121	**Reading palms**
133	**Four examples of palm reading**
153	*A testimony*
155	*Bibliography*
156	*Index*
158	*Picture sources*

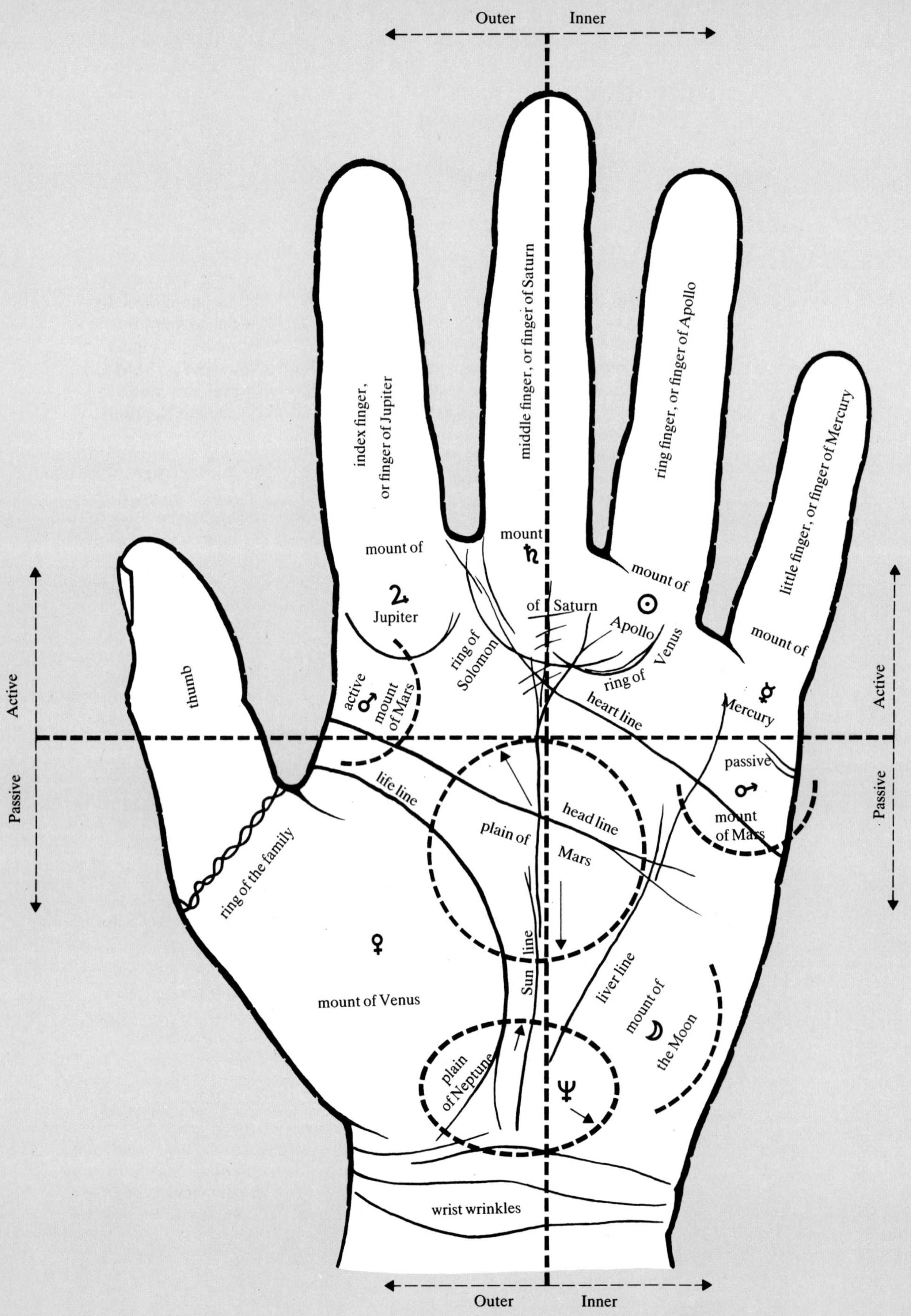

Outer
Inner
index finger, or finger of Jupiter
middle finger, or finger of Saturn
ring finger, or finger of Apollo
little finger, or finger of Mercury
thumb
mount of Jupiter
mount of Saturn
mount of Apollo
mount of Mercury
ring of Solomon
ring of Venus
active mount of Mars
heart line
passive mount of Mars
life line
head line
plain of Mars
ring of the family
mount of Venus
Sun line
liver line
mount of the Moon
plain of Neptune
wrist wrinkles
Active
Passive
Active
Passive
Outer
Inner

Introduction

There are more things in heaven and earth,
   Horatio,
Than are dreamt of in your philosophy.
William Shakespeare, *Hamlet* (I,v, 166)

The practice of reading character and destiny in the shape and, more particularly, the lines of the hand, harkens back to ancient times, claiming a solemn ancestry. In the literature of chiromancy (or chirology, or chirosophy), we find the name of Aristotle alongside references to the Bible and Hindu Vedas. Heron-Allen, the famous English palmist of the Victorian era and author of the exhaustive A Manual of Cheirosophy *(1885), gives credence to the report that Aristotle found in Egypt "on an altar dedicated to Hermes, an Arabic treatise on chiromancy written in gold letters," which he conscientiously delivered to his former student Alexander the Great. Legend, but fascinating all the same, and perhaps not without a grain of truth. In any event, it reflects a venerable tradition.*

Another Englishman from a much earlier period, Richard Saunders, author of Physiognomie and Chiromancie *(1653), lists Jews, Chaldeans, Arabs, Indians, Greeks, Latins, and Italians among the "great students and promoters of this high branch of philosophy" in the ancient world, adding that "great public figures have loved and honoured this science and made use of it. Among them are Lucius Silla and Julius Ceasar, as reported by Suetonius and Josephus, who claim that through palmistry Caesar exposed the deceitful Alexander who was passing himself off as the son of Herod."*

Almost anyone probably could add something to an anthology of successful experiences with palmistry. It is certainly not surprising that men accustomed to risking their lives in the field of battle would be receptive to whatever instrument might foretell the future, particularly in classical antiquity, when augury was a function of the state. However, there are numerous instances much more recently of reliance on the reading of fortunes.

When Napoleon married Josephine Beauharnais, he apparently took over her card-reading fortune teller and palmist Marie-Anne le Normand, described by some as the most famous charlatan of the nineteenth century. When he was still just General Bonaparte, rich only in hopes and ambitions, le Normand took an imprint in ashes of his hand and from it predicted marriage to a beautiful woman with two sons (Josephine), the command to which he aspired (of the Republican army in Italy), and "sufficient glory to make him the most illustrious of all Frenchmen." Le Normand recorded these events afterwards, but a friend of Napoleon's who was an eyewitness confirmed that she had made these predictions.

We need not dwell on the skepticism expressed at times, one citation of interest is enough: in 1530 Henry VIII of England issued a decree denouncing gypsies as people "who use ingenious and subtle means to deceive persons into thinking that through the reading of palms they can foretell the future of men and women." The decree made no distinctions among gypsies and amounted to wholesale persecution. It was not repealed until the late eighteenth century, during the reign of George III. In effect it decried a mischievous practice without addressing the essential issue. We can but return to Hamlet, *"There are more things...."*

The reader will find Maria Gardini to be an authoritative guide to the fascinating secrets of palm reading, presenting the possibility of experimenting personally with this art. She opens with an explanation of the basic terms chiromancy, chirognomy, *and* chirology, *as well as a history of our subject. The seven sections of the book address the general principles of palmistry and its techniques, focusing first on the general shape of the hand, the different hand types, and the conclusions that can be drawn about each. Then, in a more analytical examination she considers the different parts of the hand: the fingers, each one related by ancient tradition to a star; the mounts and the plains of the palm, with their mythological names; and the signs and lines, with their all too revealing names: life, heart, head, fate, marriage. In the final sections the author demonstrates her considerable and wide-ranging professional skill in palm reading and tells the exciting stories of four actual case studies.*

The following observation by the psychologist Carl Jung strikes an encouraging note of balance: "The global concept of modern biology, based on data from an amount of observations and research, in no way rules out the possibility that hands—whose form and function are so closely allied to the psyche—provide clear and therefore easily interpretable evidence of psychic characteristics, which is to say the human character."

The Editor

The study of the hand and its history

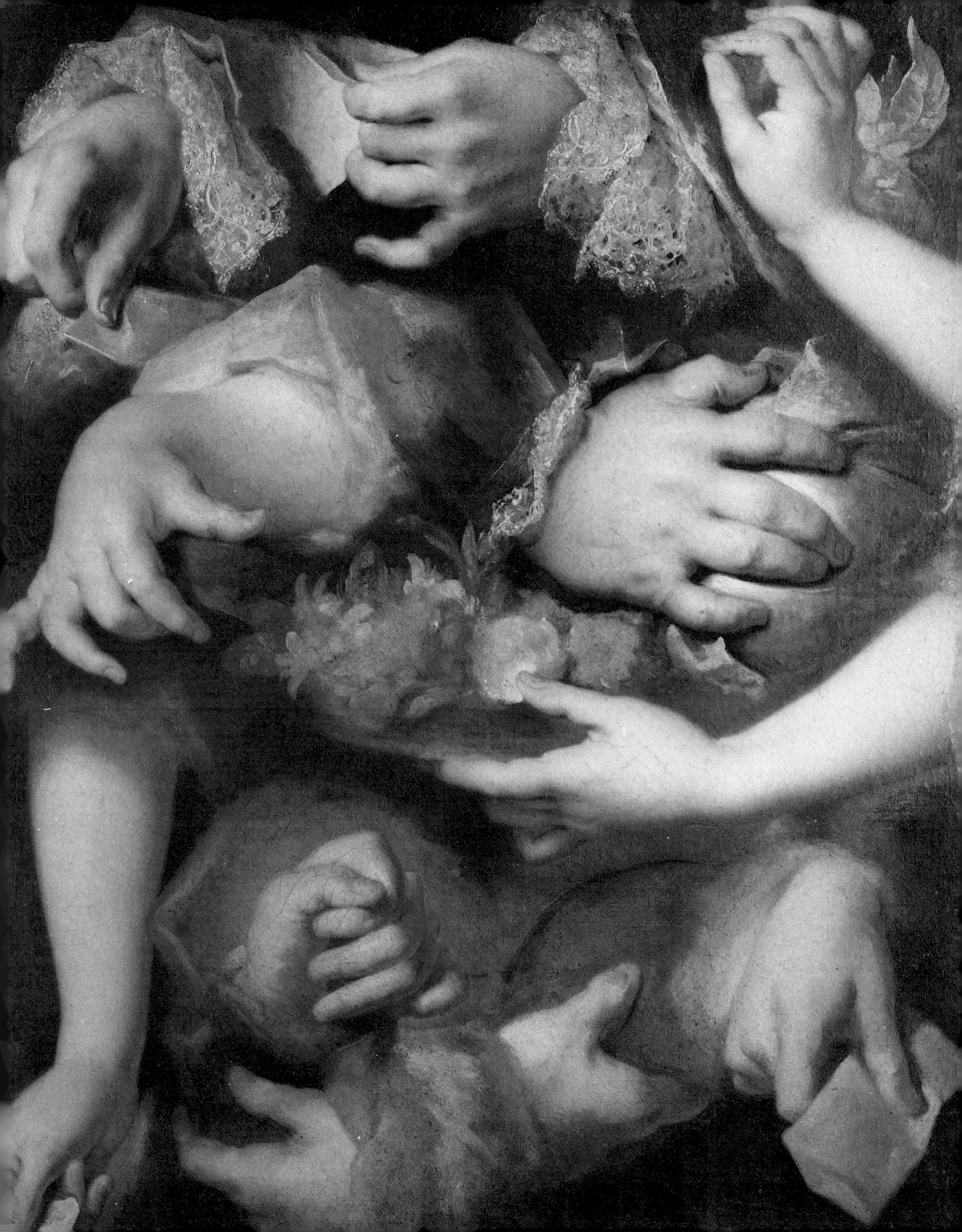

Chiromancy, Chirognomy, and Chirology

The word *chiromancy* comes from two Greek words: *cheir* meaning hand, and *manteia* meaning divination. According to some it is a science (or, in any event, an art) that requires extensive study and diligent training in order to be applied properly. Is it really possible to predict the future through palmistry? Careful examination of the whole hand by an expert can reveal a given subject's personality, events in the past and the effect on character, the illnesses he has had or may be prone to, and tendencies in general. On the basis of such preliminary information it is then possible to predict what his behaviour will be in the future.

In fact each of us has only one past and one present, but unlimited possible futures—any number of paths leading from point *A*, representing the present, to point *B* in a fairly distant future. It is logical to suppose that some of these futures are more probable than others, taking into account what the personality and past behaviour of the subject suggests.

The word "destiny" thus enters our discussion almost surreptitiously. The course of our lives has already been determined; what must happen will happen. If we believe that, there is no chance of changing anything. What point is there in finding out what is going to befall us? A legitimate question, but it contains a basic error: it discounts the existence of free will, the possibility of dealing with certain situations so as to modify their effects, reducing dangers or heightening advantages depending on the particular case.

There are many reasons why an individual may fail to handle important problems rationally, the most common being an imperfect state of health. It clouds one's sense of judgement so that decisions and reasoning lack objectivity; depression and enthusiasm are disproportionate to circumstance. Very often a simple remedy is all that is needed for the person to regain his equilibrium, but unfortunately he is sometimes unaware of the illness or considers it unimportant, or does not believe that it can lead to certain consequences.

Another frequent cause of bewilderment when one is faced with life's problems is lack of experience or lack of self-knowledge, as is often the case with young people. A competent palmist could rapidly give the subject a knowledge of himself that would be beneficial.

Predicting the future by means of palmistry is logically possible, with a margin of probability that in some cases exceeds eighty per cent. But if we know the future, can we change it? Let us be quite clear on this point. The power of a palmist to change what fate has already decided is minimal. The palmist can exert influence within a very restricted framework and this limitation leaves the general plan defined by the signs on the palm unchanged. Yet the subject's knowledge of the future allows him to prepare himself spiritually for what is to come by accepting the inevitable—to avoid being taken by surprise and to soften what would otherwise be a painful encounter with reality. How could it be otherwise? For example, a car accident involving no risk to life can be averted or its effects minimized, thus avoiding pain and injury. However, if destiny has decreed a fatal accident, the palmist's prediction cannot change the outcome.

The term *chirology* is used today to define the series of studies and experiments that constitute a complete examination of the hand. It consists of two distinct but closely related disciplines: *chirognomy*, the study of the shape of the hand, its consistency, colour, and suppleness; and *chiromancy*, the study of the lines on the palm and fleshy parts of the fingers. A complete hand analysis has to take into account many diverse elements which must be compared and interpolated. This requires interpretative abilities utilizing intuition, intelligence, and a talent for organization.

A complete analysis must establish with maximum accuracy the events of both the past and future that represent the main events of the subject's entire life: birth, loves, serious illnesses, vital encounters, death. Some of these events are obviously unalterable; others, as we have said, can be avoided, attenuated, or even enhanced with the appropriate behaviour. The complexity of all this is obvious, and indeed palmistry is among the most difficult of arts, but one that is apt to give great satisfaction to those who practise it.

Study of Hands *by the French painter Nicolas de Largillière (Paris, 1656-1746).*

Docebo Vos Per manum DEI.
Iob. 27. v. 11.
Ecce in Manibus descripsi te
Et in sinistrâ Eius divitiæ et Gloria.
Pro. 3. v. 16.
Longitudo dierum est in Dextrâ illius
Fautor utroque tuum Laudabit Pollice Ludum.
Horat. Ll. Epist. 18. v. 66.
ΣΥΝ ΘΕΟΥ ΠΑΛΑΜΑ
METOPOSCOPICU
LUDICRUM CHIROMANTICUM PRÆTORII
Vsus habet Laudem:
Sed abusus crimina gign
Cheiromantica:
Hic omina certa.
Chiromantice:
Cichainer_tom.
Quod est Inferiô est sicut id quod est superius.
Experimentum proprium docuit Chiromantiam esse veram
DERISORES huius artis Contemplentur saltem locum ♀ in manibus propriis. etc.
IOHANES AB INDAGINE
RODOLPHUS GOCLENIUS

A brief history of palmistry

The history of palmistry is entirely a history of chirosophy—a store of knowledge about the hand acquired together with an infinity of superstitions. The accumulation of many thousands of experiences, nevertheless, has provided the basis for a theoretical framework which, divested of all unfounded speculation, is still essential today in the art of modern palmistry. However, the origins of this art are lost in the mists of time, primarily because the knowledge of it was transmitted orally for so long, its genesis being of an esoteric, even religious, nature. Those who practised it tended not to divulge their experiences but kept them secret for the chosen few. Thus the invention of this art has been attributed from time to time to the different peoples of antiquity without any confirming documentation. Even in light of present-day knowledge we cannot say where or when palmistry began.

In all likelihood it originated in the East. It was practiced in India almost two thousand years before the birth of Christ, substantiated by a clear reference in the *Vasishtha*, an ancient Vedic text. It was a very widespread and respected art, indicated by the fact that the ancient bronze figures of the gods exhibit diagrams of the principal lines on their palms.

Palmistry is mentioned in the Bible. In the Book of Job it is written: "It is He who places a sign on the hand of each man indicating the choices he must make."

In China there are texts on palmistry dating from before the fourth century B.C. with information that is surprisingly similar to the most modern knowledge of this art. However, on reading these ancient texts one gets the impression that they are derived from knowledge and experience of times already long past and that the real golden age of palmistry is lost somewhere in prehistory.

Palmistry reached the West through contact between ancient Greece and the East. The first written evidence goes back to Aristotle, whose references are rather vague, but we are left with the understanding that palmistry was held in high esteem by the Greeks. It was practiced by people of great standing whose fame has reached us by reason of their excellence in other disciplines: Hippocrates, Plato, Galen, Aristotle. But we are not dealing with actual texts, which is understandable since palmistry focuses on predictions of the future and has itself therefore always been shrouded in mystery, a factor that seems to confirm its esoteric origins. The painstakingly acquired ideas were transmitted orally over the centuries, retaining—and probably contributing to an increase in—the aura of magic that gave rise to superstitions still rife today. For this too there are reasons.

The prediciton of future events by a palmist has never caused a great stir, as have biblical prophecies or those of a seer

Opposite, detail of the frontispiece of Ludicrum chiro chiromanticum *(Jena, 1661).*
Right, an illustration from the introductory page of Die Kunst Chiromantie *published by the German Johann Hortlich around 1475.*

On this page, an interpretation of some of the signs of the hand by Bartolomeus Coclés in his L'art de la chiromancie *(1560).*
Opposite, a palmist's map of the hand (seventeenth-century tantric art).

like Nostradamus which concerned whole populations and historical periods. Palm reading, although more accurate and logical, is limited to the experiences of a single person and it is the outcome of an exchange between two people, the subject and the palmist, which is destined to remain secret, particularly if it is an important person whose palm is being read. To this should be added that it is difficult to put into words and record all of the subtle phases in the complex procedure of comparisons, considerations, and intuitions that make up an exhaustive examination of a hand.

The first European manuscripts devoted entirely to palmistry date from the early fourteenth century. Their contents as well as their nomenclature are so similar to those still in use that it is clear that they are not simply an account of a given author's personal experience—perhaps extensive but limited nevertheless—but rather are drawn from an incalculable fund of knowledge derived from studies by ancient chiromancers whom we know neither by name nor date.

These first texts deal principally with the main lines of the hand which today we call the lines of life, head, and heart. Only later in the fifteenth century did the mounts, triangles, and references to the general proportions of the hand and shape of the nails appear.

As a point of interest the first text on palmistry was printed in 1475, entitled *Die Kunst Chiromantie*, written a few decades earlier by the German Johann Hortlich. During the next two centuries palmistry spread throughout Europe, attracting as much interest among the erudite as alchemy and astrology. However, while the latter disciplines evolved under the impetus of the new rationalism into the fields of chemistry and astronomy, palmistry remained apart, and it was not until this century that it became more technical and gradually gained scientific credibility.

Among the works on palmistry that have earned incontrovertible prestige is *Chiromantia, opus rarissima de aedem chiromantiae* by Andrea Corvo, or Corvaeus, who also called himself Bartolomeus Coclés. A famous palmist from Bologna, Coclés lived at the turn of the fifteenth century.

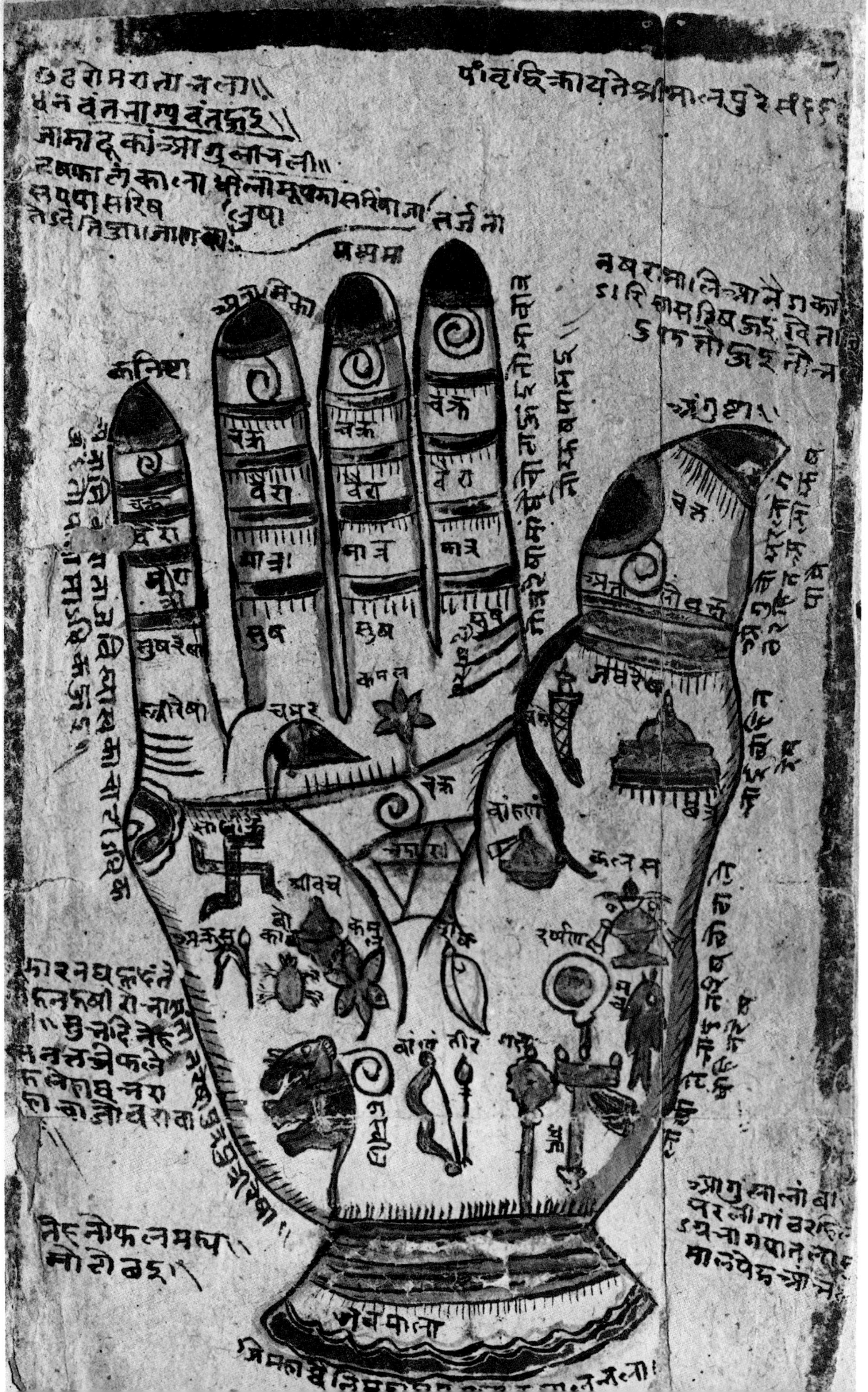
कनिष्ठा
तर्जनी
चक्र
कमल
चमर

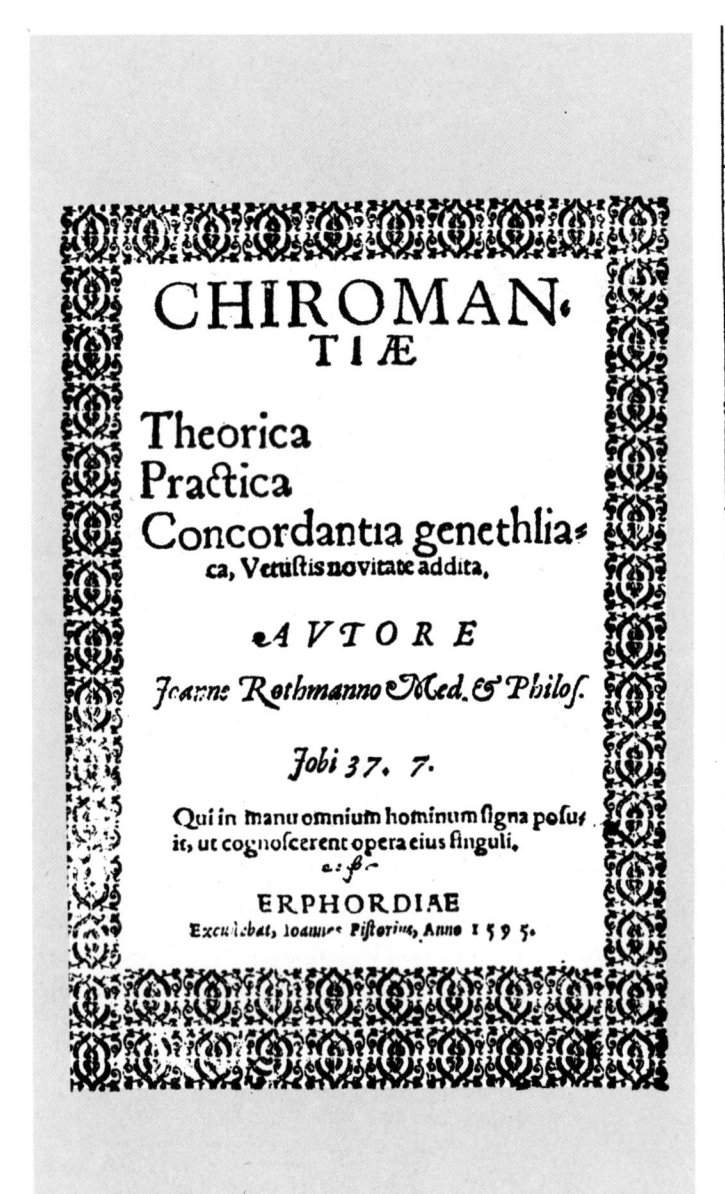

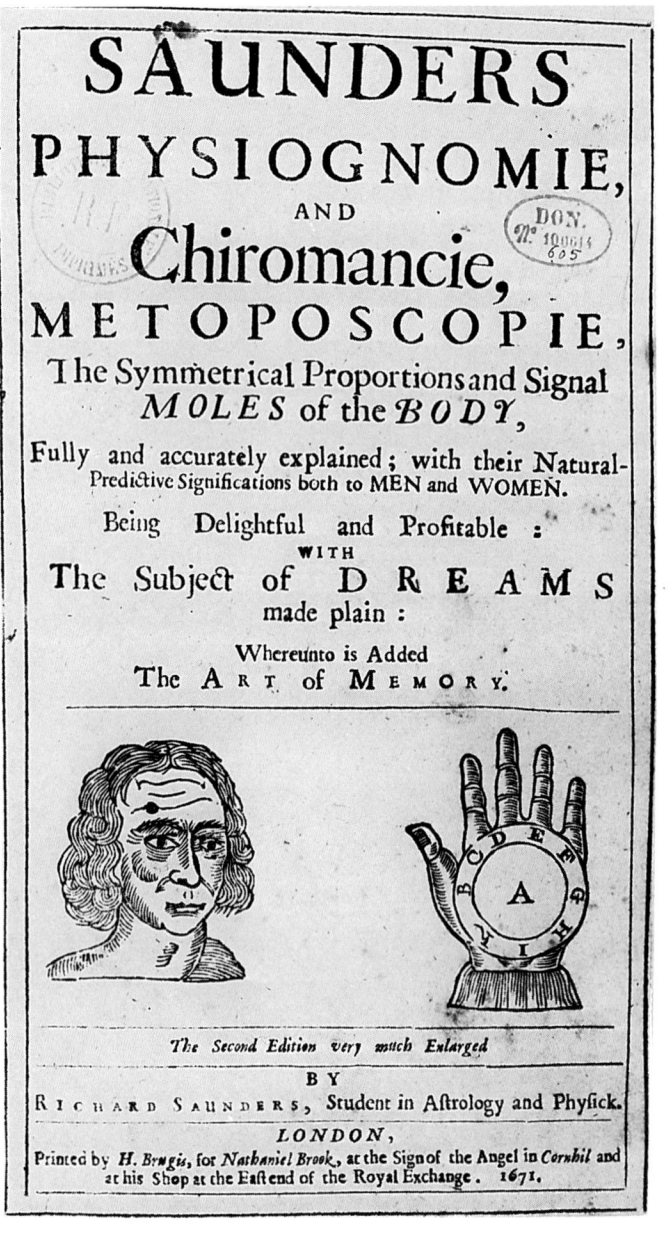

Above left, frontispiece of Chiromantiae *by Johann Rothmann (1595); above right, frontispiece of the second edition of* Physiognomie and Chiromancie, Metoposcopie *by Richard Saunders (published in London, 1671).*
Opposite, detail of The Peasants' Dance *by Peter Bruegel (Vienna, Kunsthistorisches Museum).*

His work is highly readable, which is perhaps the reason for its success. Well below the standard of other less known texts of the period (for example, *Chiromantie medicinal* by Ludwig Heinrich Lutz), it is a work clearly inspired by the diagnoses of Paracelsus which were based on palmistry.

Another book worth mentioning in this rapid excursion through the history of palmistry dates from 1653, *Physiognomie and Chiromancie, Metoposcopie* written by Richard Saunders. It gives serious consideration to palmistry as well as other sciences such as physiognomy, and metoposcopy, the study of the lines of the forehead. This work is more than just a reputable compendium of the knowledge of that period; it is regarded as the first serious contribution to modern palmistry. As in other works of the time, many comparisons are drawn between palmistry and astrology and indeed Saunders was first an astrologer, then a palmist.

No doubt some rather interesting links exist or can be drawn between the two

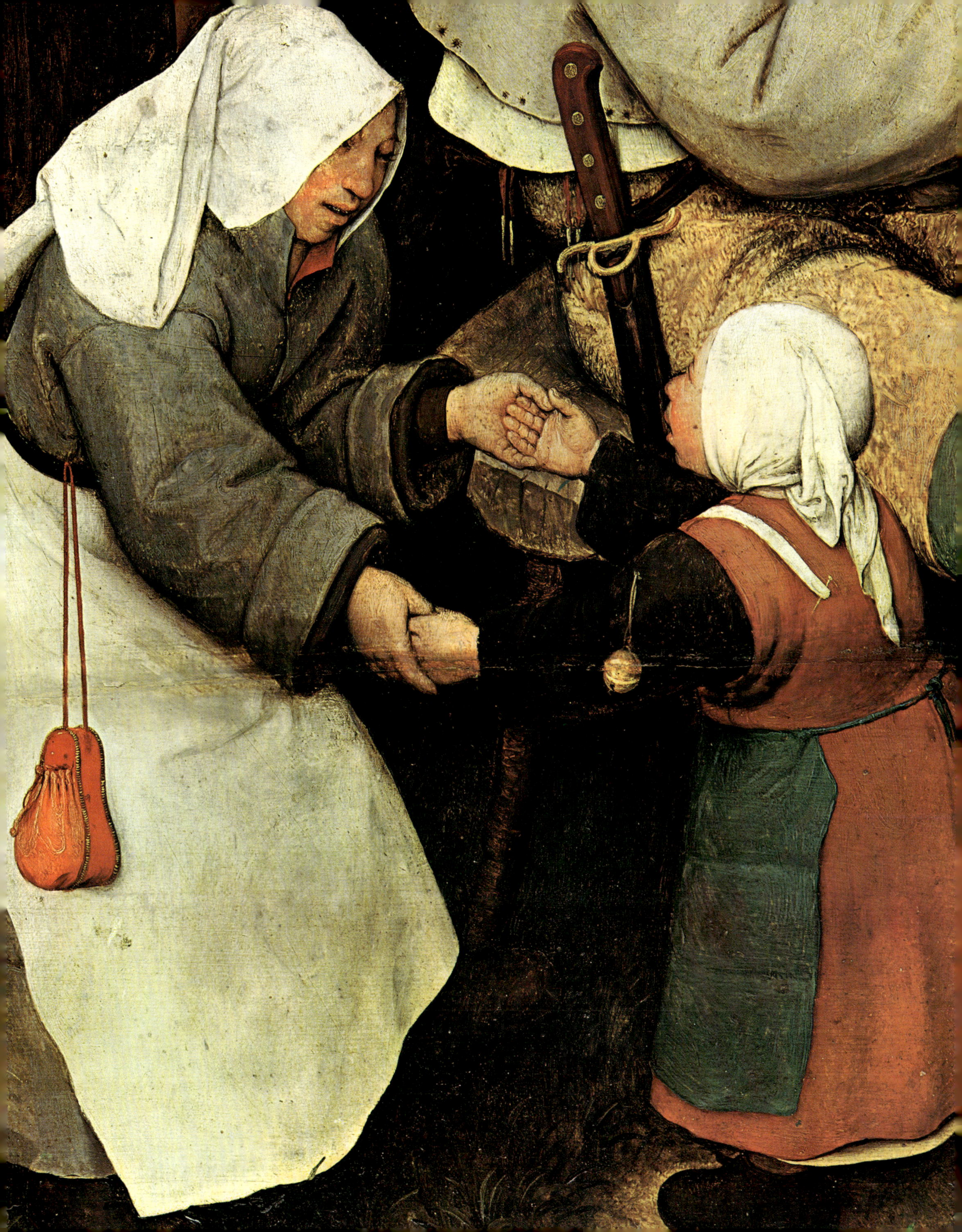

בְּיַד־כָּל־אָדָ֥ם יַחְתּ֑וֹם לָ֝דַ֗עַת כָּל־אַנְשֵׁ֥י
מַעֲשֵֽׂהוּ אִיֽוֹב ל״ז

QVI IN MANV OMNIVM HOMINVM SIGNAT, VT NOVERINT SINGVLI OPERA SVA IOB XXXVII

Right, an illustration of different types of hands from Physiognomische Fragmente zur Beförderung der Menschenkenntnis und Menschenliebe *(1775-1778) by Johann Kaspar Lavater, with the collaboration of Herder and Goethe who collected characteristics of hands from studies.*

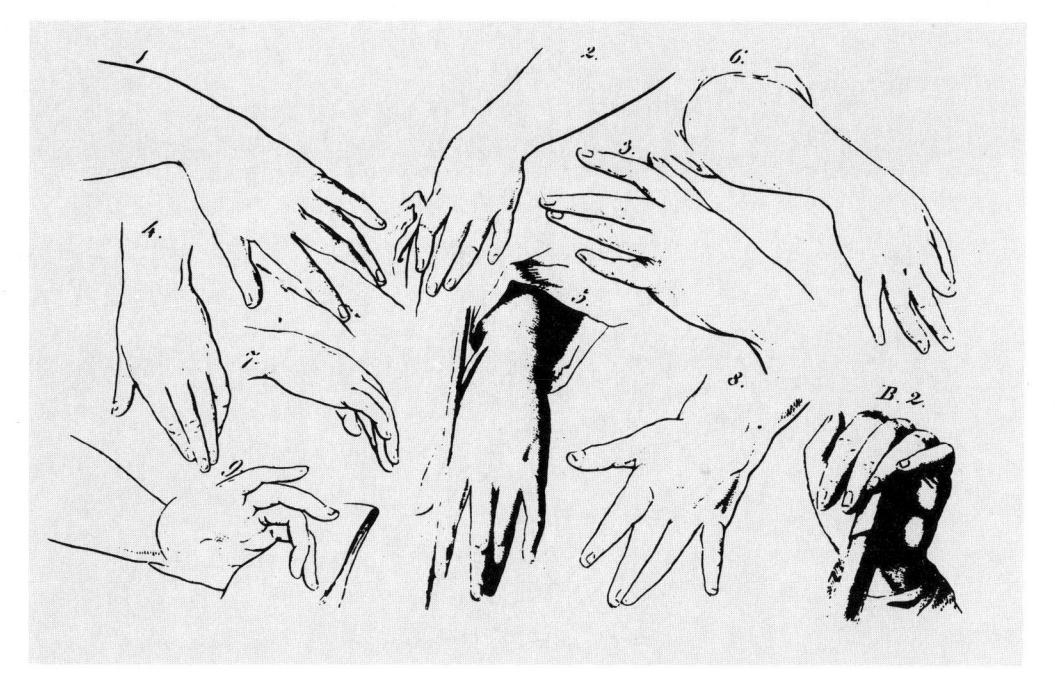

Left, hands and a chart of hands of Victor Alfieri by the French painter François Xavier Pascal Fabre (Burcardo Theatrical Collection, Rome).

disciplines; moreover, the mounts of the palm have the names of some of the planets (Jupiter, Mercury, etc.), indicating that in the past these affinities were more strongly felt and universally accepted. But the subject of this linkage is too vast and important to be resolved with a few passing remarks and deserves a more thorough treatment at another time.

With the advent of the scientific method in the eighteenth century, palmistry underwent a long period of decline. During those years there were no enlightened palmists who could bring to their art the discipline that would have placed it in a different light within the framework of knowledge of the time, as happened, for example, with physiognomy in the work of Lavater. This brilliant scholar's contribution to palmistry was too slight and his findings, fascinating though they were, were not collected until many years later in the nineteenth century. It was not until 1800, thanks to the work of two French scholars, Count Casimir D'Arpentigny and Adrien-Adolphe Desbarolles, that palmistry began to emerge from the mists of superstition.

What Lavater did for physiognomy D'Arpentigny did for palmistry. He was the father of palmistry and although some people today believe that his theories and classifications of hands into seven basic types is outdated, for the time and considering what experiments were possible then, his studies were of an unquestionable validity and brilliance.

Desbarolles's work is of a different sort. An extremely able man, a writer and painter, a famous palmist, the author of many works, the credibility of modern palmistry owes much to his theoretical research into the symbols of this art. Yet the title of his first book on palmistry, *Les mystères de la main*, published in 1859 to a resounding success for that epoch, reveals the limitations of this gifted man. His interest in the occult, the cabala, and astral influences lent a mysterious quality to his research on the abstract values of palmistry, thereby obscuring—for those not engaged in such studies—his quite valid theory of planetary types. It is accepted, however, that his studies have influenced the investigations of almost all later palmists up to the present day.

In this rapid march across the centuries we have done little more than mention the names of distinguished individuals who, with passion and diligence, devoted their lives to this complex study without the support of the scientific community. What was lacking was a systematic and rational study that could bridge the gap between the lines of the palm and the human psyche.

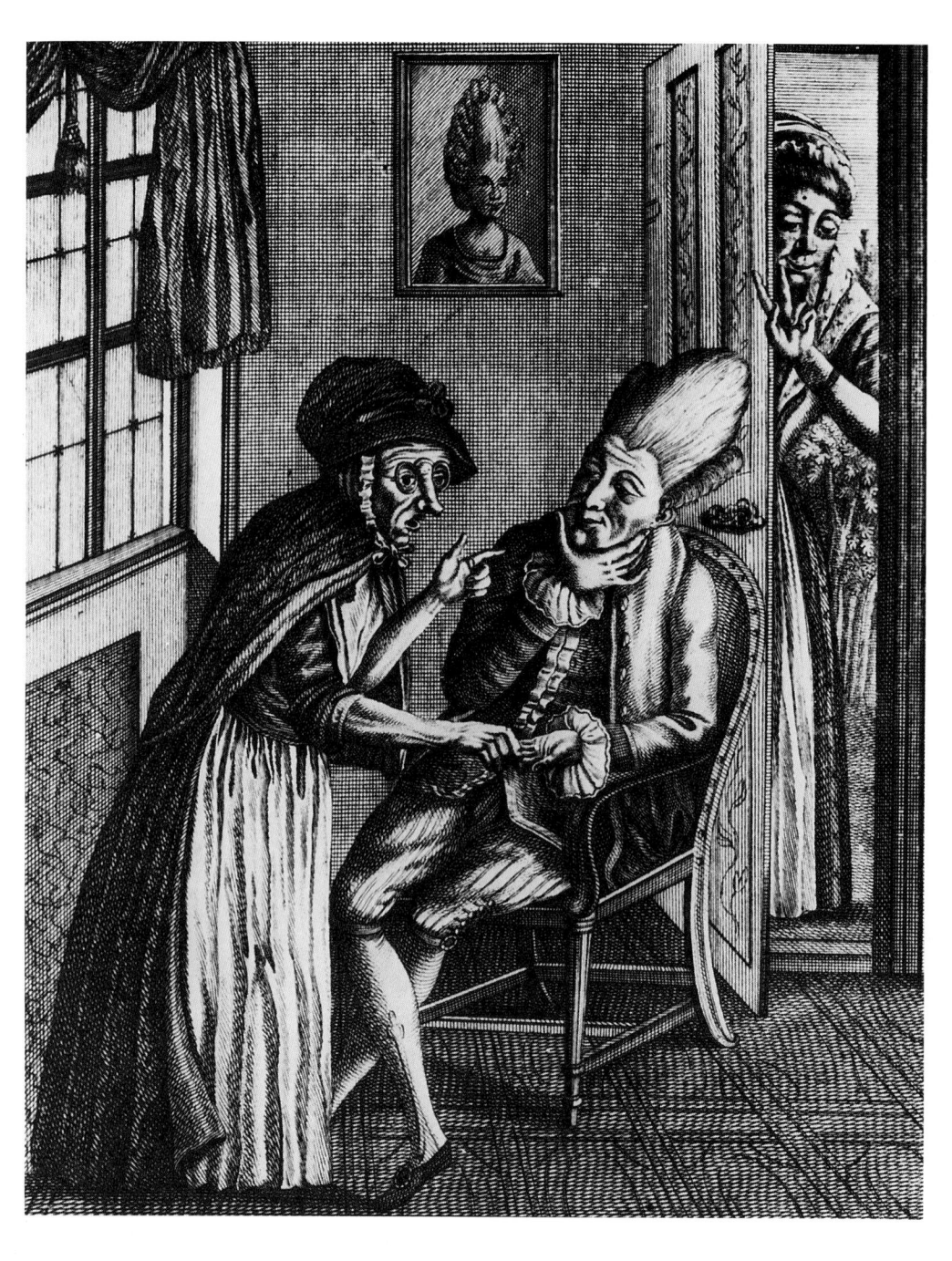

German caricature of palm reading (eighteenth-century engraving).

A last point. The term *chirology* was coined in the nineteenth century to describe the two disciplines of chirognomy and chiromancy. But it is not precise. It is derived from two Greek words, (as we saw earlier) *cheir* meaning hand, and *logos* meaning speech; and it means the ability to make oneself understood and converse with a deaf-mute using special hand movements.

An increasing number of doctors are in fact relying on chiromancy to confirm their diagnoses, and psychiatrists are interested in chiromancy in order to identify deep traumas. Modern palmistry has at its disposal sound methods of inquiry, although it still lacks the wide endorsement that would allow better use of the possibilities it presents for investigating the innermost areas of human nature.

The shape of the hand

Maria magdalena
Index · cognitio
Pollex · voluntas dei
Si voluntatem dei scis ·
Agnosce malum vitiantes ·
Si malum egisti · doleas ·
Si vere doles · confitearis ·
Si confessus es · satisfac ·
Pollex signat voluntatem dei ·
Index significat cognitione ·
Medius digit⁹ sigt ctritione ·
Medicus significat ofessionem ·
Auricularis satisfactione ·

The hand and its different types

Let us begin with some important general remarks for the prospective student.

Everything that is given as fact in palmistry is the result of careful observation that has been checked thousands of times over the course of centuries. Therefore today we can state with a high degree of probability that certain signs or groups of signs correspond to a certain aspect of character or an event in the future much in the same fashion and with the same degree of success as a doctor who makes a diagnosis by comparing data deduced from a patient's symptoms.

The idea of using fingerprints as a reliable and easy method of identification comes from palmistry. It has always been known by those studying the fleshy part of the fingertips that these marks are different for each person and remain totally unchanged over the years, unlike the lines—or most of the lines—of the hands. Fingerprints appear on the fetus in the twentieth week and remain for life. This observation probably gave rise to the exhaustive but not very diffused field of learning called *dactyliomancy* which, noting the uniqueness of fingerprints, proposes to determine character through their study.

Certainly every hand taken as a whole is different from every other, and each person's destiny is likewise different, even if the lines are similar. How do these lines form? Are they always the same or do they change with time?

To begin with, hand movements have a minimum effect on the formation of lines. Again, the most visible lines, the principal ones, form before birth and are retained, with only the slightest changes, for life. However, the capillary lines are also very important for a thorough reading of the hand, and some reliable theories have been advanced regarding their identification. One theory is based on the observation that the many thousands of nerve endings located in the palm of the hand are linked across the fissure of Roland to the frontal lobe of the brain, wherein the conscious impulses of thought, memory, and imagination reside. From this observation comes the hypothesis that arousal of this area of the brain, connected as it is with the nerve endings of the palm, can determine the formation of capillary lines. Given their short duration, they are useful in ascertaining such things as the present state of a person's health or a minor psychological upset.

Is there a precise order to be followed when reading a palm? Experience has shown that order is very important, and a specific procedural sequence is prescribed so that an orderly arrangement of information gradually emerges.

We begin with the general appearance of the hand (*chirognomy*), then a comparison of the two hands. We take the hand *measurements* and look at *shape, colour,* and *consistency*. Next we examine the fingers and each phalange of each finger, as well as the fingernails (*shape, colour, hardness, transparency,* and the like). Then we come to the actual study of the mounts and the lines of the hand (*chiromancy*). When speaking about palm reading we traditionally use the singular, but since we have two hands every good palmist knows that both hands must be examined. As a rule both hands are similar in shape and in the details of the lines, except in unusual cases which we shall take up later.

Why is it advisable to examine both hands if the difference between them is usually minimal? To establish what the difference is and to what extent it manifests itself. And then there are other more important reasons having to do with interpretation.

Two plausible theories exist as to the values to be attributed to the lines on the left hand as opposed to the right. According to one theory, the left contains the unconscious ideas that are with us from birth, the right reveals changes resulting from our experiences in life. Another, more modern theory maintains that the left hand expresses brain impulses stimulated directly by the subconscious, allowing us to investigate the more private side of the subject's personality, while the right expresses brain impulses stimulated by the external world, thus revealing our reactions and subsequent adaptations to the world around us. The difference between the two theories is more a matter of form than substance and in the light of present-day knowledge both are considered credible.

The hand as a mirror of salvation (German engraving, 1466).

We all know that right-handed people use their right and left hands differently, and the above observations apply to them. But in the case of a left-handed person does the opposite hold true? No, logic does not apply in this instance and other factors must be examined to answer this slight puzzle. In cases where the left and right hands show marked differences in the lines and mounts, a very extensive examination is necessary because then we have a person with contradictory tendencies and an unstable personality.

By now it is accepted universally that there exists a fairly precise and constant relationship between an individual's physical appearance and his psychic characteristics, tendencies, and personality. This forms the basic principle of physiognomy, the study of character from a person's features, and is even more the case with chirognomy, which studies the form, dimensions, and other aspects of the hand in order to establish important facts indispensible for a complete palm reading.

Chirognomy is a very ancient field of study. Plato mentions it, citing ideas and concepts that were old even in his time, all starting from the principle that "if the outward forms are the visible aspect of interior patterns, it is possible from the study of certain external characteristics to go back to the psychic causes to which they are related." Axiomatic to this principle is that outward appearance is the mirror of an interior reality, and as the outward form of a hand is unique, so clearly demonstrated by fingerprints, it follows that every one has a unique interior form that is distinct from anyone else's. In other words every human being is complete in himself. He constitutes a unique microcosm reproducing every law in himself that regulates the greater macrocosm, that is, the universe. Chirognomy and chiromancy aim to comprehend the universe by starting with the smallest element—man. (Astrology applies the opposite theory: beginning with the cosmic, it seeks through that means to establish man's place in the universal scheme of things.)

Since the hand is the means by which the palmist conducts research, it is logical to correlate the different shapes of hands that are most commonly found with the seven basic types into which palmists have divided humankind since the earliest times. This system, re-examined in light of contemporary psychological techniques, has proven surprisingly valid and accurate.

Basic types of hands

The father of modern chirognomy is the Frenchman Casimir D'Arpentigny. In scrupulous studies carried out at the close of the nineteenth century he was the first to classify hands into the seven distinct types now accepted and used by all palmists: *elementary* (1), *spatulate* (2), *psychic* (3), *square* (4), *knotty* or *philosophic* (5), *conic* (6), *mixed* (7).

Before we go into this study in depth, let us look briefly at other factors that can be useful in our investigations and which we can become aware of on first contact with the subject whose palm is to be examined simply by shaking hands. Rapid and very precise deductions allow the person who is reading the hand to make an initial classification of the subject. Skin *quality* is very important because it can give sound information about the subject's sensitivity. If the skin is delicate and soft, the person is highly sensitive, tends to be emotional, and has little taste for physical labour. A hard, rough skin indicates the opposite tendencies: little sensitivity and a strong practical sense. (Of course, it is important in this case to take into account the type of work done by the subject.) Finally, there is an intermediate elastic or springy skin that is frequently found with professional people (doctors, lawyers, businessmen). This type is typical among those who have the ability to put their own ideas into practice. When making these preliminary deductions surprises will occur only with a subject forced to undertake an uncongenial line of work.

A careful glance under normal light conditions will suffice to establish the skin colour of the hand and obtain information which does not strictly belong to chirognomy, but which nevertheless makes a valid contribution to the general picture. If the hand is particularly white—usually a female hand—and not because of a pallor but by nature, this person will not hesitate to use all the arts of deceit and flattery to

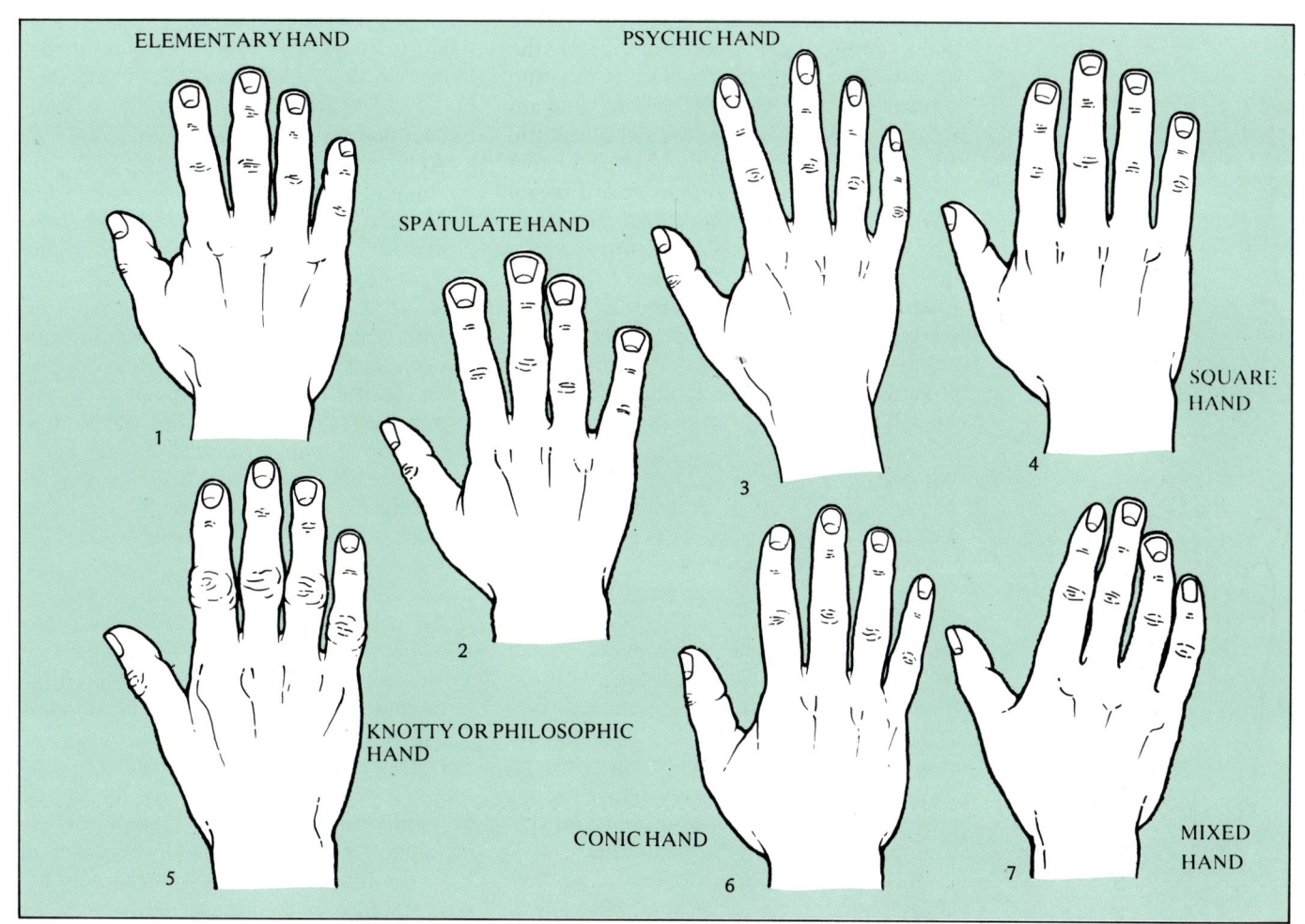

The basic types of hands: elementary (1), spatulate (2), psychic (3), square (4), knotty or philosophic (5), conic (6), mixed (7).

achieve personal aims. This is an egoist who is not without cruelty. If the palm of the hand is a deep pink colour, then we are dealing with someone who is fairly gifted as a medium.

There is another piece of information that can be learned from a handshake: the *firmness* of the grip can indicate the amount of energy the person has. If the hand feels flabby and offers no resistance, it means that the person is unable to turn his own fantasies and dreams into reality and tends to lie even to himself. If the hand has a slight firmness, the person lacks impulsiveness but not the ability to act, which is frequently characteristic of ill people. A handshake offering slight resistance is very often accompanied by light perspiration. Contact will not indicate from what illness the person is suffering, but it does invite further investigation.

A hand that reacts readily to a handshake with muscular firmness belongs to an active person whose inner energy is spontaneously translated into creative energy. Last we have the *hard* hand, actually very rarely encountered, belonging to the individual with a great store of energy which can be discharged only through physical work or sport; this person tends to be withdrawn.

Another important factor here is the *suppleness* of the hand (page 34). If the fingers can be bent backwards easily, it indicates a personality rich in nuance, intuition and mental agility, perspicuity, and organizational ability. The more rigid or less supple the hand is, the simpler the person's character and powers of discernment.

There is an ancient practice of palmistry called "the three worlds of the hand" (8). According to this centuries-old tradition, the *rationabilis* area is represented by the

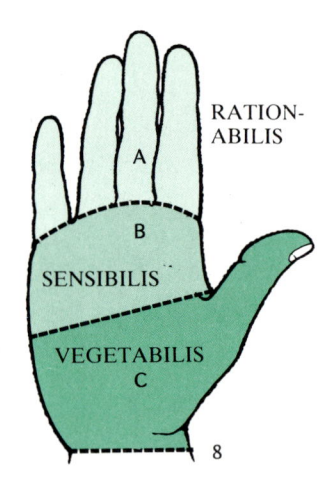

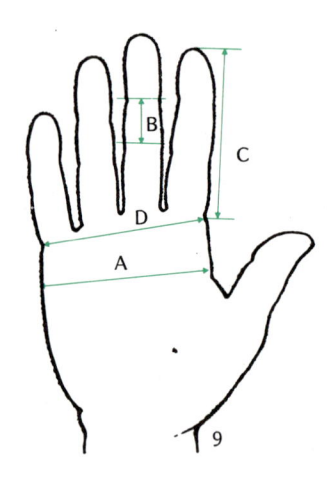

The three worlds of the hand (8): A *"rationabilis,"* the fingers; B *"sensibilis,"* the upper part of the palm; C *"vegetabilis,"* the lower part of the palm. A perfectly proportioned hand (9): A = 4 × B; C = D.

fingers from the point where they join the palm. The longer and more agile the fingers, the more spiritual, artistic, and refined the subject is. If the fingers are short and stumpy, the subject has little ability for analysis and reflection. The next area, the *sensibilis,* extends from the arc (the name for the line marking the juncture between the fingers and the palm) to a line that approximately follows the head line, joining the two mounts of Mars. The wider this space is, the greater the practical abilities of the subject, and this makes it possible to identify the extent of the person's ambition—the desire for social success, money, and power. Below this area is the section called *vegetabilis* in which a person's deepest instincts can be identified. The more these instincts are controlled by the intellect, the smaller the area will be.

By comparing the three areas and interpreting them correctly, we gain an overall picture of the subject's personality, which will provide a useful guide for the investigations that follow. The predominance of one of these areas over another denotes the subject's preferences and tendencies. In recent times, extensive scientific testing has confirmed the exceptional accuracy of this traditional means of interpretation.

Another important point, before we look at the palm, is the size of the hand, which should be judged in relation to the subject's build and not independently. If the hands seem small, then we are dealing with a person who is quick to make decisions (sometimes too much so), who has a fairly clear, broad view of issues, and who tends to overlook details. If the hands seem rather large in relation to build, then the person places great importance on detail, from which he makes an overall assessment. He is reflective and almost slow in making decisions out of a need to examine matters thoroughly and confirm his findings; he is also very observant.

We can conclude these general observations with a point of interest: the measurements of what is regarded as a well-proportioned hand (9). The width of the hand should be four times the length of the second phalange of the middle finger; the length of the index finger should correspond to the distance between the attachment point of the index finger and that of the little finger. It is very rare to find such a hand and the person who has it will have many good qualities: courage, incorruptibility, goodness, and health.

At last we come to chirognomy itself, the evaluation of the hand and its classification into one of the seven types established by Count D'Arpentigny. Despite its considerable value and serious scientific approach, this system is somewhat outdated, and the count's deductions no longer fulfill present-day requirements. Rapid changes of customs, attitudes, and habits due to the society in which we live require that palmistry be brought up to date too. The parameters of 1850 within which D'Arpentigny based his experiments are no longer valid, although certain basic psychological insights still hold true. For this reason palmists almost always use a simpler but no less effective classification, with recourse to D'Arpentigny's system in cases of doubt.

The German Carl Gustav Carus, another late-nineteenth-century palmist, divided the hand into four basic types (*10, 11, 12, 13*). They may seem few when one thinks of the incredible variety of hands that are to be found, but numerous interpolations can be made between two or three different types so that in practical terms the number of types may be increased greatly. Bear in mind that our examination is not just to do with chirognomy but chiromancy as well. The level that we are at now is provisional and the information obtained here will then be considered in the light of what is learned later from the palm lines, mounts, and so on. Carus's classification is eminently useful in providing a framework on which to add refinements and finishing touches. In any event, the information from an accurate interpretation of Carus's classification is based on very rigorous criteria and therefore very reliable.

Carl Gustav Carus's four types

According to Carus there are two types of hands, each of which is divided into subtypes. The *prehensile* hand is built for an effective grip on objects and has two subdivisions: *elementary* (*10*) and *motoric* (*11*). The second type, *tactile,* is better suited to perceiving things through touch; it

The four types of hands, as defined by Carl Gustav Carus: elementary (10), motoric (11), sensitive (12), psychic (13).

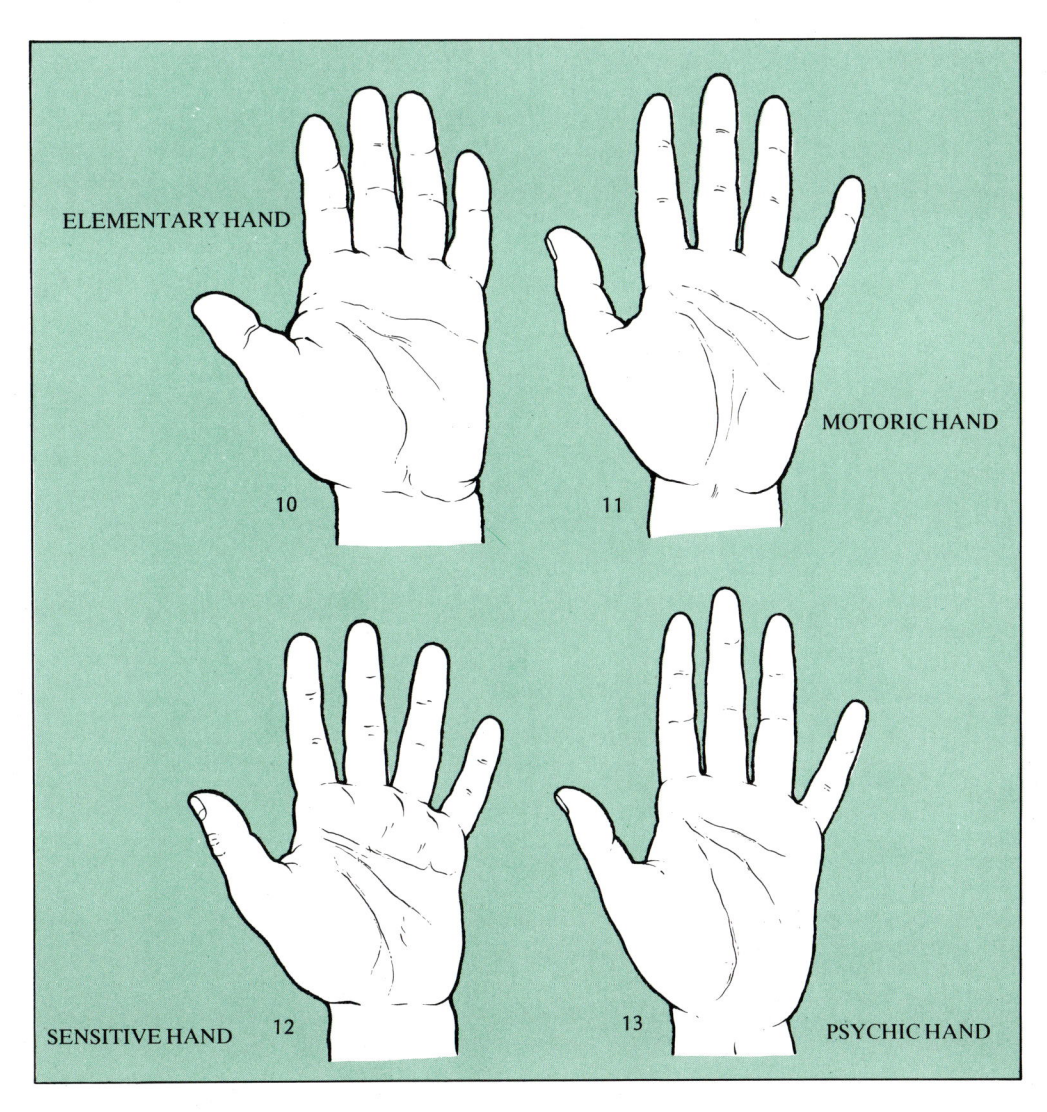

ELEMENTARY HAND 10

MOTORIC HAND 11

SENSITIVE HAND 12

PSYCHIC HAND 13

has two subdivisions: *sensitive* (*12*) and *psychic* (*13*).

The elementary hand (*10*). Its shape is sturdy with rather short fingers that are not very supple. It gives the impression of considerable energy. A person with an elementary hand is practical-minded, serious, and highly intelligent, with a marked orientation towards concrete things. He is highly adaptable. This hand usually belongs to extroverts, very prone to extremes of enthusiasm and depression. This kind of temperament, in terms of astrology, is close to Saturn. A similar Chinese subdivision calls this hand an *earth hand*.

There is a tendency in modern chirology to draw on astrology. Some palmists, interested in this relationship, have devised a new classification of hands which, without losing sight of the accepted and tested elements of chirology, establishes a parallel with the four basic elements of pre-Aristotelian philosophies: *fire*, *air*, *water*, and *earth*, which are also groups of astrological signs. This is a very subtle connection with some scientific validity and one sees significant confirmation in the correlation between the theory of the four elements and the four temperaments of Galen and current trends in psychology (as can be found in the studies of Salomon Diamont, for instance).

The motoric hand (*11*). Also prehensile, but thinner than the elementary, with longer fingers and softer, more supple skin. The palm has more lines than that of the elementary hand, denoting a more emotional nature. A motoric hand indicates an

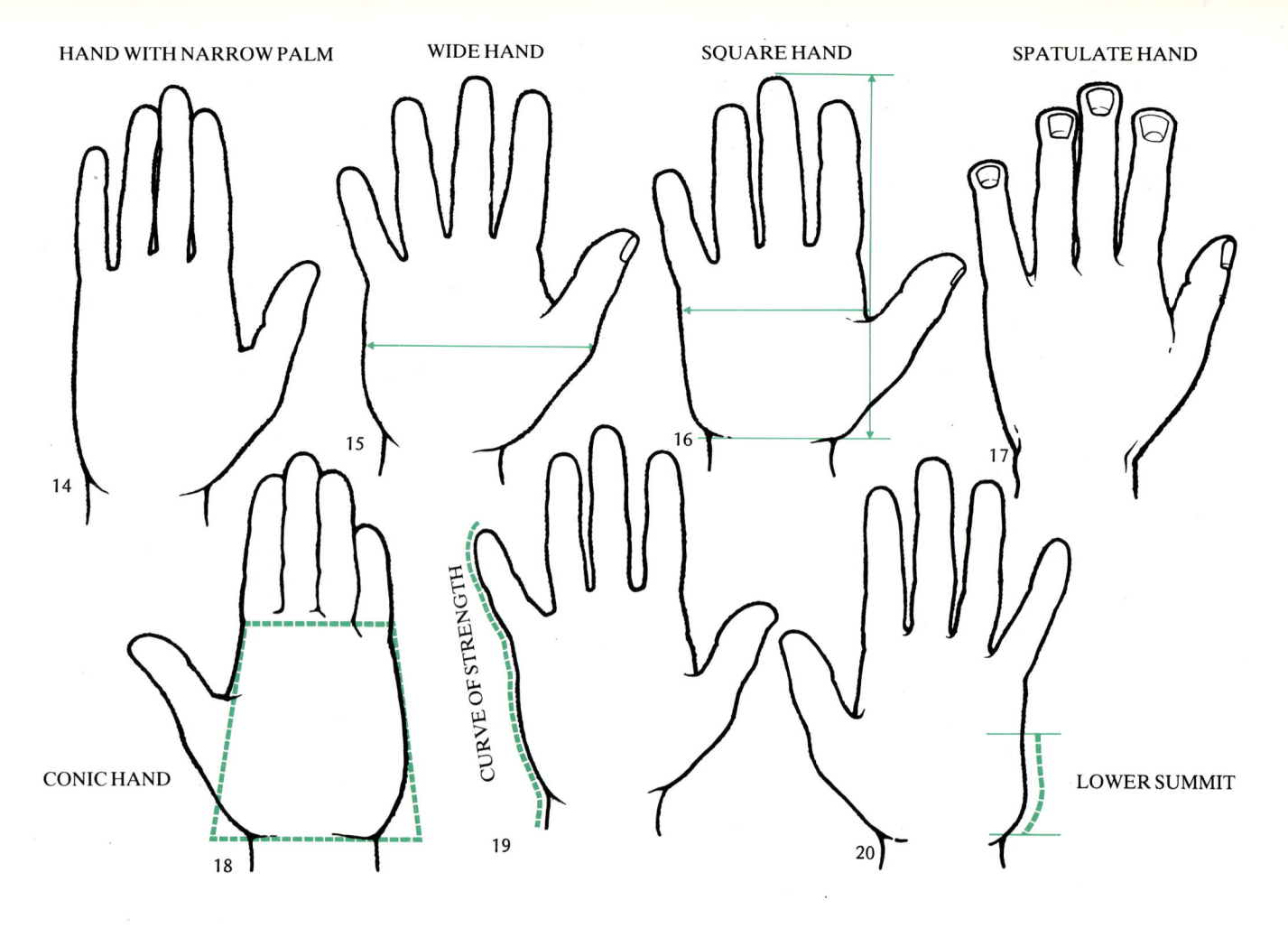

| HAND WITH NARROW PALM | WIDE HAND | SQUARE HAND | SPATULATE HAND |

Classifications and characteristics of hands: hand with narrow palm (14), wide hand (15), square hand (16), spatulate hand (17), conic hand (18), the outer edge of the hand (19) (as it is commonly but incorrectly called; its technical name is "curve of creativity" or "curve of strength"), lower summit (20).

extrovert and hedonist type, able to appreciate and enjoy beauty. Despite his potential egocentrism, he is broad-minded and his basic skills are eminently practical. This type of hand is typical of people who strive for success and power, such as military men, sportsmen, people in business, and very often opera singers. In China it is called a *wooden hand*; in astrology it is comparable to the planet Jupiter.

The sensitive hand (*12*). This is one of the tactile types in Carus's classification. It is usually rather small compared with the person's body. The fingers are slim, movements agile, and it transmits nervous energy that while very emotional is not without a practical side. The palm lines are numerous and fine, overlapping in many cases, and they suggest a tendency toward instability. The sensitive hand is common among actors, ballerinas, graphic artists, and publicists. These people are actually less superficial than they pretend to be and it is better not to believe their promises even when made in good faith. The Chinese call this type of hand a *water hand*; astrologically it is close to Mercury because of its quickness and versatility.

The psychic hand (*13*). This is the fourth and last type. It is easily recognized by the long, tapering fingers, emphasized by a very small, supple thumb. This hand is extremely soft, sometimes to the extent of seeming insubstantial. The palm lines are very fine, complicated, and not easy to interpret; they show great imagination to the extent that the subject loses his sense of reality. Persons with this kind of hand are completely lacking in business sense and tend to escape from the hardships of life through daydreams. However, even these seemingly defenseless people, if they embark on the right course, can reach the highest peaks of success. The Chinese call this the *metal hand*; it has astrological affinities with Venus.

Other types

More types may be added to Carus's classification for a study in greater detail. We will concentrate on the structure of the

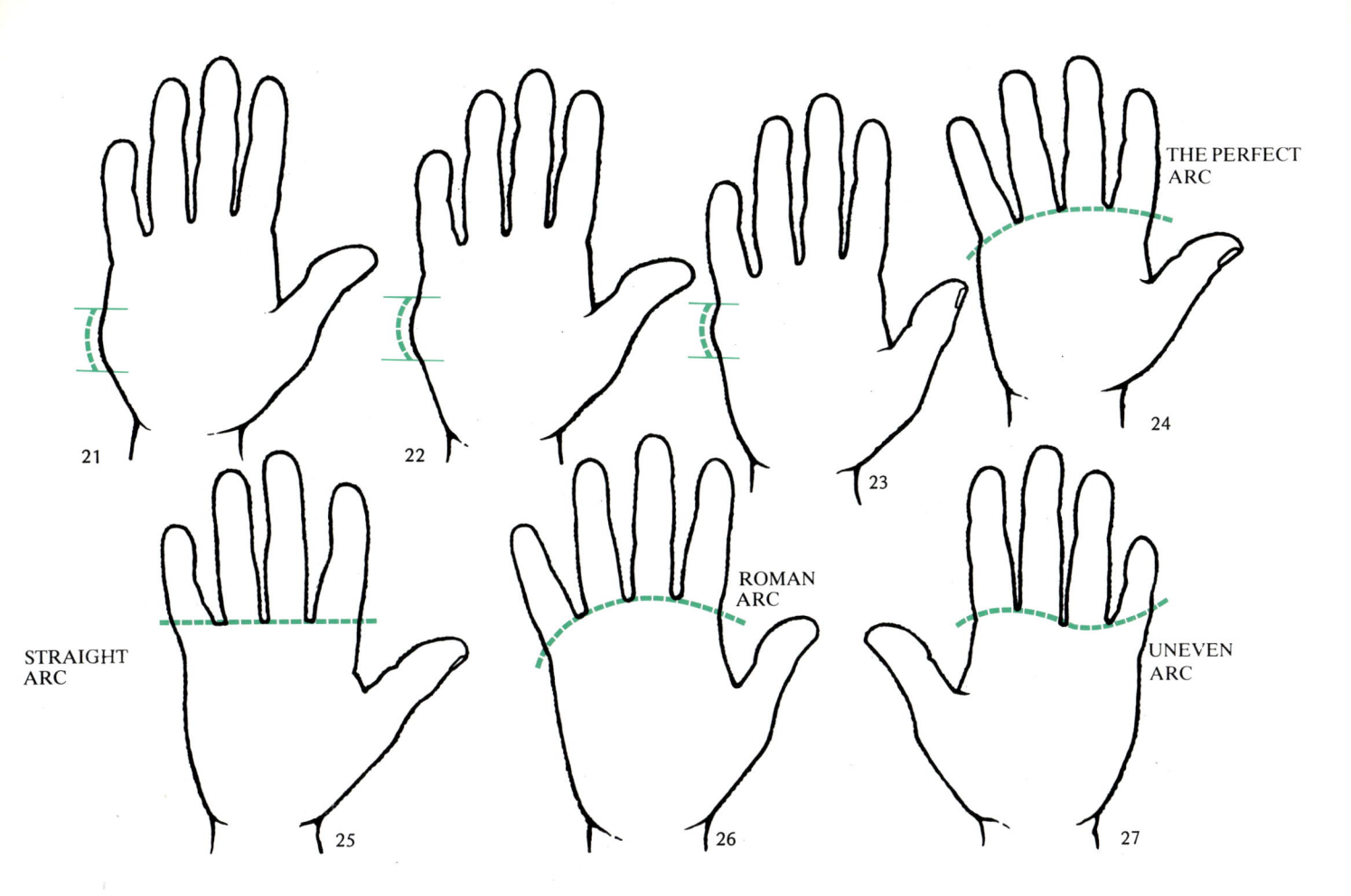

Summit beneath the passive mount of Mars (21), summit coinciding with the passive mount of Mars (22), summit above the passive mount of Mars (23), the perfect arc (24), straight arc (25), rounded or Roman arc (26), uneven arc (27).

palm, the shape of the fingers, and the relationship between the fingers and the palm. These types, together with the four types of hands described already, will help to extend our knowledge with appropriate interpolations and comparisons.

The narrow hand (*14*). This is how we describe a hand with a markedly long and narrow palm regardless of the shape of the fingers. It belongs exclusively to the psychic or motoric hand, and denotes a tendency toward solitude and working alone rather than in a group. Persons with a narrow hand instinctively avoid crowded, noisy places. They possess qualities that allow them to achieve real success though it may cost them much effort.

The wide hand (*15*). This is the opposite of the preceding type and is found only among elementary and sensitive hand types. It is indicative of a generous nature, a love of the countryside, and of good food. People with wide palms are rarely shy and are often in trouble because they put too much trust in their neighbours. These are people who are almost always well liked and tend to assume protective, paternalistic attitudes. They need to be active and busy and they cannot tolerate prolonged periods in stuffy, restricted places.

The square hand (*16*). The palm of this hand is almost a perfect square: the distance between the attachment point of the middle finger and the base of the palm is the same as the distance between the base of the index finger and the little finger. This hand can be found in each of Carus's four types or categories. It denotes a lively wit and sense of responsibility. Persons with a square palm can represent security and a guarantee of continuity. They are open and loyal.

The spatulate hand (*17*). The palm of this type of hand is shaped like a trapezoid whose upper side, at the base of the fingers, is the longer. It is typical of people who live on nervous energy and always make the maximum effort, displaying unexpected endurance. Their behaviour often causes annoyance, resulting in arguments and incomprehension.

The conic hand (*18*). In this case the palm is

shaped like an upside-down trapezoid when compared with the spatulate hand. The longer side is at wrist level. This hand denotes a lack of imagination and a near inability to break away from a very concrete, realistic attitude. These people are usually energetic in their work, dynamic, but not very enterprising. In fact they are excellent executors and organizers, but rarely originators.

The curve of creativity

Another important aspect of the palm which deserves mention is the shape of the *outer edge* (*19*). By outer edge we mean the curved outline of the hand extending from the tip of the little finger to the wrist, just skirting the mount of the Moon. There is, of course, an outer edge for both the left hand and the right. This line, also called the *curve of creativity* or the *curve of strength*, can be very or slightly pronounced and its most prominent point is called the *summit*. The significance of the summit varies according to its location.

1. If the summit is located on the lower part of the palm near the mount of the Moon (*20*), it means that the person's strength and energy take a predominantly physical form.
2. If the summit is higher, but below the passive mount of Mars (*21*), the subject shows a good balance between physical and moral strength, and is gifted with endurance and authority. He lacks a sense of fairness, however.
3. If the summit coincides with the passive mount of Mars (*22*), this means that the subject possesses remarkable strength of character, but lacks physical energy and does not bear up under pressure.
4. If the summit is above the passive mount of Mars (*23*), the subject's energy is purely psychic; he loses himself in an elaborate fantasy world and has almost no practical sense.

In comparing both hands one frequently notes differences in the location and prominence of the summit of the curve of strength. If the summit is more apparent on the left hand, the subject has more psychic than physical energy, and this can serve to correct information already acquired. If the summit is more pronounced on the right hand, the subject has increased the practical use of his energy thanks to stimulation from the outside world.

The arc

Finally we need to look briefly at another aspect that can add some interesting information to our study. The point at which the four fingers (index, middle, ring, and little) are joined to the palm is called the arc (*24*). In chirognomy it means the imaginary line that joins the four points of intersection with the fingers. There are three types of arc.

1. A nearly *straight line* (*25*), which is not very common. It indicates a person who is very sure of himself, who does not admit that he is capable of making mistakes, and does not tolerate any opposition. He does not take account of risk due to foolhardiness, but is nevertheless able to accept discipline if it fits in with his ethical principles.
2. The so-called *Roman arc* (*26*), which is like a rounded arch. A person with a Roman arc enjoys a harmonious psychophysical balance; he tries to establish harmonious relationships with those around him and is able to bring out the best in himself. He is coherent and constant in his undertakings, but he is not conservative; in fact, his outlook is oriented towards the future. He is willing to accept innovations which he considers valid, but these are almost never the fruits of his own imagination.
3. An *uneven* arc forming an irregular line (*27*). The base of the index finger and that of the little finger are not on the same line. This irregular arc is found in subjects who are not very objective in their opinions, never quite sure of themselves, and often doubtful about their own abilities. They are, however, able to go against the tide, which is typical of people who are not well balanced. They sometimes achieve success with great effort.

The fingers

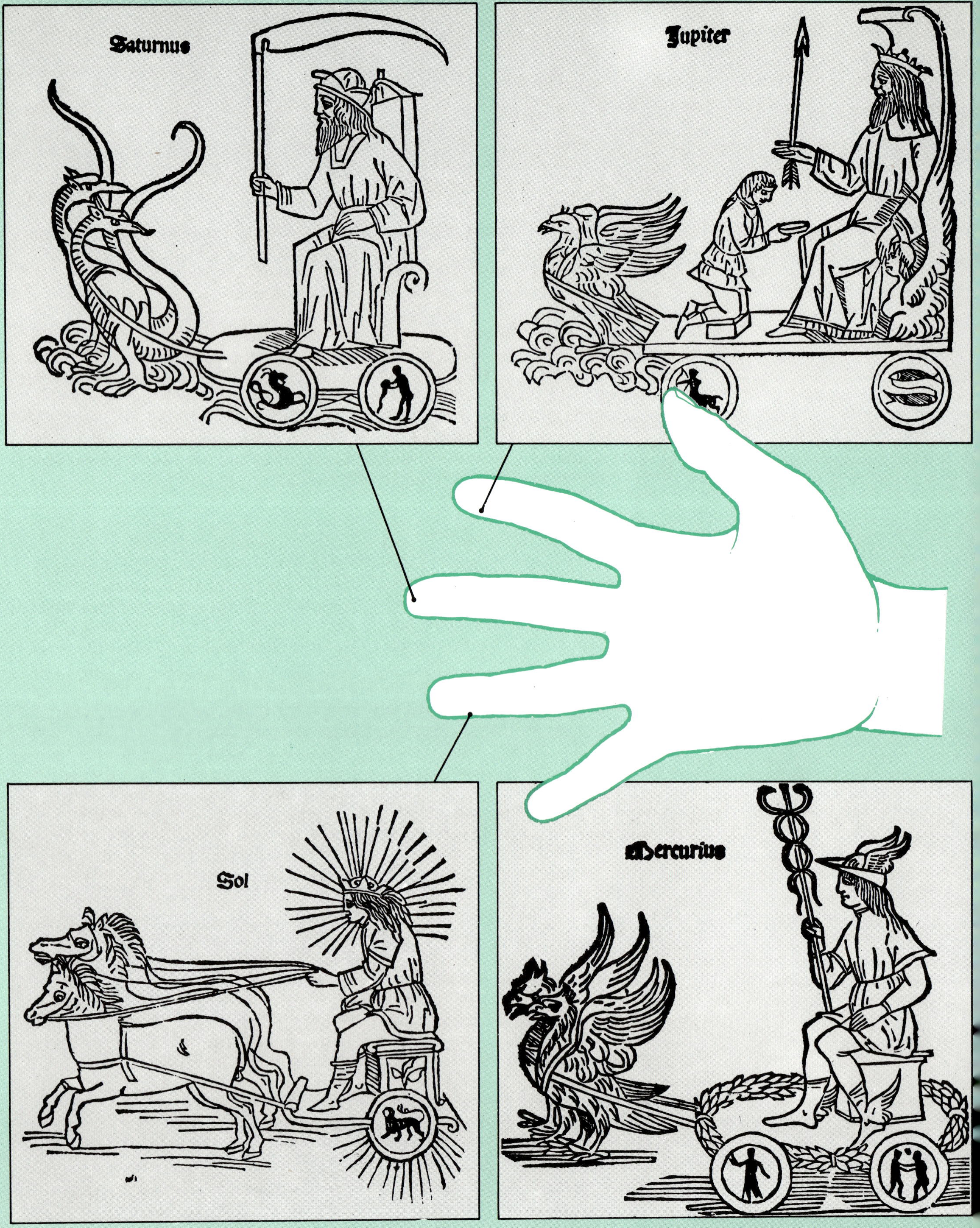
Saturnus
Jupiter
Sol
Mercurius

The fingers and the world of reason

The fingers represent a key element in chirognomy. A thorough knowledge of them is essential to the study of palmistry and allows easy and reliable access to ideas of great importance. Studying the fingers is not easy because the differences between the various shapes are not as clearly defined as one might expect. One can make mistakes, especially if one lacks experience. This chapter should therefore be read with care.

In dividing the hand into *three worlds*, the fingers quite rightly represent the first, the spiritual world, the area devoted to reason. Only in mankind have the fingers reached a spiritual level of development, differentiating humanity from all other life forms. To make this study more logical and easier, we shall lead off with a classification that allows a clear view of this very sensitive area and gives answers that are almost always valid. We say "almost always" because we may *interpret* wrongly, which can occur with any aspect of the hand. The basic theoretical information is never wrong—it is our ability to evaluate it that is sometimes faulty. Indeed, as we now enter a fairly exacting phase of palmistry we must bear in mind the possibility of error, the danger of giving a reckless or hasty opinion and the likelihood of having neglected or underestimated a detail that could prove important. Although these anxieties ought not actually stifle one's initiative, they should prevent too lighthearted an approach. Always remember that the person having his palm read, whether he appears to be open-minded or claims to be cynical about the value of the reading, will somehow be affected, perhaps even swayed, and awaits the palmist's words with a mixture of curiosity and awe.

If one wishes, one could, even at this stage, attract attention in a drawing room or among a group of people by putting into practice the ideas set forth thus far. One could make some surprising pronouncements about someone in the group by rapidly observing some of the more obvious characteristics of that person's hand. It might be entertaining but it is not advisable, especially for someone who intends to take up the art of palmistry with any degree of seriousness. As a game or pastime it can create a certain impression, but a facile, superficial approach risks disappointment and association with the gypsy atmosphere unjustly attributed to palmistry, one which we would like to dispel.

For us the hand has five fingers, but for the palmist it has only four; because of its importance the thumb requires special consideration of its own. According to William Benham, author of some very important books on palmistry, "The thumb cannot be called a finger because it is much more." Moreover its significance in the evolution of man is so fundamental that an entire book would be needed just to define it in the broadest terms.

Let us then first look at the other four fingers. They are: the *index finger*, also called the *finger of Jupiter*, the *middle finger* or *finger of Saturn*, the *ring finger* or *finger of Apollo* or *the Sun*, and the *little finger*, also called the *finger of Mercury*. These names again reinforce palmistry's relationship to astrology. In fact in chirognomy the astrological name for each finger corresponds to the precise meaning of the planet whose name it bears. (The relationship between palmistry and astrology could be explored in a more detailed and complex manner, but that would take us beyond our subject.)

In concise terms, the sphere of the personality belongs to the thumb; ambition to the index finger; cerebral activity, travelling, and knowledge to the middle finger; impulses of the soul and the sphere of propriety to the ring finger; and parental and sexual love to the little finger.

But before analyzing each finger in detail, let us add some general remarks about the fingers collectively, which will recapitulate, or in some cases expand, points touched on previously.

Flexibility

To determine whether the fingers are flexible, and to what extent, the subject should stand and place his fingertips on a flat surface (if he is seated, the wrist cannot rotate freely). Pressing lightly, begin to rotate the wrist until the palm rests flat on the surface. Note flexibility in the joints: between the first and second phalanges (*a*);

An allegorical representation of the four fingers of the chirologist (the thumb is considered to be much more than a finger): the index finger, or finger of Jupiter; the middle finger, or finger of Saturn; the ring finger, or finger of Apollo or the Sun; the little finger, or finger of Mercury.

Examples of suppleness: top, normal suppleness; center, very supple; bottom, slightly supple. Opposite, an example of total suppleness.

On page 36 top left, the right hand of Saint Nicholas, *tempera on wood, an icon from the early sixteenth century from the Monastery of Curtea de Arges in the Valacca region of Rumania (Bucharest, Museum of the Monastery of Antim); top right, the hand of God in a fresco originally from St. Clement of Tahull, now in the Museum of Art of Catalonia, Barcelona; bottom left, detail of hands from* St. Matthew and the Angel, *painted by Caravaggio, in the church of San Luigi dei Francesi in Rome; bottom right, hand pointing to the dead Christ on the cross, detail from the* Crucifixion *by the German painter Mattias Grünewald (Colmar, Unterlinden Museum). On page 37, detail of hands from the* Madonna of the Magnificat *by Raphael (Florence, Uffizi).*

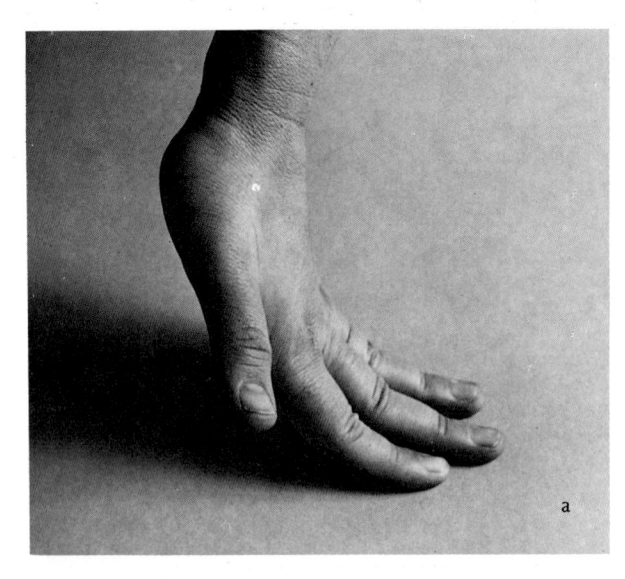

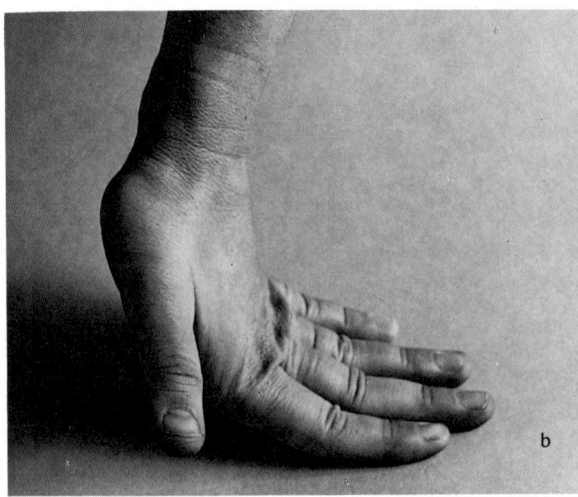

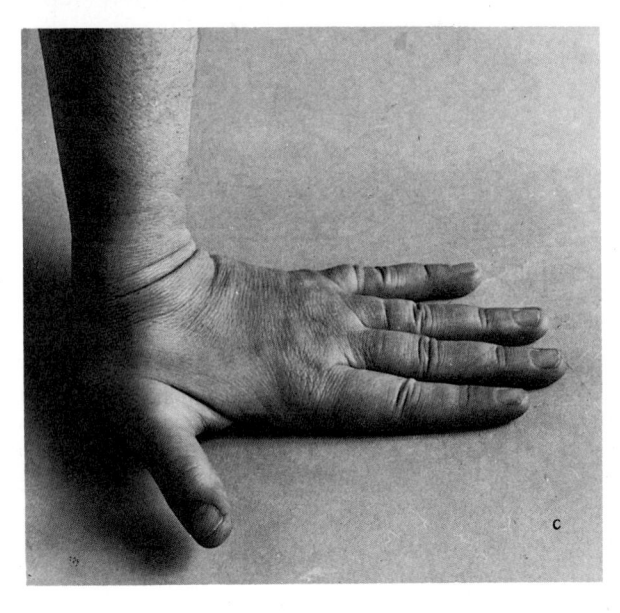

between the second and third phalanges (*b*); last, at the line of the *arc* (*c*). Flexibility in position (*c*) indicates that the subject is potentially well balanced and very adaptable. Will power is not his outstanding trait, but he is not necessarily weak-willed. Flexibility in position (*b*) signifies that the subject has a lot of common sense. In position (*a*), when there is flexibility between the second and first phalanges, we can say with considerable certainty that the subject is open-minded, receptive to new ideas, and willing to experiment. If flexibility is particularly evident in the ring finger, this means that the subject has a highly developed artistic sense.

As for fingers that are not flexible, see the preceding pages.

Length

Fingers are measured in relation to the palm, which is measured from the base of the middle finger to the wrist joint (*28*). If the fingers are longer than eighty per cent. the length of the palm, they are considered *long*; if they are less than eighty per cent., they are considered *short*. These measurements should not be taken as hard and fast. In questionable cases an overall evaluation, supported by other data drawn from the rest of the reading, will resolve any doubts. With that in mind we can classify the fingers thus:

Long and slender (*29*): these are typical of persons in whom idealism, imagination and superficiality predominate over the material and practical.

Long and thick (*30*): the subject has strong idealistic tendencies, with visionary aspirations, and a poetic view of the world, but is tempered by a certain realism that takes into account the advantages of material comforts.

Short and fat (*31*): indicates a total lack of idealistic aspirations and is typical of people who place the highest value on the material pleasures of life, such as comforts and good food. If they achieve their aims or riches, they may become art collectors, not just because it represents a good investment but because ownership of beautiful and rare objects fills them with such pride and satisfaction that they feel important and cultured.

Short and thin (*32*): this type of person is

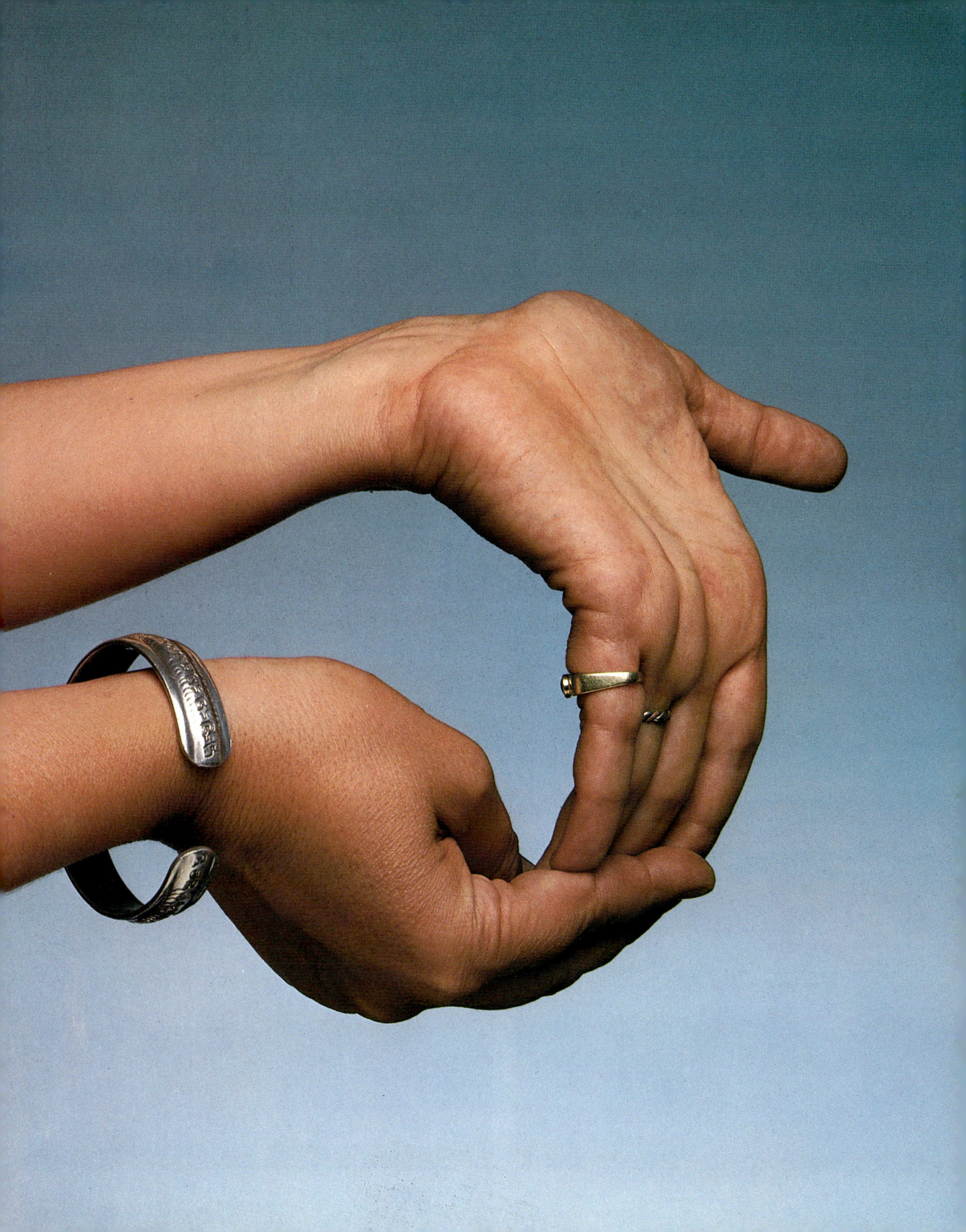

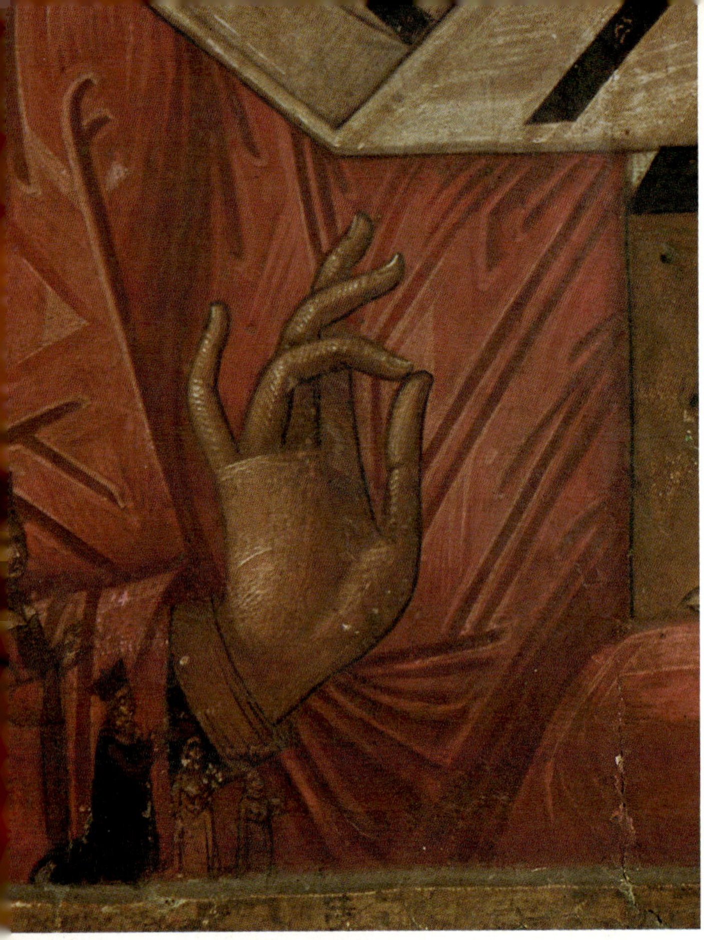

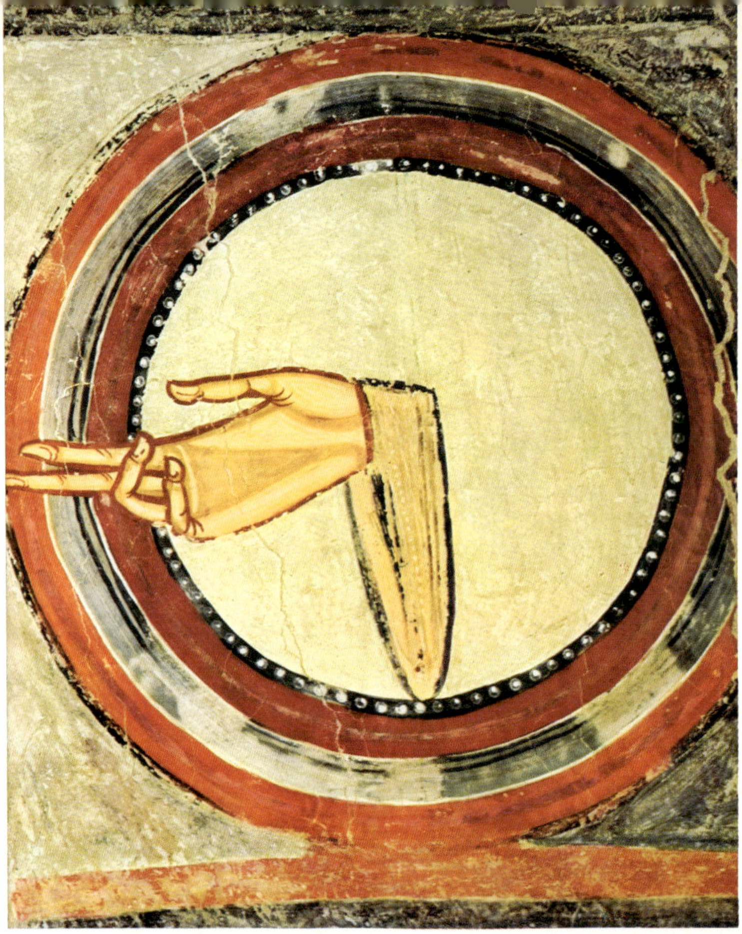

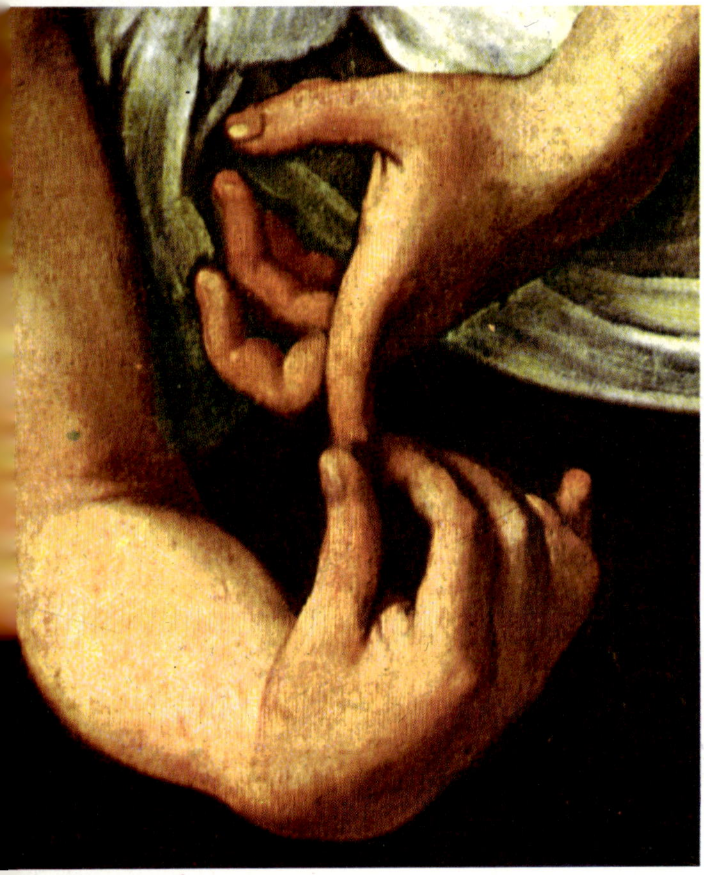

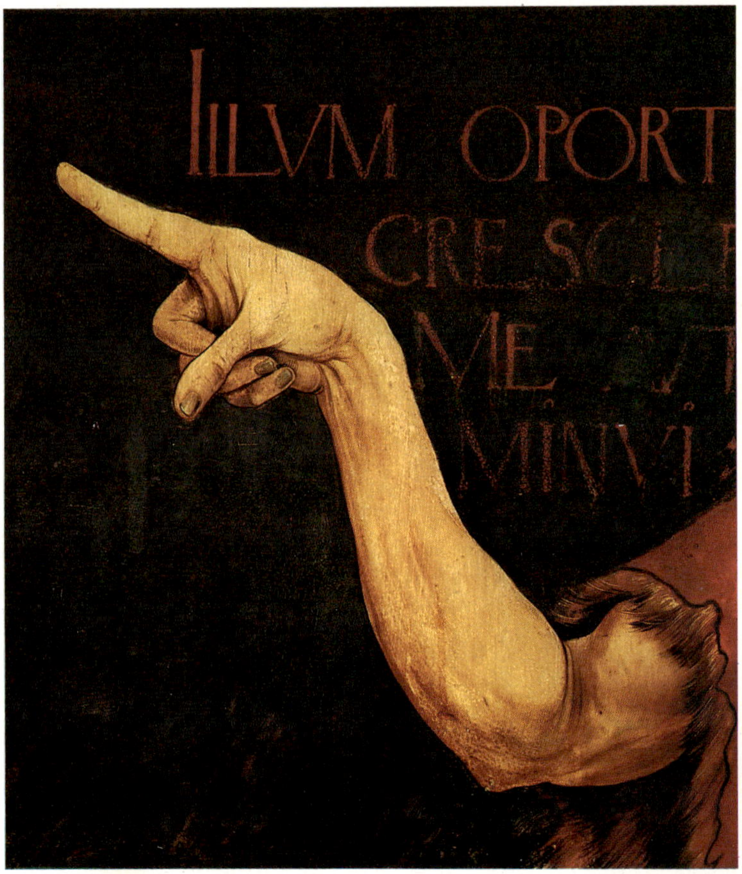
ILLVM OPORT
CRESC
ME
MINVI

Magnificat a[n]i[m]a
mea d[omi]ni...
...avit sp[iritu]s...
salutari m[eo]...
humilita[tem]...
...ecce e[ni]m...
...me dicent om[nes]...

Quia

LA MAIN PUISSANTE ❋ LA MANO PODEROSA

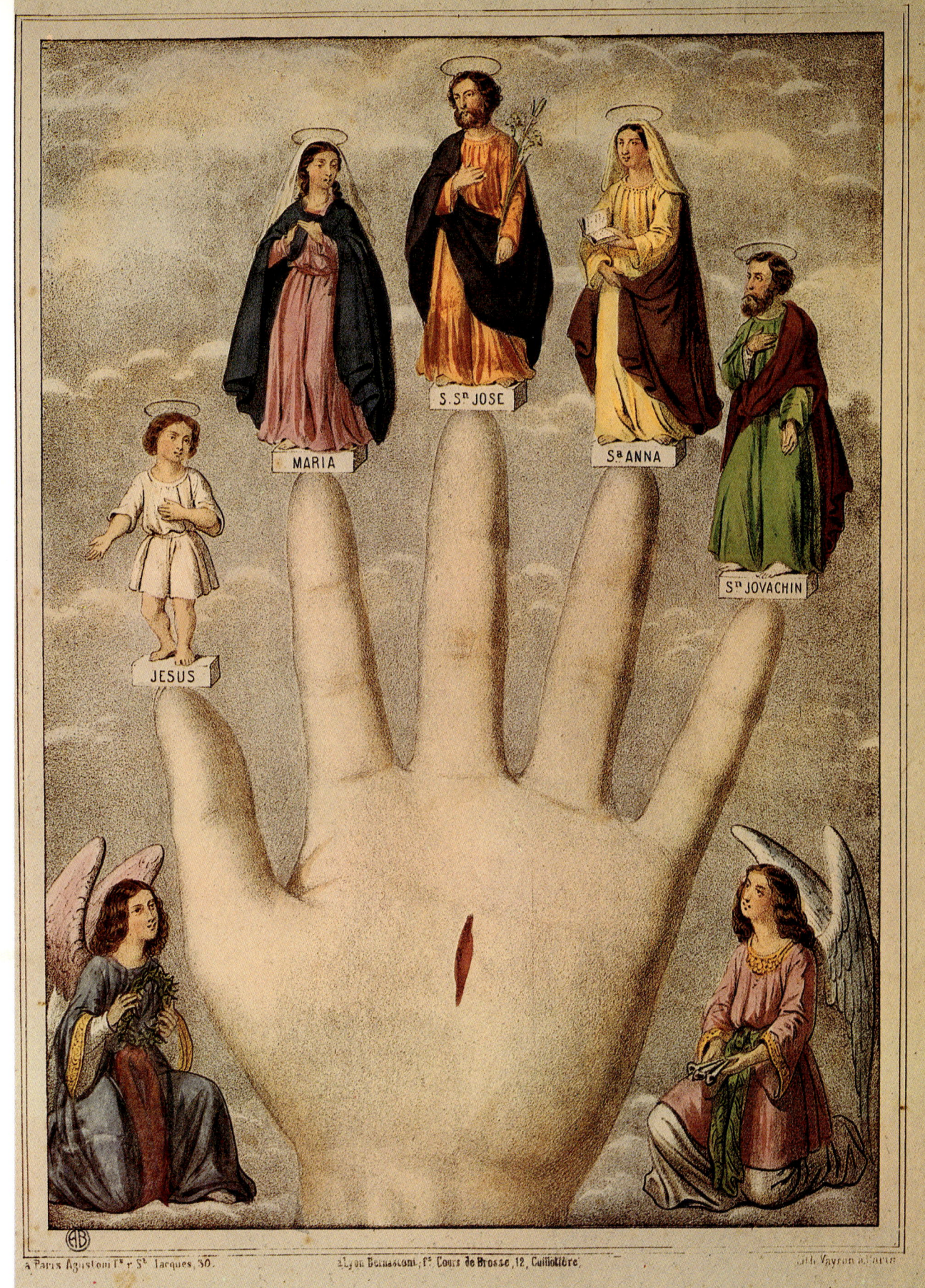

La Mane Potenta

The Mighty Hand, a popular print published in Rome in 1825 (Civica Raccolta delle Stampe "Bertarelli," Milan).

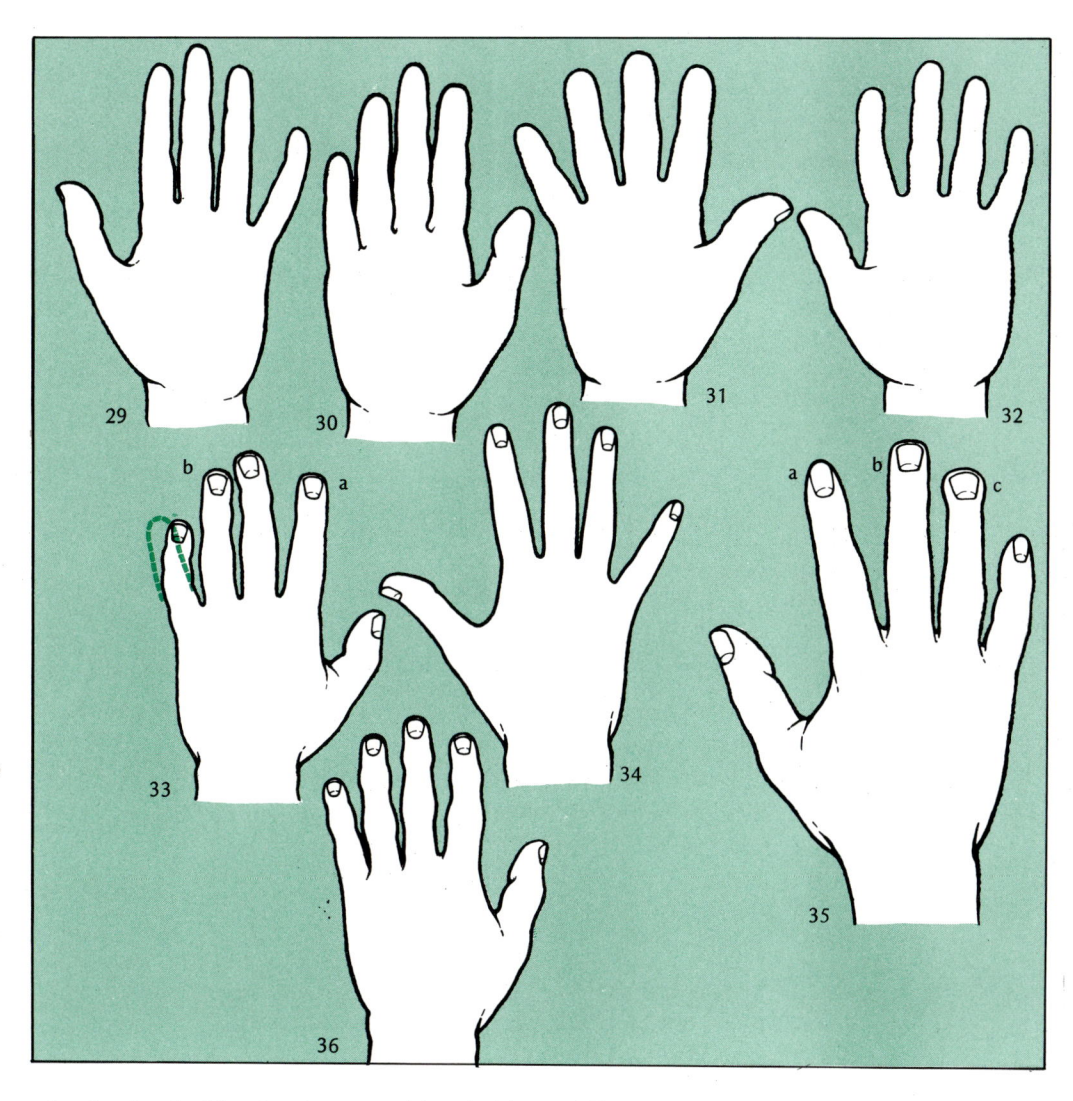

Length of fingers (28): for fingers to be considered long, AB must be greater than eighty per cent of BC; if AB is less than eighty per cent of BC, the fingers are considered short.
Different types of fingers: long and thin (29), long and thick (30), short and fat (31), short and thin (32), straight (33a), crooked (33b), smooth (34), pointed (35a), square (35b), spatulate (35c), knotty (36).

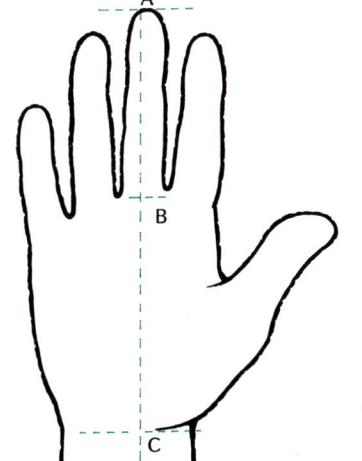

destined to hold a dominant position in his chosen milieu. He will always be able to take control of a situation and readily assume responsibility when required, and never be afraid to face critical or delicate situations.

Straight and crooked (33): this type will be discussed later in detail when we look at each finger individually, for each finger has its own special significance. Generally speaking, straight fingers are typical of people who are happy with the kind of life they have chosen, who have a good opinion of themselves, and do not see any particular reason for worry or any specific dangers. If the fingers are crooked, setbacks and short-term complications can be foreseen, the nature of which varies from finger to finger; these will be discussed later.

Fingers can also be either *smooth* or *knotty*.

Smooth fingers (34): people with smooth fingers can instantly grasp the essence of a situation, organize apparently disparate elements that when put together provide the key to a problem or relationship. Such people are endowed with intuition rather than reasoning ability and display remarkable artistic sensitivity. Frequently they are dilettantes of a very high standard. In these cases the shape of the fingertips is determinant. If they are pointed (*35a*), the subject is inclined, through laziness, to submit to externally imposed situations. If the fingertips are square (*35b*), the subject has a more practical and rational approach to life. If the fingertips are spatulate (*35c*), the creative spirit will predominate.

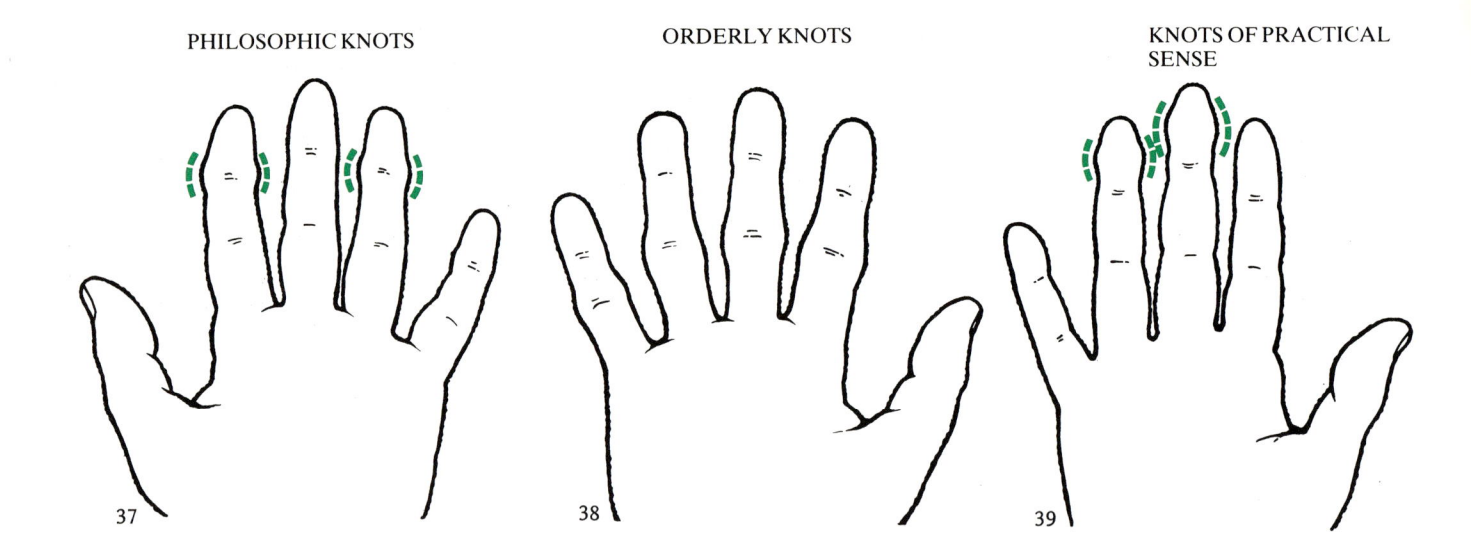

PHILOSOPHIC KNOTS   ORDERLY KNOTS   KNOTS OF PRACTICAL SENSE

Knotty fingers: philosophical (37); orderly (38), at the joint between the second and third phalanges; common sense (39).

Knots

The presence of knots in the fingers (*36*), usually at the joints, indicates a tendency to reflect, prudence, and a serious approach to situations. Hence knots are found mainly on mature or elderly people and are rather rare on the young or very young. All the fingers of a hand may not have knots, and in this case each finger has to be considered separately because the meaning of each knot depends on its location.

There are three types of knots:

The *philosophical knot* (*37*): found at the joint between the first and second phalanges. In general it indicates a tendency toward fussiness, a meticulous concern with detail, a need to verify more than once that everything is in order. This attitude arises from a distrustful nature, ill disposed toward anything new whether practical or ideological. Such people have deep-rooted convictions and it is difficult to change their opinions. If the philosophical knot is located on the index finger, it indicates a profound distrust of one's fellow man, including persons to whom one is bound by affection.

The *orderly knot* (*38*): located at the joint between the second and third phalanges. It signifies that the subject has clear ideas, an orderly and precise mind, and a good memory, sometimes even a photographic memory. This applies even when the appearance of the subject or his lifestyle is not at all orderly, which might deceive the hasty observer.

The *common sense knot* (*39*): less frequently found and located towards the tip of the finger, above the joint between the first and second phalanges. Whatever the general shape of the hand may be, the presence of this knot emphasizes the subject's practical nature and efficient, logical approach. In some cases the person has the ability to invent new techniques to improve the practical output of an activity.

The fingertips

For the most complete reading of a hand it is very important to know what significance chirognomy assigns to the fingertips. As we have already mentioned, fingers can be pointed, conic, square or spatulate. Following is a general description of each type.

Pointed fingers (*40*): these are the logical terminations of long, tapered fingers, emphasizing the refined tendencies and spirituality of the subject despite traces of superficiality that reduce the common sense aspects. If a soft, flabby hand with a weak thumb and a tendency to whitish colour has pointed fingertips, it is an indication of chronic illness, mainly rheumatic and cardiac.

Conic fingers (*41*): if the fingertip is like a truncated cone, that is, the joint between the second and first phalanges is slightly wider than the tip of the finger, which is slightly rounded, it is termed conic. It is a very positive characteristic and denotes a person of keen intelligence, a well-developed critical sense, and a good sense of humour. The conic shape is frequently found on professional people, high ranking executives and artisans with artistic inclinations. One aspect of these persons' temperaments is a marked feeling for the arts, especially music and painting, so that they are often considered amateur connoisseurs. They are refined and idealistic as well, but not to the extent of giving up the comforts of life. If necessary, they can often roll up their sleeves and do their share.

Like artists with whom they share various traits, they often have nonconformist attitudes and are intolerant of repetitive tasks and bureaucratic excesses.

Square fingers (*42*): we say square for fingertips whose shape is fairly square around the nails, when these are cut short. We are dealing here with persons whose practicality and good sense are their dominant qualities. They are disciplined and demand the same behaviour of others. They need security and stability for themselves as well as for those they love. They are methodical, but this does not necessarily mean they are boring; they have an innate sense of order and organization, and they express themselves clearly and confidently. A square finger with an active mount of Mars, which indicates physical courage, or a passive mount of Mars, which indicates moral courage, identifies a subject who can, if circumstances require, espouse the cause of freedom or the rights of the community in which he lives and identify with these ideals to the point of sacrifice. Such people are usually capable and honest administrators.

Spatulate fingers (*43*): the tip of the finger is wider than the joint between the first and second phalanges. This type of finger is found in hyperactive people, those continually on the move and continually looking for tasks that will keep them busy. Travelling is never a problem for them, and they appear not to feel tired by all their

The fingertips: pointed (40), conic (41), square (42), spatulate (43), mixed (44), the "drop of water" (45).

POINTED FINGERS

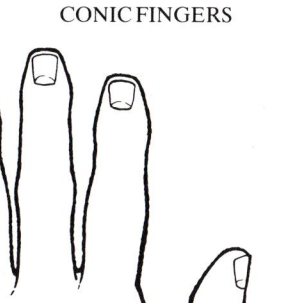

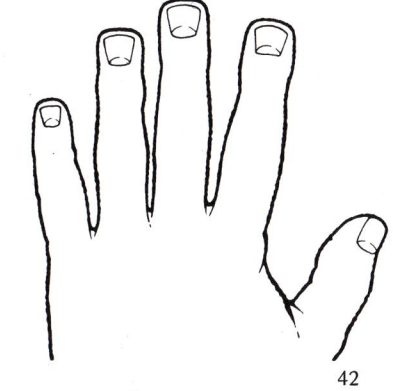

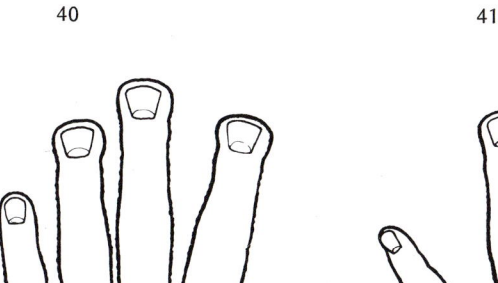

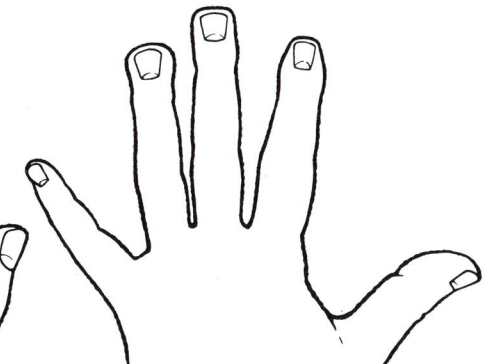

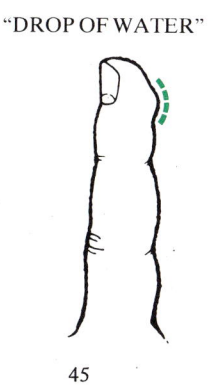

CONIC FINGERS

SQUARE FINGERS

40

41

42

"DROP OF WATER"

43

44

45

SPATULATE FINGERS

MIXED FINGER

41

activity. They usually start planning a new project before the first one is completed. They can never wait for things to happen and prefer to make the first move in order to assess a situation and possibly take control. They do not always succeed in their objectives, but this does not make them change their attitude. In extreme cases the person can constitute a danger to himself and to those around him because his love of risk and the unknown very often lead him to take unnecessary chances or to try his luck, often recklessly, at games of chance.

Mixed fingers (*44*): this kind of hand has different fingertips or is not easily classified as one of the types described above. This means the subject has multiple tendencies, although these need not cause inner conflicts. In the majority of cases it means a lack of specialization, either because of too much versatility or impatience at having only one course to pursue. These persons usually possess the ability to succeed in more than one profession and their choice is habitually left to chance or circumstance. They are naturally adaptable and therefore excel in activities that bring them into contact with other people and in which they can exercise their natural ability to evaluate other people's personalities. They can undertake a vast range of professions, from sales to diplomacy. When encountering these cases, make a very careful examination of the hand's other characteristics to establish the useful tendencies with maximum accuracy.

The drop of water
Before concluding our investigation of this one area, the first phalange, we must look at a very infrequent but rather interesting characteristic occasionally found on the opposite side of the nail, the fleshy part of the fingertip. This is usually smooth and rounded, but in some cases it forms a small cusp which, seen from the side, resembles a drop of water, hence its name in chirognomy. The drop of water (*45*) indicates exceptional tactile sensitivity. A person who has it receives a much more complete impression from contact with an object than is normally acquired by touch. In some cases these people can evaluate the authenticity of antiques, especially those made of wood, by sensing through touch the period in which they were made.

Hand symbolizing the precepts of Islam: profession of faith, prayer, pilgrimage, fasting, and charity (carved on an arch at the entrance to the Alhambra, Granada).

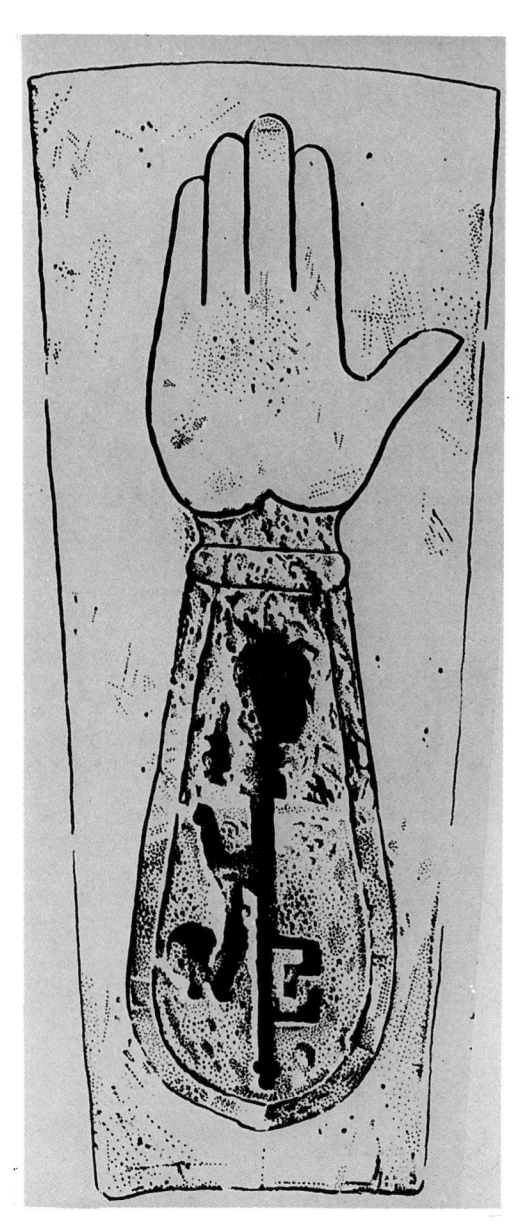

Opposite and on page 44, hand signs from a treatise on chiromancy by John Bulwer.

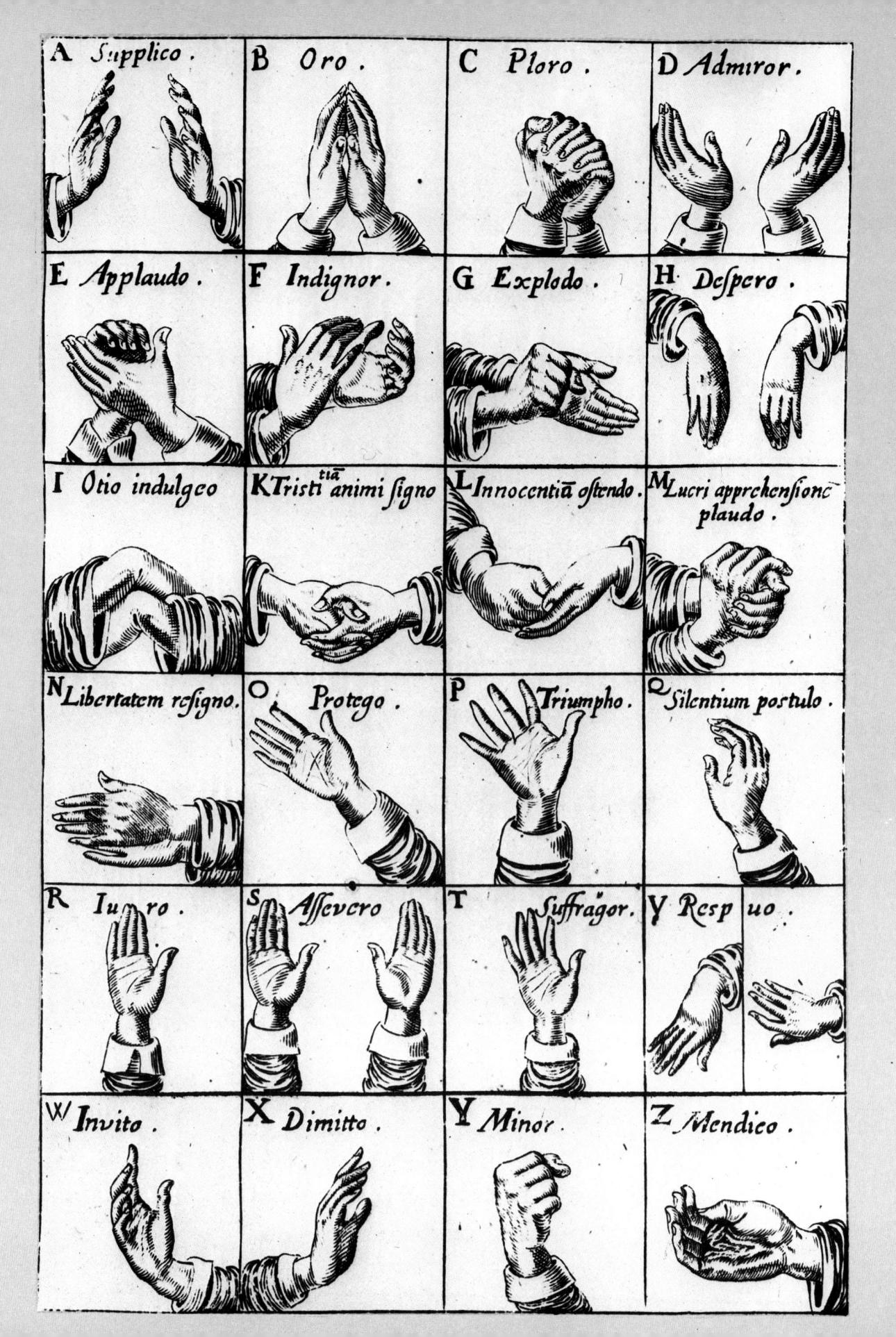

A Supplico.	**B** Oro.	**C** Ploro.	**D** Admiror.
E Applaudo.	**F** Indignor.	**G** Explodo.	**H** Despero.
I Otio indulgeo.	**K** Tristitiā animi signo.	**L** Innocentiā ostendo.	**M** Lucri apprehensionē plaudo.
N Libertatem resigno.	**O** Protego.	**P** Triumpho.	**Q** Silentium postulo.
R Iuro.	**S** Assevero.	**T** Suffragor.	**V** Respuo.
W Invito.	**X** Dimitto.	**Y** Minor.	**Z** Mendico.

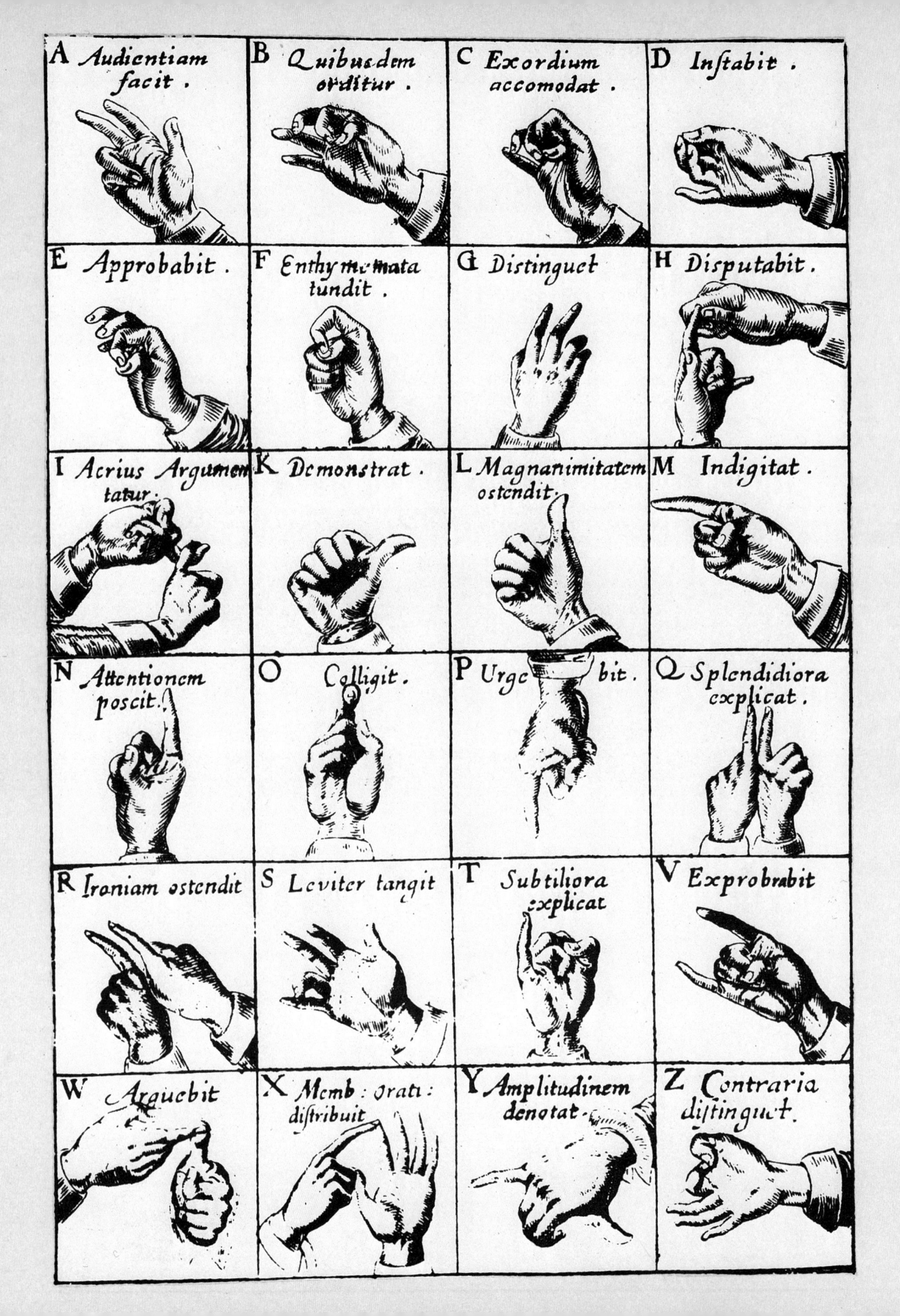

A Audientiam facit.	**B** Quibusdem orditur.	**C** Exordium accomodat.	**D** Instabit.
E Approbabit.	**F** Enthymemata tundit.	**G** Distinguet.	**H** Disputabit.
I Acrius Argumentatur.	**K** Demonstrat.	**L** Magnanimitatem ostendit.	**M** Indigitat.
N Attentionem poscit.	**O** Colligit.	**P** Urgebit.	**Q** Splendidiora explicat.
R Ironiam ostendit.	**S** Leviter tangit.	**T** Subtiliora explicat.	**V** Exprobrabit.
W Arguebit.	**X** Memb: orati: distribuit.	**Y** Amplitudinem denotat.	**Z** Contraria distinguet.

The thumb

The concepts that we have learned from our general examination of the fingers will now be applied to each individual finger. Each has its own peculiarities and brings new knowledge and information to the complex picture of the palmist's reading.

The thumb is more than a finger; we have it to thank or blame for our technological civilization. The position of the thumb—its autonomy with respect to the other fingers—and the important information it can provide have made it a subject of interest beyond the narrow confines of palmistry. As Sir Isaac Newton wrote, "In the absence of other proof, the thumb is enough to convince me of the existence of God," and according to the late-nineteenth-century French palmist Adrien Desbarolles, "It is mainly with the thumb that we absorb the vital fluid."

Of all the fingers only the thumb is autonomous, thus it has a very clear personality. We can derive information of great interest and importance from the mobility and "liveliness" of the thumb. There is little to quarrel about here; chirologists from different epochs, the most diverse localities, and with the most divergent ideas, are all in agreement over the importance of the thumb. It is interesting to note that many practitioners of chirosophy in China and to some extent in India confine their investigations almost exclusively to the thumb.

The particular importance of the thumb in describing someone's personality is confirmed by the telling fact that when a baby is born and is as yet without a personality, it holds its thumb against the palm of the hand, as do people whose intellectual development is retarded. There is also a tendency to hold the thumb this way at the moment of death.

The thumb is composed of two exposed phalanges and a third that is part of the palm and coincides with the mount of Venus (46). The first phalange, the one with the fingernail, has to do with the subject's will, spirit of initiative, and intuition. The second phalange tells about the subject's powers of logic, his judgement, and his reasoning ability. The third phalange indicates the subject's vitality and sexual drive. Even a not very expert palmist needs only a careful glance at the thumb to understand the type of person he is dealing with.

Further information can be drawn from the angle formed by the insertion of the two exposed phalanges in the palm of the hand (47). Normally the thumb can rotate in respect of the index finger at an angle of about ninety degrees. This means generally that the person is convinced of the validity of his own ideas and his own point of view and does not let himself be influenced too much by the opinions of others. However,

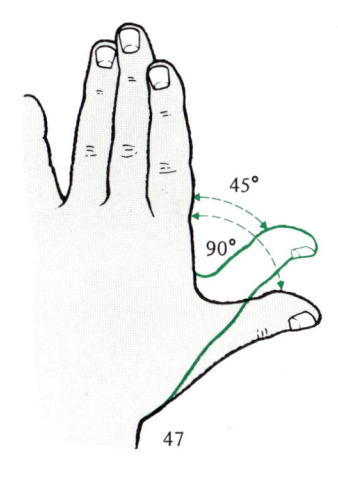

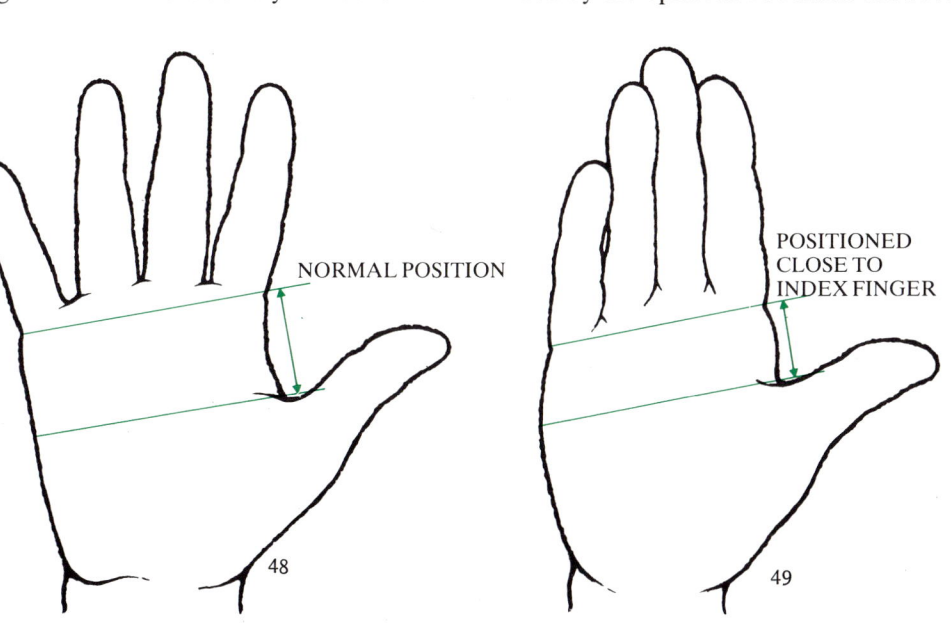

The thumb: the phalanges (46); its suppleness, determined by the angle of insertion in the palm (47); normal position (48); positioned close to the index finger (49).

Degrees of flexibility of the thumb (50): a *impulsive thumb,* b *rigid thumb,* c *flexible thumb; thumb with stiff joints (51).*

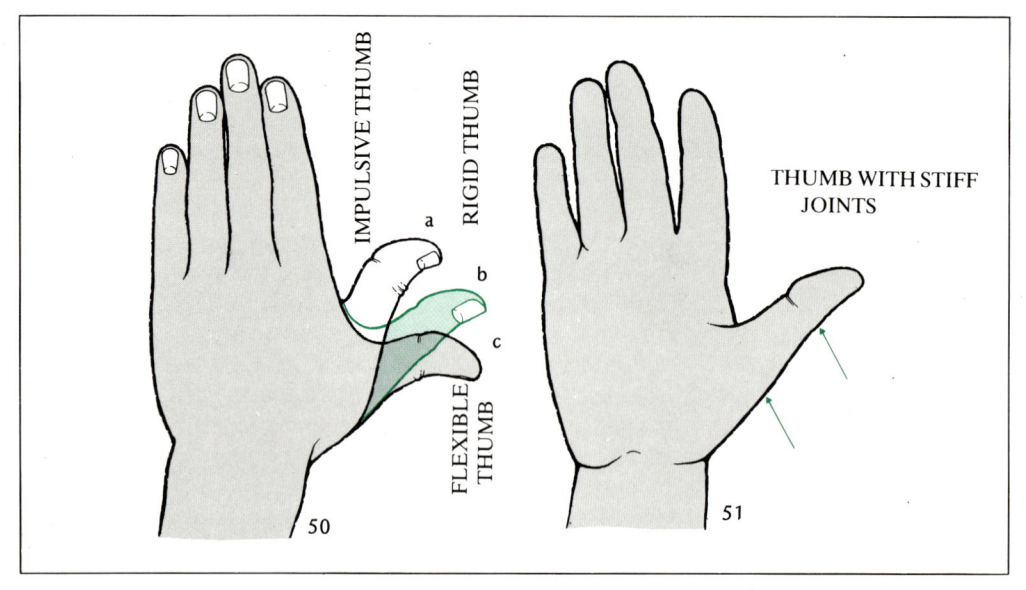

this trait, which is positive in certain respects, acts like a double-edged sword, because the subject behaves in the same way regardless of the nature of his ideas. If they are good, his behaviour is positive, but if they are bad, it is negative.

When the angle of the thumb and the index finger is less than ninety degrees, the subject is very easily influenced and may find himself swayed by another person's cogent arguments. Because the subject is very often a generous and reckless sort, he may be easily led by people with bad intentions.

Some other points concern the relative position of thumb and index finger, besides the angle that they form. The point at which they are joined can vary in distance from the joint of the index finger. If it is far away *(48),* the formation of the palm is certain to be very wide and open. Along with previously mentioned characteristics of the wide hand (page 29), we should in this case add the ability or tendency of the subject to tell others of his own view of life with whatever means are at his disposal—words, pictures, music, etc. It is a sign of egoism, even egocentrism, when the point of insertion of the thumb is very near the mount of Jupiter *(49).*

In examining the thumb, flexibility is a primary consideration; that is, the capacity to bend the first phalange backward toward the wrist. If there is little flexibility, if the thumb is rather stiff *(50),* the person is strong willed and has few scruples. If there is great flexibility in the joint between the first and second phalanges, then the subject is a potentially weak person. He is willing to accept the easiest way out of situations, with the excuse of not wanting to create problems and to please those nearest him; but the real reason is laziness or indifference. If both joints of the thumb are stiff *(51),* we have a conservative temperament, not reactionary but slow to accept innovations even if useful. These persons have remarkable tenacity in carrying out their own plans.

The next step is to determine the length of the thumb and the relationship between the two exposed phalanges. The most popular theory about the length of the thumb and its relationship in harmony with the other fingers suggests that the length should be the same, or almost the same, as that of the little finger *(52).* The thumb, therefore, will be regarded as *long* or *short* depending on whether it is longer or shorter than the little finger.

A long thumb *(53)* tends to reinforce the good points or failings that have already emerged from our other examinations of the thumb. A short thumb *(54)* always indicates weak character, someone who does not want to think for himself and who, if forced to do so, arrives at hasty and not very sound conclusions. However, these readings need to be seen in relation to the types of fingertips.

Much can be said about the relationship between the first two phalanges of the thumb, a key consideration in examining the thumb because it contains the most important information about the subject's character.

As we have pointed out, the first or nail phalange is related to the will and the second phalange to logic. If they are the same length (55), as is frequently the case, the person is fairly well balanced. Plans and the will to carry them out, desires and their realization, initiative and energy, exist in a positive relationship with good chances for success.

If the first phalange is longer than the second (56), which rarely happens, it is an indication of an authoritarianism that can become dangerous. The subject does not value logic and reason, his decisions are almost always based on intuition, with a disdain for any discussion or greater understanding. When the second phalange of the thumb is appreciably longer than the first (57), the person feels the need to reason things out. In such a case, frequent changes of mind are not due to a lack of self-confidence but to perfectionism. This attitude can impede the subject's initiative, becoming an obstacle to the practical application of his ideas.

How does this information about general character change when we take into account the shape of the tip of the thumb? Like all the other fingers, it may be:

Slender (58a): the tip of the thumb is almost the same size as the nail when cut short. It indicates great opportunism; the person in question always knows how to maneuver adroitly.

Pointed (58b): this person knows how to take advantage of opportunities and behaves diplomatically, more by instinct than by design.

Conic (58c): this type of tip signifies a lack of willpower, but only when the tip is very

Length of the thumb: perfect length (AB = CD) (52); long thumb (53); short thumb (54); thumb with first phalange (CD) the same length as second (AB) (55); thumb with first phalange (CD) longer than second (AB) (56); thumb with first phalange (CD) shorter than second (AB) (57).

The tip of the thumb (58): a *narrow,* b *pointed,* c *conic,* d *square,* e *spatulate (front view),* f *spatulate (side view),* g *bulbous (front view),* h *bulbous (side view),* i *nail phalange with well-developed knot,* j *nail phalange with short knot,* k *knot at the joint between first and second phalanges.*

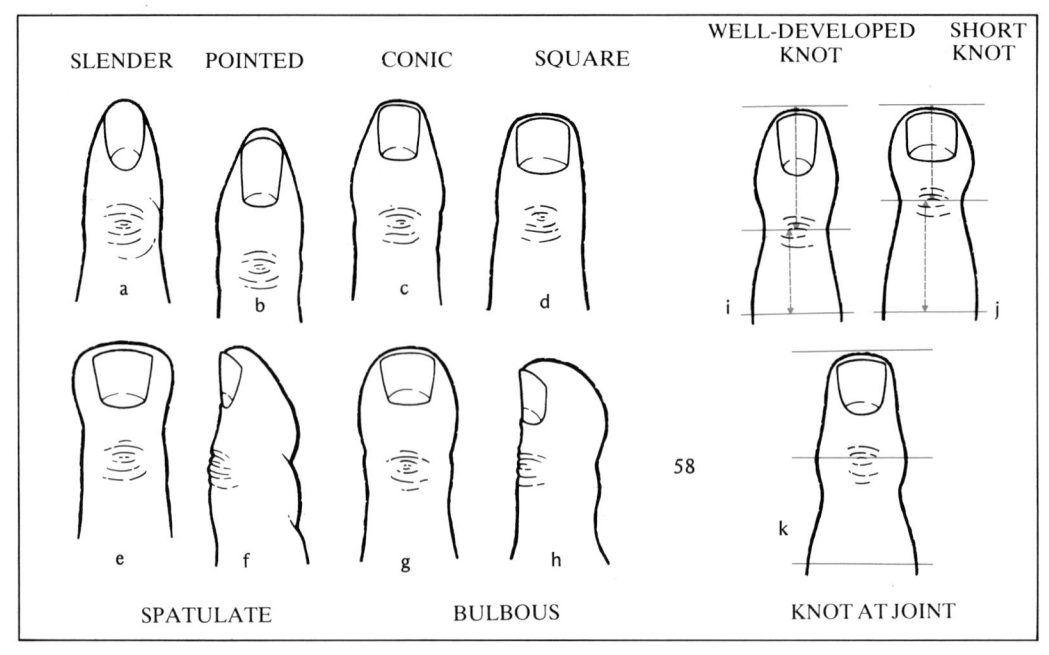

SLENDER	POINTED	CONIC	SQUARE	WELL-DEVELOPED KNOT	SHORT KNOT
a	b	c	d	i	j
e	f	g	h		k
SPATULATE		BULBOUS			KNOT AT JOINT

58

markedly conic; otherwise it does not indicate anything in particular.

Square (58d): this is rare. When the shape is very clearly defined, it signifies a propensity to stubborness.

Spatulate (58e, 58f): the traditional "potter's thumb." It is very common among those who in their profession or as artists require special tactile sensitivity.

Bulbous (58g, 58h): this type is not very common. The first phalange has a rounded shape; it is a bit stumpy, and in some cases the nail is distorted. It is a sign of obstinacy, cruelty, a tendency toward anger and violence, and a lack of reflection—the "assassin's thumb." Naturally all this can be modified by other elements that gradually emerge during the palmist's reading.

The joints of the thumb may also be important. With a well-formed nail phalange that is longer than the second phalange, an enlargement at the base of the nail (58i) indicates that the person has a high opinion of himself. Moreover, this is justified by the soundness of his insights and the determination with which he puts them into practice. If the phalange with such an enlargement is short and stumpy (58j), the subject will think too highly of his own opinions, which can sometimes result in obstinancy. In any case an enlargement of the joint at the base of the nail always means that the subject sticks very close to the facts and to his own problems, and is therefore able to make the right decisions.

Be careful to avoid any confusion with another of type of enlargement in the first phalange of the thumb. This appears at the joint between the first and second phalanges (58k), which makes it a little lower than the preceding one. In this case everything to be said about will, tenacity, and equilibrium will tend toward the extreme: The subject is often vulgar and boring, tenacity becomes stubbornness, and wilfulness turns into mulishness.

Here we must emphasize something mentioned earlier only in passing: a thorough examination of the thumb should be accompanied by an analysis of how it behaves, since the thumb has autonomous characteristics. A thumb that is agile and held away from the palm is typical of the person who knows how to adapt to life and handle situations. A thumb held close to the side of the hand denotes the opposite tendency, a person not happy with his way of life and who assumes the passive behaviour of one who would rather suffer than face the consequences of a decision. Or it may denote someone who has a disease that is coming to a head. People who frequently grip their thumbs inside their palms are very emotional and try, perhaps unconsciously, to cut themselves off from the world around them.

Opposite, the hand of David *by Michelangelo (Florence, Galleria dell'Accademia).*

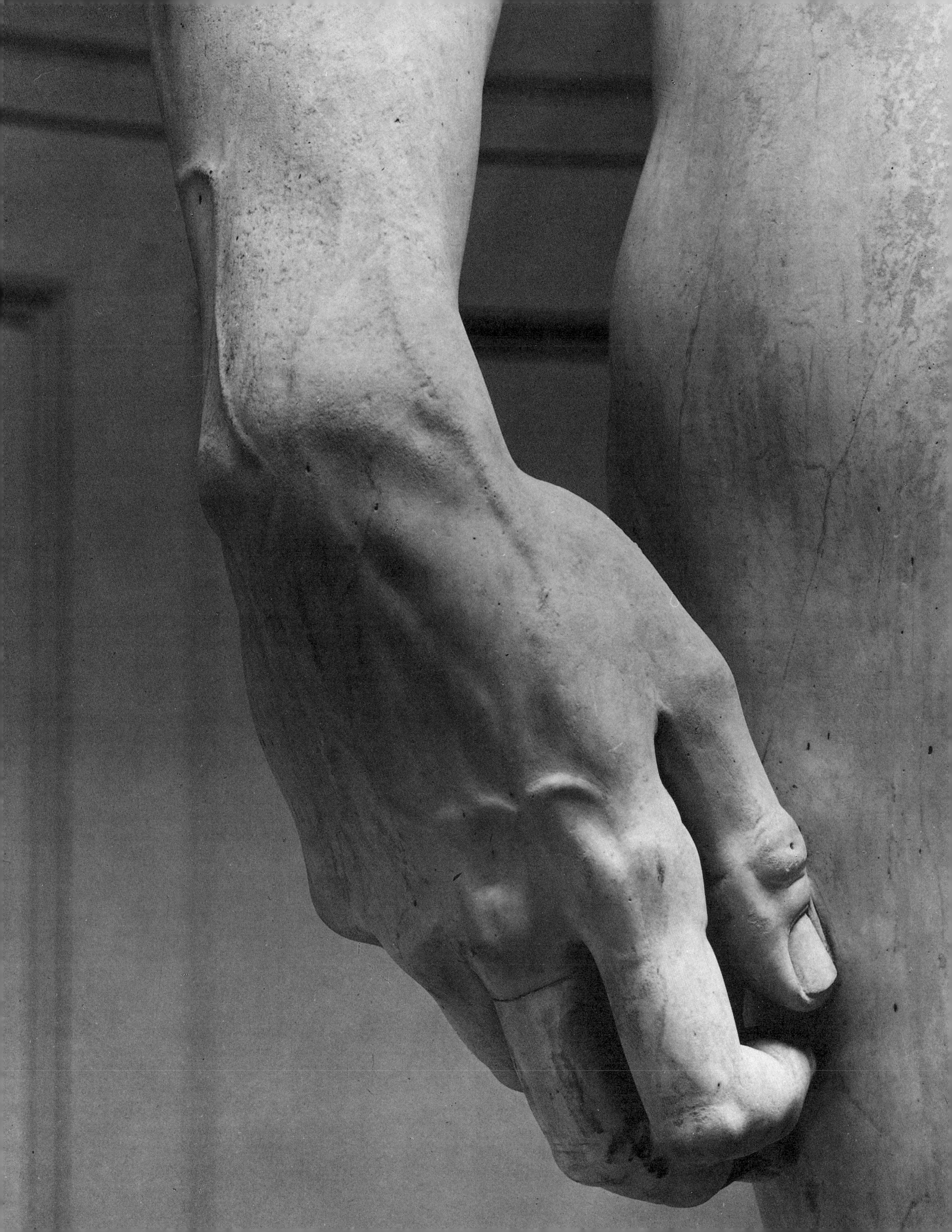

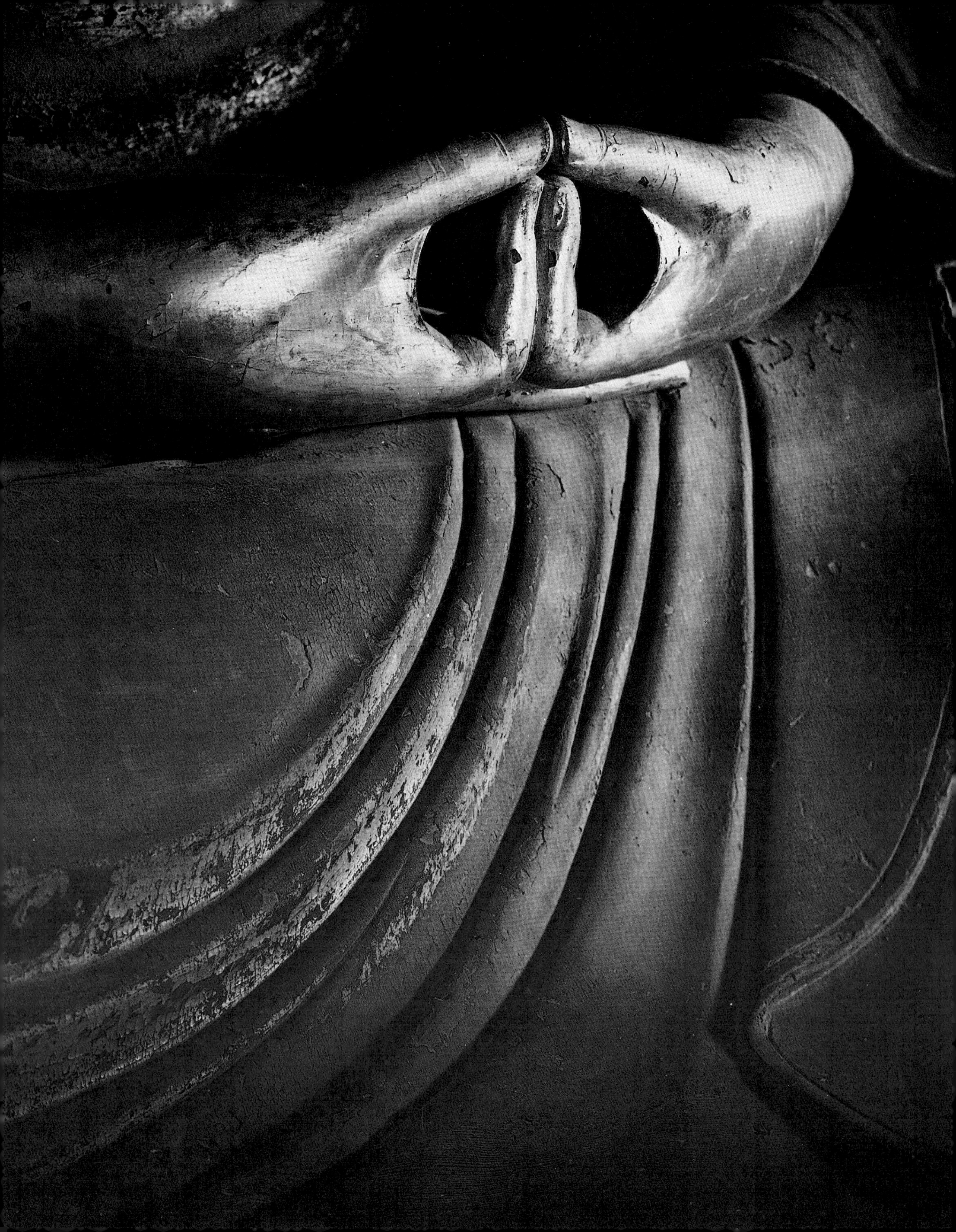

The other four fingers

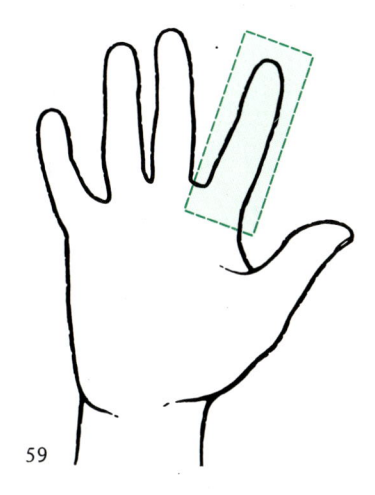

59

The index finger or finger of Jupiter or ambition (59) and the middle finger or finger of Saturn or equilibrium (60), from which can be learned, respectively, the ability of the subject to project himself outward and the degree of stability between the inner and outer selves.

The hands of Buddha Amida, statue in gilded wood by Jocho, a Japanese sculptor of the tenth century (Pavilion of the Phoenix, Uji, Kyoto prefecture, Japan).

We shall deal briefly with the remaining four fingers for two reasons. The information they provide is not vital and could be deduced from other observations. Further, through interpolation from preceding general remarks about the fingers we can obtain many very significant corrective elements for a thorough reading of the hand.

The index finger

Its name describes its purpose, which is to "indicate" the world around us. It allows us to understand how the subject, with aspirations and dreams of his own, relates to reality. In other words, it reflects the ability each of us has to project to the outside world the image we have of ourselves.

The index finger (*59*) is also called the finger of Jupiter or ambition (see page 32). We have had occasion to refer to it in our examination of the thumb because of the proximity of the two fingers. The index finger represents aspirations and tendencies; the thumb (which establishes a person's energy store) fixes the limits within which they can be achieved. Hence if the relationship between these two fingers is not harmonious, this can be the source of many psychological deviations. A long, thin index finger accompanied by a strong thumb (*61a*) means that the subject will go very far in life, depending on his aspirations. If the index finger is accompanied by a weak thumb (*61b*), the person will have difficulty in realizing his aims.

From what has been said so far it is clear that an evaluation of the index finger, like all the other fingers, must take into account the type of hand to which it belongs. The greater our understanding of the relationship between these two factors, the easier it will be to establish how successfully the subject has adapted to the demands of life.

Here then is some information about the index finger in particular that cannot be deduced from the general data already furnished.

A conic termination (*62*) suggests a greater adaptability to life than a trapezoidal termination (*63*). If the index finger has no knots, this indicates a remarkable ability to adapt to one's environment: if knots are present, adaptation has been slower owing to various reasons that can be discovered.

Similar considerations hold true with regard to the length and thinness of the index finger in comparison with the other fingers. If the index finger is very short (*64*), the subject is impatient and in a hurry to achieve the goals he has set for himself, but he suffers from a rather obvious inferiority complex and has little confidence in himself. If the index finger is very long (*65*), the subject will try to dominate situations; if it curves toward the middle finger (*66*), the subject has an immoderate desire for possessions, and should the curve be very pronounced, it can be a sign of kleptomania.

Some palmists believe that the index finger is an indication of a person's religious capacity. This theory makes sense if we understand religion as the ability of the individual to adapt to the mysteries of life. Another attribute of the index finger is that it can give us information about the state of our liver and spleen and any rheumatic

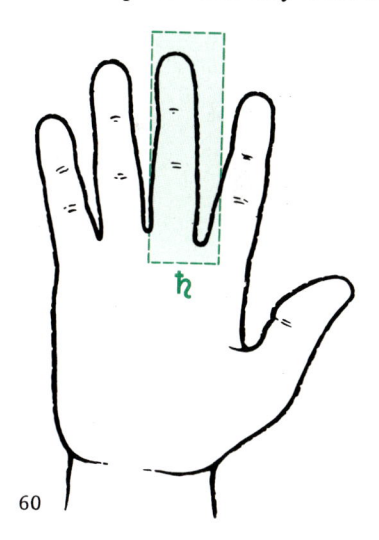

60

tendencies (*67*), through a dark pink colour on the outside edge or slightly enlarged joints respectively.

The middle finger

The middle finger (*60*) is called the *finger of Saturn*. Saturn, which according to astrology expresses a person's reflective nature and the turbid, dark, bad side, is better suited than any other planet to describe a

51

NARROW INDEX FINGER WITH STRONG THUMB AND WEAK THUMB

CONIC INDEX FINGER

TRAPEZOIDAL INDEX FINGER

SHORT INDEX FINGER

61

62

63

64

LONG INDEX FINGER

INDEX FINGER CURVED TOWARDS THE MIDDLE FINGER

HEPATIC AND RHEUMATIC INDEX FINGER

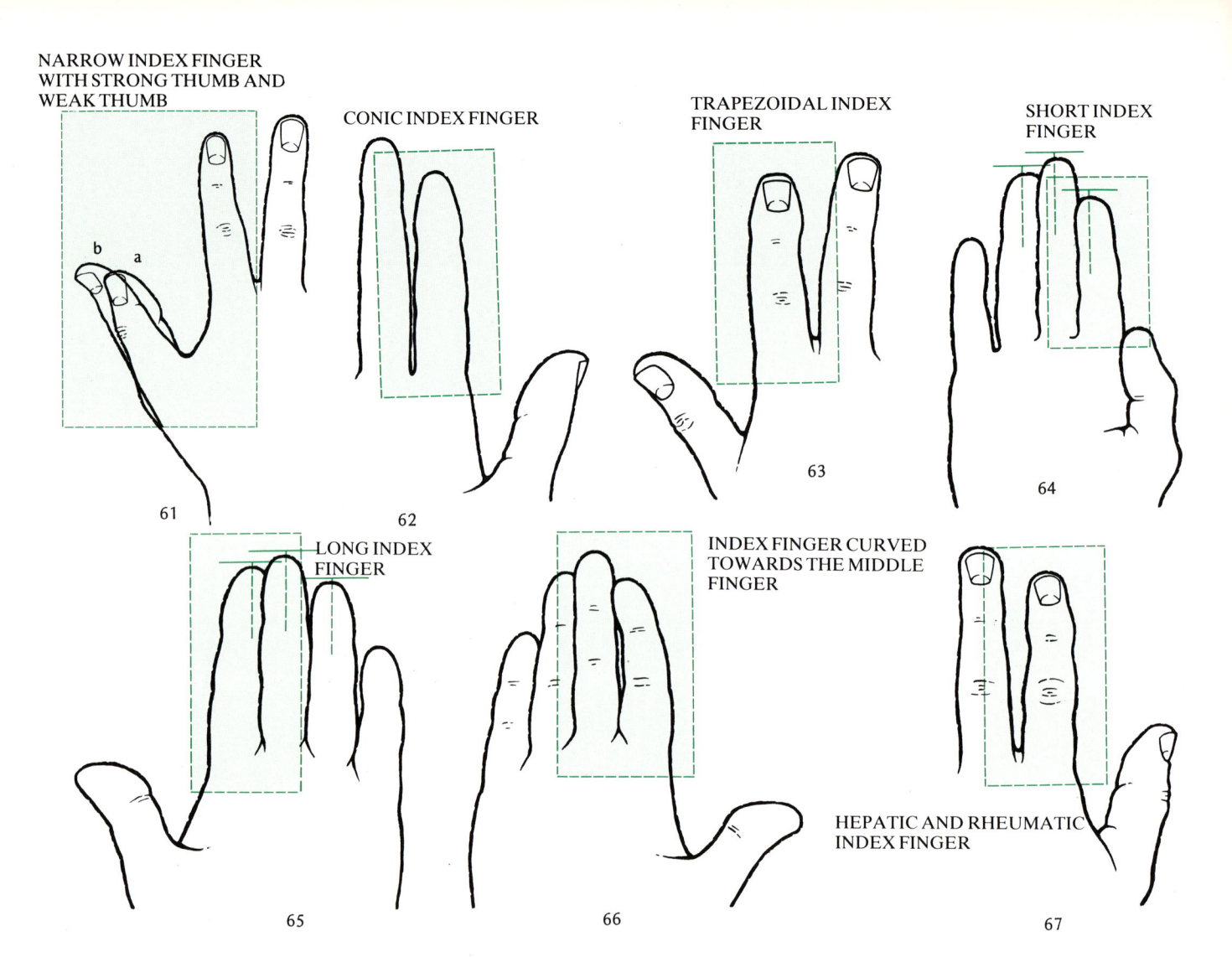

65

66

67

Narrow index finger (61), with a strong thumb a, and with a weak thumb b; conic index finger (62); trapezoidal (63); short (64); long (65); curved toward the middle finger (66); hepatic and rheumatic (67); ring finger or finger of Apollo (68).

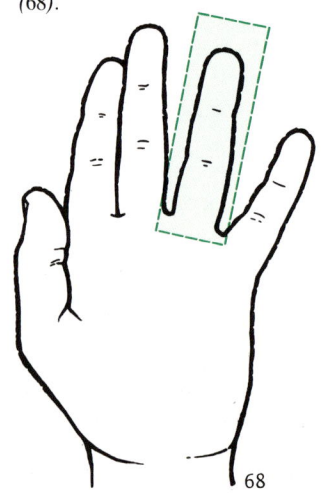

68

finger whose characteristics have been a mystery for a very long time.

The latest theory, which I have in part developed, assigns the middle finger a balancing role between the subject's inner and outer worlds, between the unconscious and awareness of reality. Any abnormality in the middle finger, too long or too short, corresponds to a fairly serious organic or psychological imbalance.

Thus we can regard the finger of Saturn as the needle of a scale that indicates an individual's stability, especially in his relationship with his family and professional life. The middle finger can provide information about intestinal illnesses, whose presence would be indicated by a curving of the first phalange toward the fourth finger (69). A clearly visible cross in the center of the first phalange on the fleshy part of the fingertip is often a sign of sterility in women.

The fourth finger

In palmistry the fourth finger is usually called the *finger of Apollo* or *the Sun* and expresses a person's creative ability. It can reveal how emotional people are and, hence, the way in which they react to external stimuli. It also indicates artistic potential. A well-shaped finger of Apollo, harmoniously proportioned in relation to the whole hand, is a sign of emotional stability. This data can then be interpolated with the ideas provided in this chapter on the shape of the fingers in general. However, we must look at a few special details.

When the finger of Apollo curves toward the middle finger (70), there is a strong possibility of conflict between the subject's sense of duty and search for happiness. If the fourth finger and the middle finger tend to draw apart (71)—though it is much more usual to find these two fingers closer

RING FINGER INCLINED TOWARD THE MIDDLE FINGER

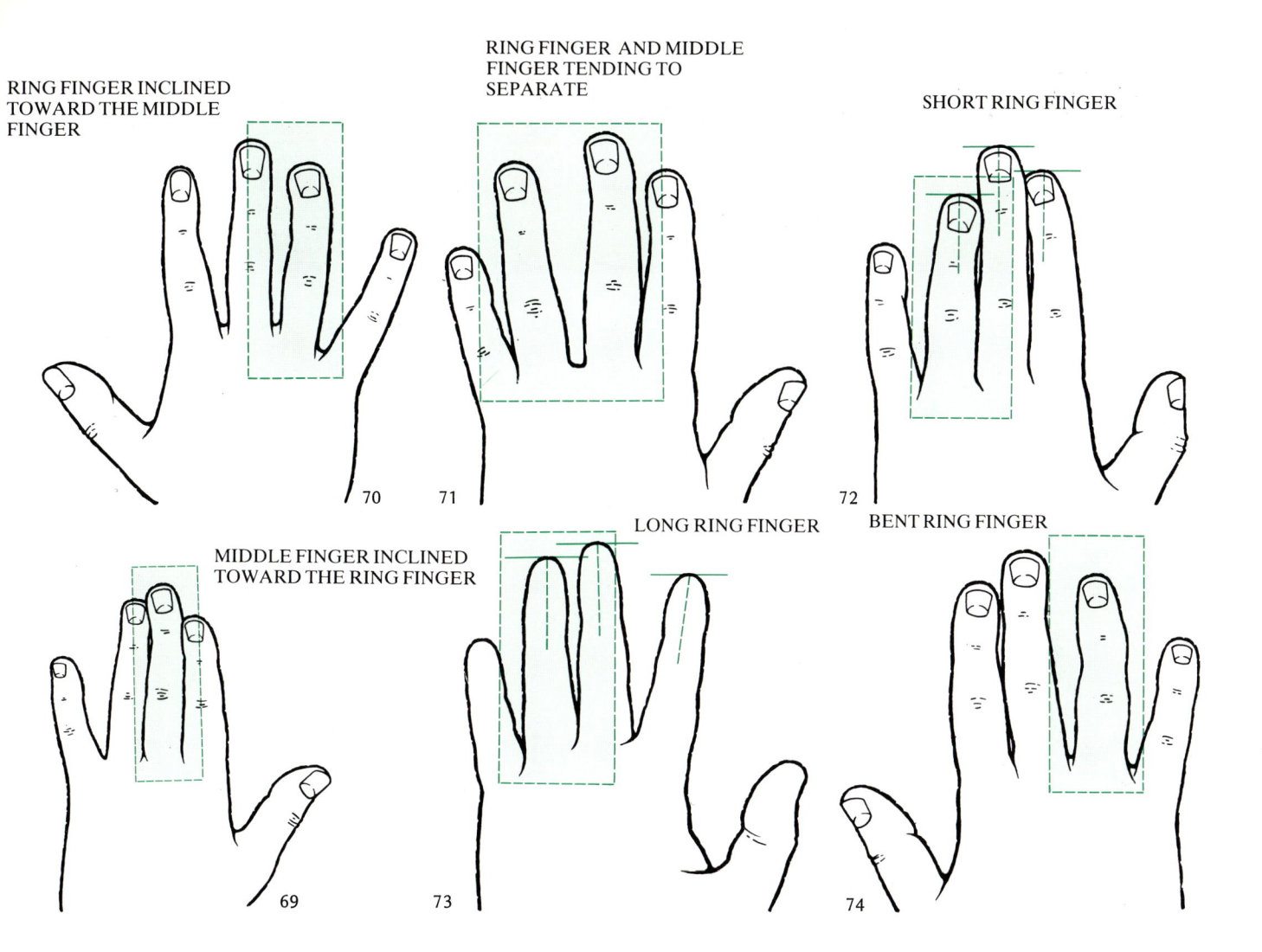

RING FINGER AND MIDDLE FINGER TENDING TO SEPARATE

SHORT RING FINGER

MIDDLE FINGER INCLINED TOWARD THE RING FINGER

LONG RING FINGER

BENT RING FINGER

Middle finger inclined toward the ring finger (69); ring finger inclined toward the middle finger (70); ring finger and middle finger tending to separate (71); short ring finger (72); long (73); bent (74); little finger or finger of Mercury (75).

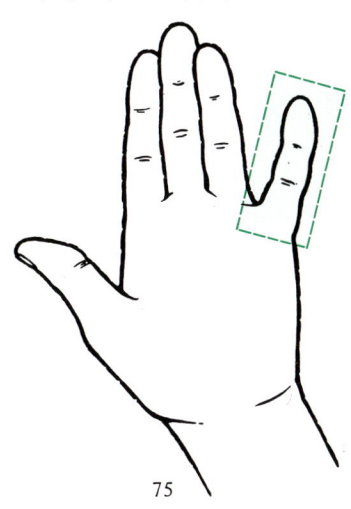

together than any other fingers—it means that the subject has a strong sense of independence and adventure, but not to the extent of rebelling against generally accepted rules. As to length, if the fourth finger is very short (72), which is highly unusual, it is an indication of emotional instability that should find confirmation in the information gathered from the little finger and the mount of Venus. Similarly, a very long fourth finger (73) indicates emotional instability in the opposite direction—towards a form of introspection which, if not kept under control, can lead to serious and irreversible disturbances of the psyche.

Modern as well as traditional palmistry believes that there is a very close link between the fourth finger and the heart. A bent finger of Apollo (74) is a clear indication of possible heart disease, present or future, the nature and intensity of which would have to be determined by other examinations.

The little finger

Also called the *finger of Mercury*, the little finger (or pinky) presides over all those emotions that do not belong to the finger of Apollo. It tells us in particular about our parental, family, and sexual relationships. It provides a clue to our vocal and verbal abilities in their many manifestations. The most significant information supplied by the finger of Mercury has to do with sexuality. It is in this context that the general information already given on the shape of the fingers should be interpreted and studied for any variations that may appear. However, the following data concerns only the finger of Mercury.

If the little finger tends to remain separate from the other fingers (76), one of the subject's main problems is bound to be of a sexual nature, and there is potential for

53

LONG AND SQUARE LITTLE FINGER

ISOLATED LITTLE FINGER

LITTLE FINGER INCLINED TOWARD THE RING FINGER

KNOTTY AND INCLINED LITTLE FINGER

LONG LITTLE FINGER

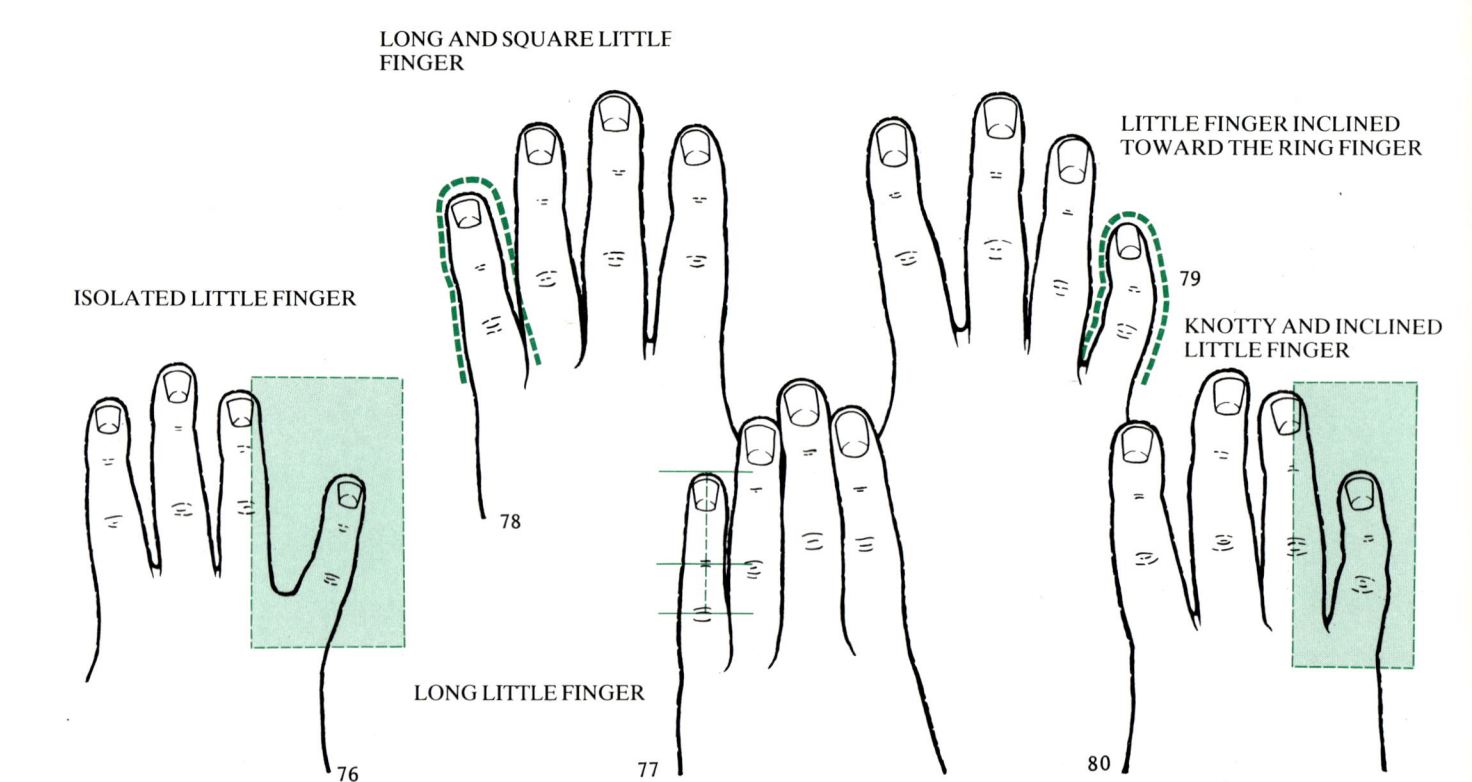

Aspects and characteristics of the little finger: isolated little finger (76); long (77); long and square (78); inclined toward the ring finger (79); knotty and inclined (80).

Opposite, the crossed hands of the Virgin in the Annunciation *by Carlo Crivelli (London, National Gallery).*

marital discord. Further investigation will allow us to define more precisely the nature and degree. A long little finger (*77*) due to a very developed first phalange indicates a love of knowledge and study and a vocation for teaching. If such a finger has a square tip (*78*), we have a person with an exceptional gift for public speaking.

The traditional practice of assigning the qualities of frankness and sincerity to the little finger is also endorsed by present-day theories. If the little finger bends toward the fourth finger (*79*), it is certain the subjects tends to play with words and tell little white lies; accompanied by prominent knots (*80*), we can assume that lies are being told for fraudulent purposes.

The medical world has long recognized that manifestations of cretinism are always accompanied by malformations of the little finger; however, malformation does not always connote cretinism. We can learn some interesting things from the little finger about the functioning of the kidneys, the reproductive organs, and the bladder. Bladder problems in particular are suggested by the absence of a half moon on the little fingernail, but other information would be necessary to substantiate this.

The nails

We devote a separate section to nails because of their importance in chirology. It would be a serious mistake in the reading of a palm not to consider the very relevant information supplied by the nails, which are secondary details in appearance only. The data furnished by the nails come from two sources: shape, which relates mainly to the subject's character and temperament; and colour, which relates to health, particularly the functioning of the nervous system and glands. Clearly a more extensive study than we are able to undertake is warranted, and the possibility exists for anyone to delve deeper into this fascinating aspect of chirology.

While there is an infinite variety of nail shapes, they can all be classified according to certain basic types. However, it is very rare for all the nails of a hand to belong to the same type; there often will be at least two or three types, and the significance of each relates to the particular finger to which it belongs.

Nails can be *large*, *small*, *wide*, or *narrow*. A nail is considered large (*81b*) when it occupies almost all of the width of the

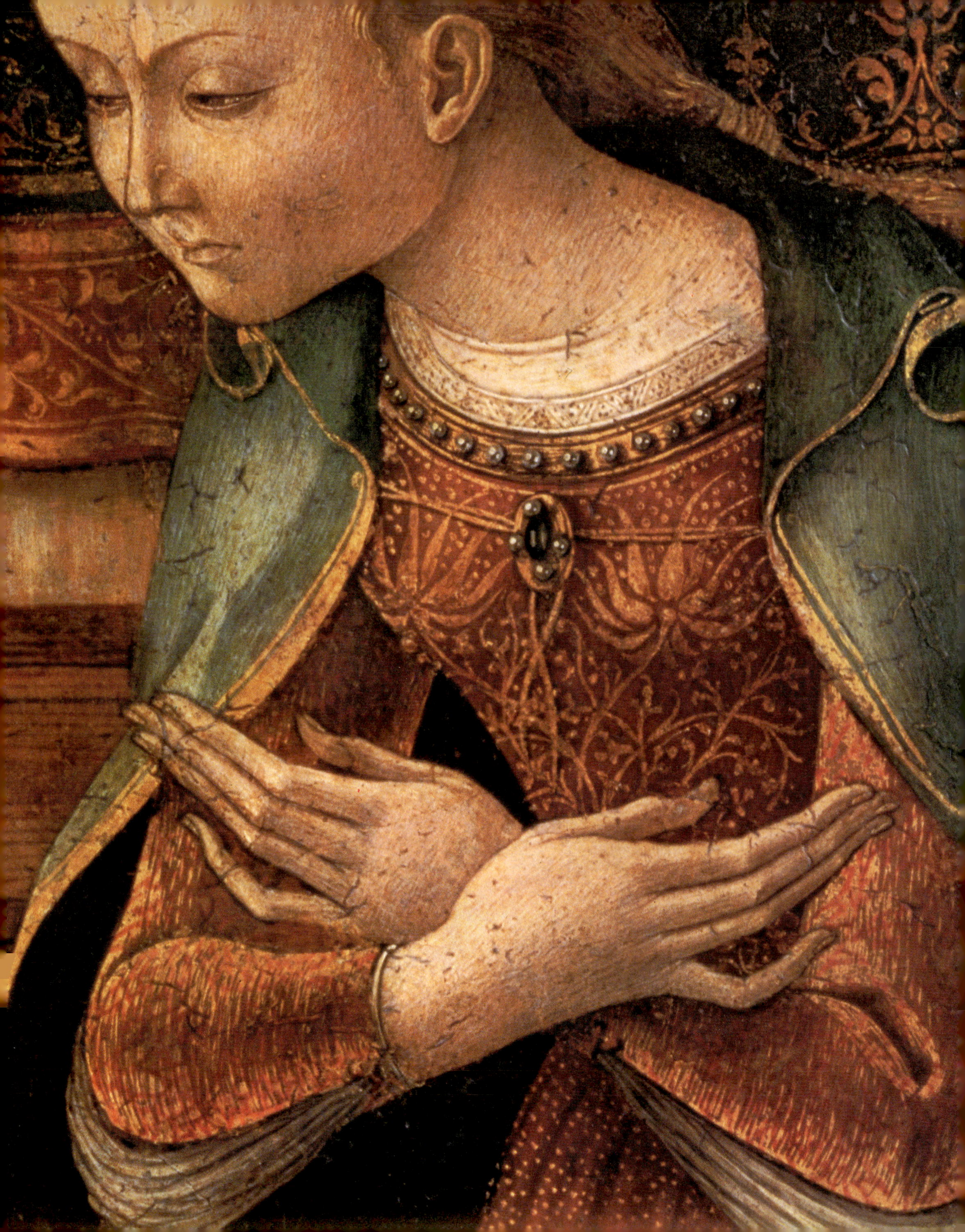

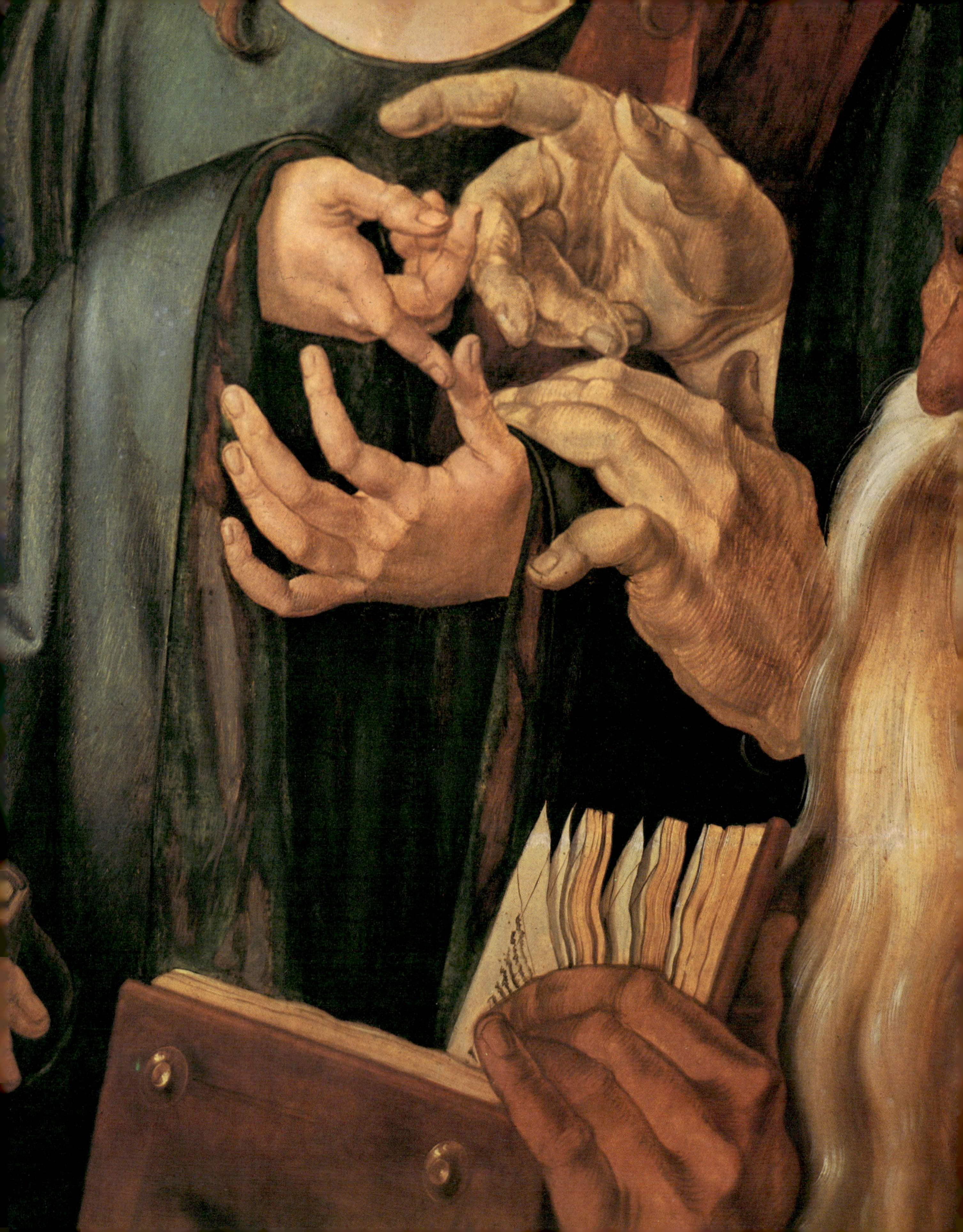

first phalange, and small (*81c*) when it is framed by a large amount of flesh which in some cases appears to engulf it. A nail is considered wide (*81e*) when its shape resembles a rectangle, the horizontal sides being longer, and narrow (*81d*) when the vertical sides of the rectangle are longer.

When it comes to *colour*, it is not possible, even with the most-up-to-date techniques, to describe the gradations, and so we must limit ourselves to a somewhat less than complete description. Nail colours generally range from nearly white to deep pink; sometimes there are shades that verge on yellow or mauve. If we bear in mind that the darker the colour, the clearer and more emphatic its significance, it is easy to determine through interpolation the importance to assign it. Good health is indicated by a fairly dark pink colour contrasting with the white of the half moon (the white half-circle sometimes found at the base of the nail). To produce this contrast, the best method is to press the fingertip from underneath so as to slow down the flow of blood. The colour of the nail and the half-moon will be clearly differentiated. Make sure your nails are clean and free of polish.

What constitutes the *perfect nail* (*81a*)? Colour has already been discussed; as for shape, the conventional characteristics can be summed up in a few words. The length of the nail, measured from the half-moon to the end of the rose-coloured area, should be equal to half of the first phalange. The width should be about three quarters of the length. A nail with these measurements is not only attractive but evidence of the subject's excellent psycho-physical equilibrium. This person is able to apply logic with conviction, has clear ideas, and is objective in his judgements. Unfortunately nails of this sort are rather rare. The nearest we find to the ideal shape are described below.

The *square nail* (*81f*) differs from the perfect one in being wider, while its length conforms to the rule given above. As its name indicates, its shape approaches a square. A person with this kind of nail is short tempered but able to control himself. Colour indicates the degree of self-control. If the nail is pale, the person has a colder temperament; with a heightening of colour there is a greater tendency to explosions of temper. The impassioned types usually "live" their nervous outbursts and may as a result damage their circulatory system. This sort of information can prove very useful to a doctor.

The *small square nail* (*81g*) is not a positive sign. This nail is often an indication of narrowmindedness, a limited field of action, and sometimes pettiness. It is frequently found on people who embrace an idea with fanaticism and are unable to discuss certain subjects calmly. Their behaviour, much like that of fanatic football fans, benefits neither the individual nor society. These persons frequently have problems of a sexual nature, and are capable of sudden explosions of jealousy. In this case the colour of the nail is unlikely to be pale; the darker it is, the more it is an indication of danger. The subject may even become suicidal under unusual or violent stress.

The *nail shaped like a hazelnut* (*81h*) is rarely encountered by palmists. It looks like a normal square nail but with an attractively rounded base. It has an elegant and functional appearance which relates directly to its significance. A person with this kind of nail always tries to reduce gestures and actions to a minimum, choosing in every instance the most rational course, the necessary action. Naturally all this is the result of an intellectual process. The person will express himself in an exact and concise manner, his thinking will be logical and coherent. This kind of behaviour, which saves energy without sacrificing results, is often mistaken for laziness. When required, however, these persons know how to enter the fray with rapid and timely initiative. They are not passionate, they do not have wild enthusiasms; they are analytical and methodical, whether for good or evil purposes. A pale colour in this type of nail indicates considerable coldness and is often found on someone who, if planning revenge, knows exactly how to carry it out no matter how long it takes. A darker colour means a more normal type of person; we are still dealing with the non-passionate type of person who loves quiet and wants to be left in peace.

Hands in Jesus and the Doctors *by Albrecht Dürer (Lugano-Castagnola, Thyssen-Bornemisza Collection).*

The *almond-shaped nail* (*81i*) looks like a square nail at the base but becomes a rather narrow oval at the other end, hence its resemblance to an almond. It is quite a positive sign and indicates refinement, elegance, and sensitivity, combined with a sense of diplomacy. The latter can often be excessive to the point of hiding part of the truth, but one must verify and confirm this sign in light of what emerges from other parts of the hand.

The *elongated almond-shaped nail* (*81j*) resembles the preceding one except that both ends are rounded, giving the appearance of a rather elongated oval. It is obvious that not all the nails of a hand can have this shape; it is usually reserved for the finger of Apollo. Contrary to what one might think, the elongated almond-shaped nail is not a sign of marked artistic ability, despite its elegance, which makes it particuiarly appropriate for female hands. Unfortunately this type of nail very often indicates an endocrine malfunction, frequently found in women, or cardiovascular problems.

For a complete analysis of the nails it is necessary to look at the profile, which may be *convex*, *normal*, or *concave*.

A nail with a normal profile curves slightly at the sides, while the center part tends to be flat (*81k*). The nail is termed convex when the curvature is pronounced and the profile appears very curved (*81n*). When this curvature is exaggerated, it leads to the *claw-like* nail (*81l*), similar to the claws of birds of prey.

Whereas the convex nail denotes a tendency to pulmonary problems (the information supplied by the colour may prove vital), the claw-like nail has a more precise, not very flattering meaning. It is found in possessive, egocentric persons who have an imperious manner and tend to dominate the people around them.

The *concave nail* (*81m*) has the opposite characteristics of the nails described thus far and is not very common. It usually indicates a lack of certain mineral salts in the body, either due to bad diet or a fault in the metabolism. A pronounced concavity of the nail indicates a worsening of the problem; treatment is needed as soon as possible to prevent complications that could be serious.

Sometimes instead of being smooth and homogeneous, nails have deep vertical ridges. This irregularity is most commonly found in young children and the elderly. In the first case it is a sign of physical exhaustion; in the second, nervous disorders related to old age.

Until quite recently it was usual to see nails with very elegant, white half-moons at the base of the nail. Over the past twenty years or so they have been disappearing. The reason is not very clear, but it is probably linked to a change in the kind of food we eat. Actually they can still be found with the same frequency in people from underdeveloped countries. Other anomalies found in nails: white spots that disappear when the new nail growth appears used to be thought to signify good news in the "area" of that particular finger; and black spots had an unhappy significance, or were supposed to be synonymous with general bad health.

From what has been said thus far and from what everyday experience tells us, we can state that as a rule there is a relationship between the finger and its nail that is not only aesthetic but logical as well. They are, as the old expression goes, "made for each other." The problem arises when the relationship is one of disparity. That is both strange and unusual, and it is necessary to try to understand what nature is saying with this kind of arrangement. Those who study palmistry are all too aware that nothing happens in nature as a result of chance.

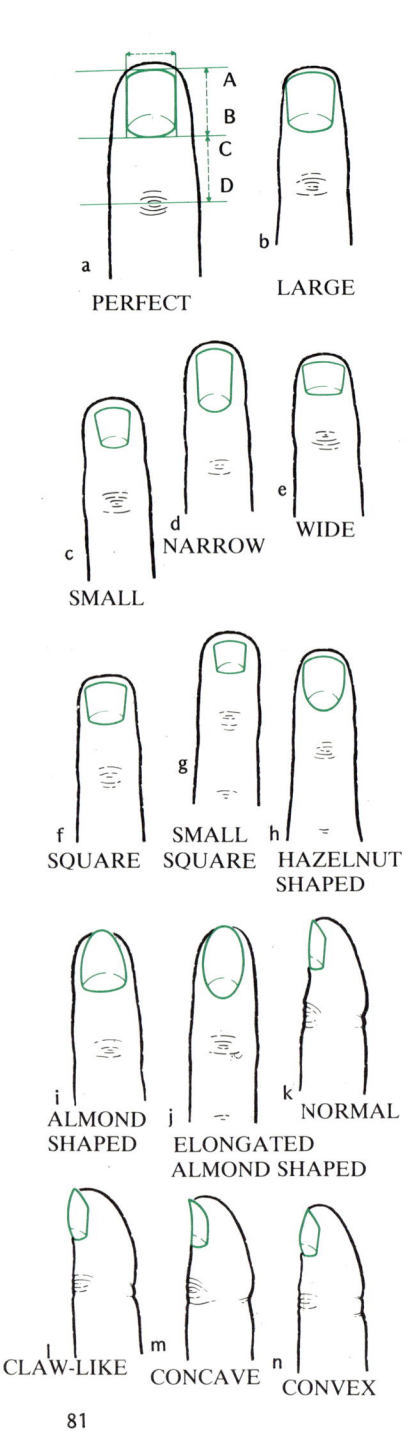

Aspects and characteristics of the nail (81): a *perfect nail (AB = CD)*, b *large*, c *small*, d *narrow*, e *wide*, f *square*, g *small square*, h *hazelnut shaped*, i *almond shaped*, j *elongated almond shaped*, k *normal*, l *claw-like*, m *concave*, n *convex*.

The palm and the mounts

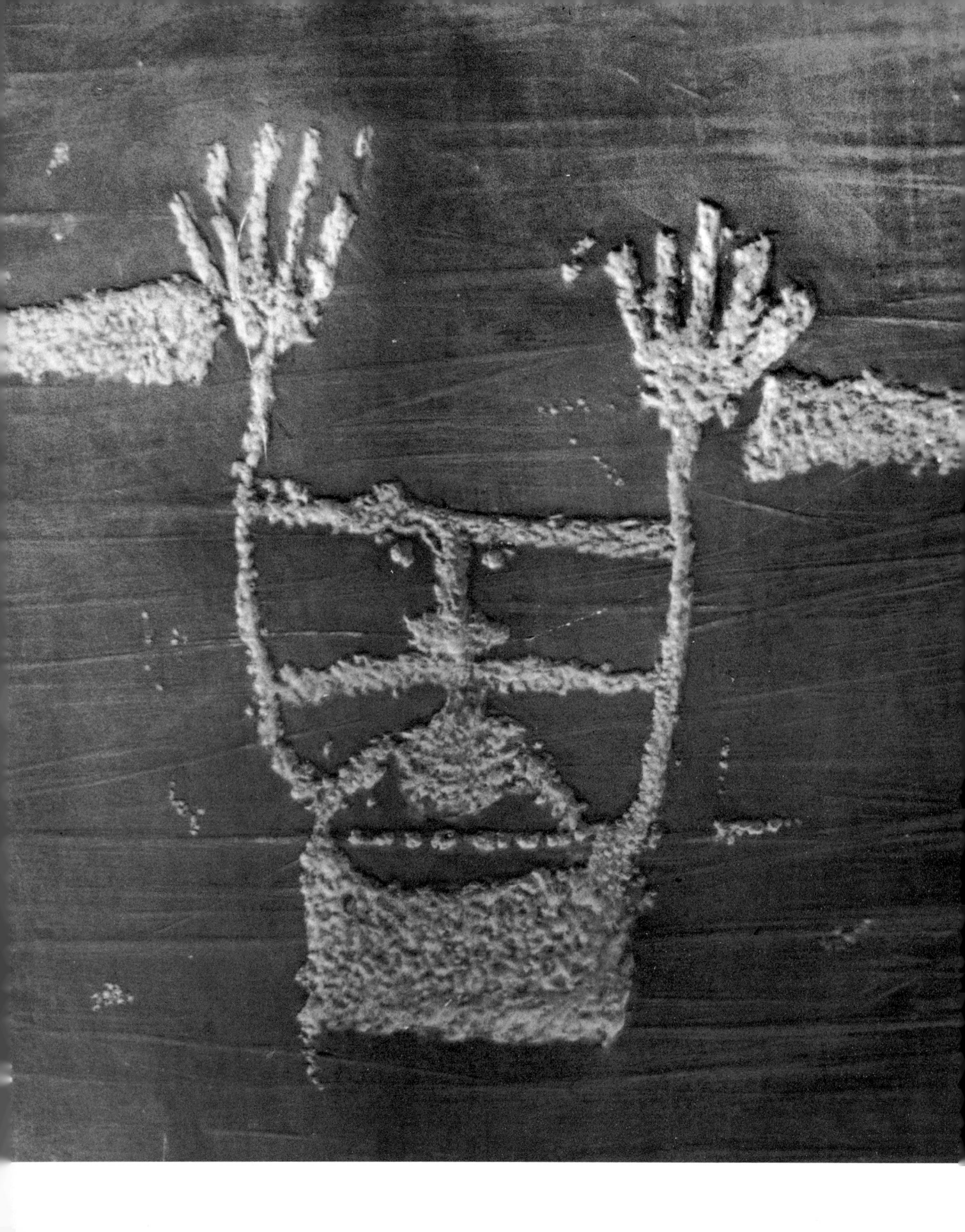

The palm

Having studied the hand in general, its shape, fingers, and nails, we shall now concentrate on the palm, the main concern of palmistry. Still, we shall often refer to the preceding material because it is only by careful comparison of all available data that the palmist can give an accurate reading.

The most important details in the palm are the mounts, plains, principal lines, secondary lines that appear only on some hands, and special signs. We shall begin with the signs, as these often figure in discussions of the other details.

Special signs are particularities equivalent to capillary lines and almost always found on lines, plains, and mounts; their presence can change the significance of the element on which they are located. When they take the form of a *square* (82), the meaning is decidedly positive; the square appears for the most part on principal lines. When a special sign is shaped like a *kidney* or an *island* (83), the meaning is rather negative: there are obstacles or difficulties to be faced, and these will be surmounted only with great difficulty. Island formations too are located mainly on lines.

A *short line* or bar is a special sign consisting of a secondary line that cuts across a main line or a mount (84). It represents an obstacle, a barrier to initiative, and often suggests the need to find another route to reach a goal. (The interpretative ability and experience of the person reading the palm will play a vital role in discovering the sign and its exact nature.) The *grille* (85) can appear on any part of the palm and always signifies a slowing down, a temporary obstacle lasting for a period of time that can be calculated with some accuracy. *Crosses* and *stars* (86) are signs of sudden change, often drastic, and have a positive or negative value depending on their position.

In the same way that one glances over a preface before beginning a book, it is advisable to look at the palm as a whole before undertaking a reading. Its appearance can provide information that will prove useful when formulating an opinion or an answer.

We know from what has already been said about the shape of the hand that the palm may have many or few lines distributed evenly or chaotically, with clear or ambiguous signs plainly marked or hidden by a thick net of capillary lines that create a confused picture. Nevertheless, every hand can be assigned to one of the following categories:

Flat palm with few lines (87). This is typical of the person with few but very precise ideas, very little sensitivity to physical pain, and a fairly rudimentary nervous system.

Palm with orderly and well-drawn lines (88). This indicates a good psycho-physical balance, and as a rule belongs to a well-balanced person. If the lines are very light, we have a personality that is easy to influence. Heavily marked lines indicate a nervous temperament, someone very caught up in personal problems and therefore fairly self-centered and prone to nervous exhaustion.

Palm with seemingly very complicated lines (89). Here we have a person whose personality is not easy to interpret because of its complexity and frequent contradictions. It will require a thorough examination to unravel the tangle. If the hand is also very pale and the principal lines are submerged in a web of capillary lines, then the person has probably reached the limit of his emotional endurance.

The dating system

One of the most frequently asked questions of palmists is, "Will I live a long life?" It can be answered, but it is not always advisable to do so, and honesty in these cases should be tempered by certain considerations. The subject's disposition and possible reactions must be taken into account. It is usually best to stick to general remarks, avoiding a precise answer, and not make unrealistic predictions. It is important for the palmist to place certain events in the life of the subject within the correct time period; for that can seriously affect the interpretation.

Expert palmists have spent many years working on dating and have achieved reasonably satisfactory results. There are four methods currently used to determine the most important dates in a person's life.

1. *The oriental method.* An arc is drawn to encompass the whole of the life line and is divided into four equal sections (91), each

Prehistoric hands carved on rock in the Maritime Alps. Our Stone Age ancestors made cave drawings of animals and various signs, and for man they drew the hands first to indicate their supremacy over the other parts of the body.

SQUARES

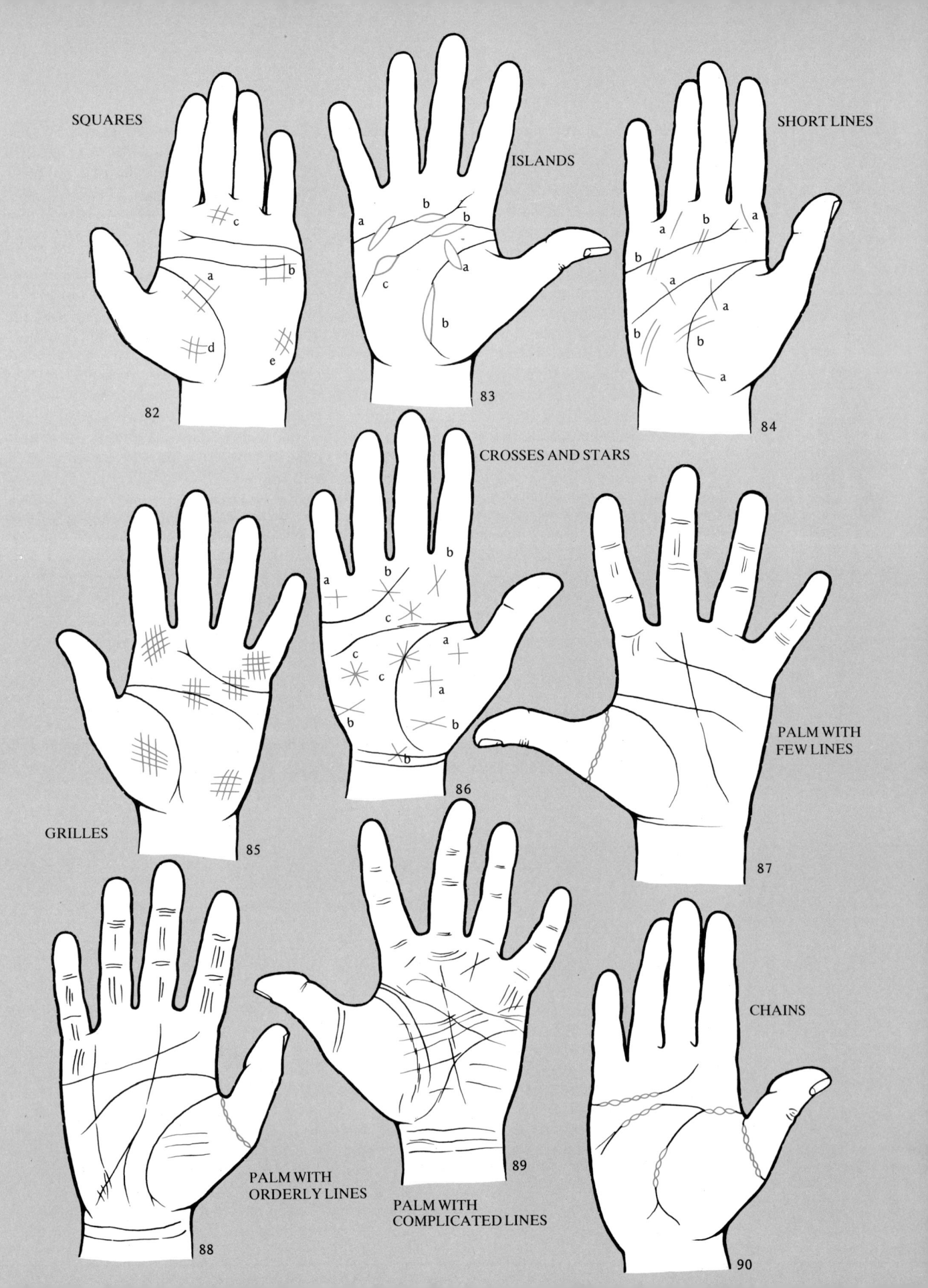

ISLANDS

SHORT LINES

82

83

84

CROSSES AND STARS

GRILLES

85

86

PALM WITH
FEW LINES

87

PALM WITH
ORDERLY LINES

88

PALM WITH
COMPLICATED LINES

89

CHAINS

90

Special signs on the palm of the hand: squares (82): a, b on lines, c, d, e on mounts; islands (83): a diagonal, b vertical, c kidney-shaped; simple short lines (84a) and double short lines (84b) on mounts and on lines; grilles on mounts and lines (85); crosses and stars (86): a Latin crosses, b, crosses of Saint Andrew, c stars; palm with few lines (87); palm with orderly and well-drawn lines (88); palm with complicated lines (89); chains on different lines (90).

of which represents twenty-five years. Further divisions will allow the palmist to determine dates within a period of ten years or less. It is an easy, quick method but not very reliable; it is more accurate when the life line is very long. Problems arise when it is short. It should be made absolutely clear at this stage that the length of the life line has nothing to do with length of life, not in this or any other case.

2. *The amended oriental method.* This is a perfected form of the above method; it is more complex but does not fundamentally improve the reliability of the first method. It is advisable only if a fairly clear imprint of the palm is available. Having divided the life line into four sections, as explained above, one draws a straight line from the center of the base of the middle finger to the beginning of the wrist (*92*). This line, so it is believed, represents eighty years on a hand with a square palm and ninety years on a long palm (as described earlier). The line is divided into eight or nine sections, depending on the palm, equivalent to about ten years each. At the point where this line is nearest to the life line a line is drawn at right angles. The point where it intersects is numbered to correspond to the straight line and the other number referents for the life line are figured from there.

3. *The Anglo-Saxon method.* This is based on the same principle as that of the oriental method, but is very complex and not innovative enough to merit extensive discussion.

4. *The French school.* Originated by Desbarolles, this method has been perfected in recent studies made by Papus. Here too a very clear imprint is needed. It establishes three probable periods of time in the subject's life and then finds the arithmetical mean (*93*). We begin with the head line (or its logical extension) and draw three vertical lines starting from the center of the base of the middle finger, ring finger, and little finger, respectively. This delineates three periods corresponding to twenty-five, fifty and seventy-five years, respectively. We then proceed in a similar fashion with the heart line, (or logical extension) so that it is intersected by the same three vertical lines now also indicating periods of twenty-five, fifty and seventy-five years on the heart line. Now take the fate line, which will cut into the head line at a point corresponding to twenty years, into the heart line at forty years and into the Sun or Mercury line at around ten to twelve years. If the fate line extends to the base of the middle finger, it will indicate seventy-five years. If it extends beyond the middle of the third phalange, we are into one hundred years.

For an example of how this system works, suppose that the heart line ends at the seventy-year-point, the head line ends at about sixty-five, and the Sun line ends at seventy-five. We take the average of these three ages (70+65+75=210÷3=70) to get the age the subject will reach (with a ninety per cent chance of probability, according to Papus). I rarely use this method, although

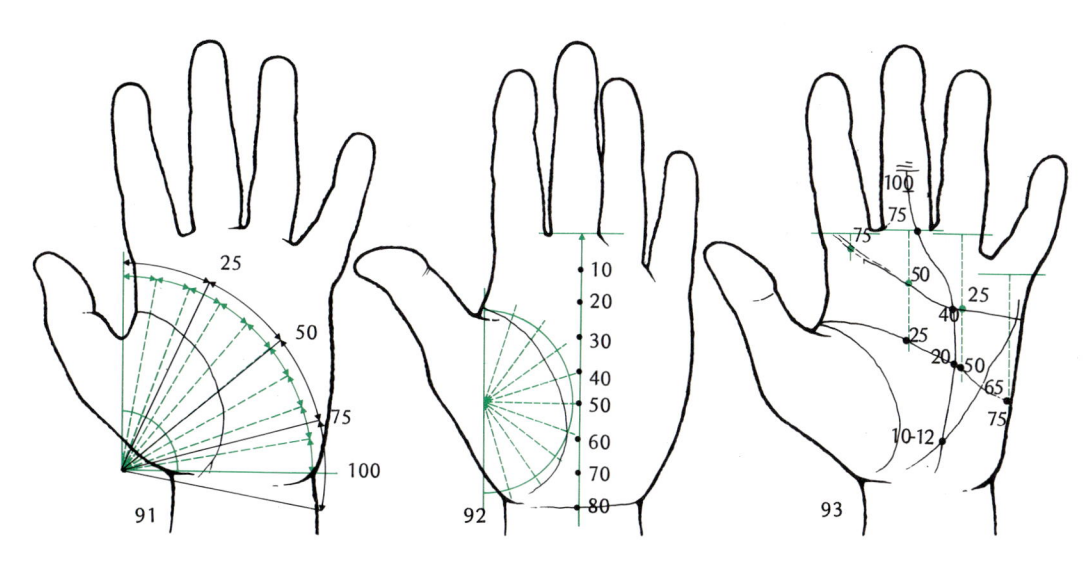

Principal methods of dating: oriental (91), amended oriental (92), French (93).

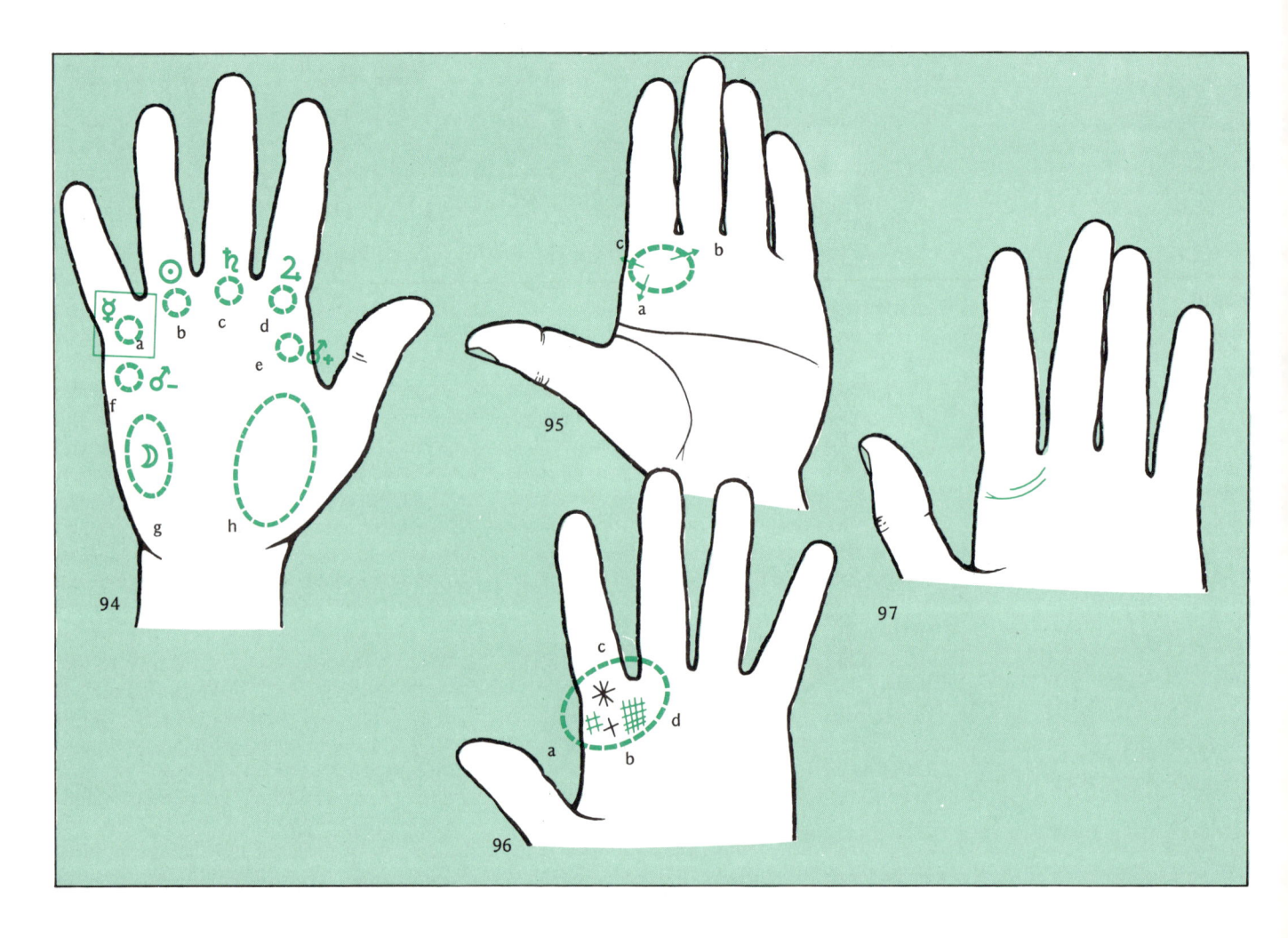

The mounts of the hand (94): a Mercury, b Apollo, c Saturn, d Jupiter, e active Mars, f passive Mars, g Moon, h Venus.
The mount of Jupiter (95) with different types of summits: a facing downward, b toward the Mount of Saturn, c facing outward; and its special signs (96): a square, b cross, c star, d grille. The ring of Solomon (97).

The mounts

Opposite, four French postcards from the early twentieth century.

it is considered effective and reliable, but instead employ the classic oriental method. With the other data supplied by a reading of the hand, it allows for a sufficiently accurate evaluation of the facts that are of interest.

We are now ready to examine the mounts, the raised parts of the palm whose significance depends on their prominence. They may be very pronounced, or appear not to exist at all, but even then whatever signs are present in that area designated by palmistry as the mount should be properly interpreted.

There are eight mounts (*94*) and they have very exact locations. Four are to be found below the bases of the four fingers and are named correspondingly: the *mount of Jupiter* for the index finger, the *mount of Saturn* for the third, the *mount of Apollo* or the *Sun* for the ring, and the *mount of Mercury* for the little finger. In the area between the thumb and the index finger, below the mount of Jupiter, is located the *active mount of Mars*. It is necessary to distinguish between it and the *passive mount of Mars,* located below the mount of Mercury on the other side of the hand. These two mounts are situated just above either end of the head line, and below either end of the heart line. The last two mounts, the *mount of Venus* and the *mount of the Moon* are very important. The first is formed by the third phalange of the thumb, which is submerged in the metacarpus; the second is found between the wrist the passive mount of Mars, lying on the outside

LIGNE de VIE FINE — Goût des Sports	**ANNEAU DE VÉNUS** — Ménage Heureux et Uni
MAIN CHARNUE — Goûts Champêtres	**MAIN AVEC LIGNES BIEN MARQUÉES** — Caractère Rêveur

edge of the hand and forming part of the profile of the hand.

The mount of Jupiter

As shown in figure 95, it is located at the base of the index finger and indicates the conscious side of the subject's personality, particularly with regard to life and the world around him. The more prominent the mount of Jupiter, the stronger the personality. The high point of this mount, represented by a small cusp, (fairly evident in well-developed mounts) should be carefully scrutinized. If the summit faces downward (95a), toward the head line, the subject expresses his personality in the service of others, not out of love but to make himself needed. When the high point of the mount of Jupiter faces the mount of Saturn (95b), it means that the subject has a remarkable practical sense and will direct every effort to achieving goals that can be useful to him. If the summit of the mount faces outward (95c), the subject is very ambitious and has such a strong spirit of adventure that he loses sight of his own social duties.

The presence of special signs on this and other mounts can produce considerable variations. A well-drawn square (96a) signifies the ability to communicate one's own wisdom and knowledge to others; this is typical of teachers and the best executives. A clearly marked cross (96b) anywhere on the mount of Jupiter means a marriage of love that may meet with opposition but will not be prevented if a capillary line cuts into the vertical line of the cross. A star (96c) on the mount of Jupiter indicates rapid and sometimes unexpected success in work, even though it does not necessarily mean the achievement of riches. During certain periods in the life of particularly sensitive and apprehensive individuals, one can observe a grille (96d) on the mount of Jupiter, caused by anxiety of having committed an act that may be judged in a negative light.

Another interesting sign on the mount of Jupiter is the *ring of Solomon* (97), a curved line, whole or divided in two, that circles the base of the index finger. Depending on its clearness, it is possible to establish how sensible the subject is, that is, his ability to evaluate situations and give sound advice. It also indicates the need for solitude and meditation, especially in old age.

The mount of Saturn

This has the same significance as the middle finger under which it is located (98). It gives information on the nature of the subject's relationships in his work and social environment. The intensity of these relationships is indicated as always by the degree of prominence of the mount.

If the high point of the mount is located in the center toward the base of the middle finger (98a), the meaning is positive: excellent ability for planning and carrying out business transactions. If the summit is lower down towards the head line (98b) this ability tends to be less strong to the point of disappearing altogether. However, if the summit of the mount of Saturn faces toward the mount of Apollo (98c), the meaning is negative: little business acumen and sometimes a tendency to spend beyond one's means.

A prominent cross (99a) on the mount of Saturn, especially if the lines of the cross are of equal length, signifies sudden and violent death, almost always by accident. The prominence, clarity, and colour increase the probability: the darker the colour the nearer at hand the event is.

The *ring of Saturn* (99b) can be found on the mount of Saturn. It is a rather rare and often temporary mark whose significance is never favourable. When it is particularly evident, it indicates a continual and often inexplicable lack of success in work.

The mount of Apollo

Located below the ring finger or finger of Apollo (100), it bears this name because it too represents the person's innermost abilities—his emotional and creative nature, particularly in the artistic sense. It is not always well defined and is often confused with the two adjacent mounts of Saturn and Mercury. That notwithstanding, an investigation for any special signs should be done in the relevant area defined in the illustration.

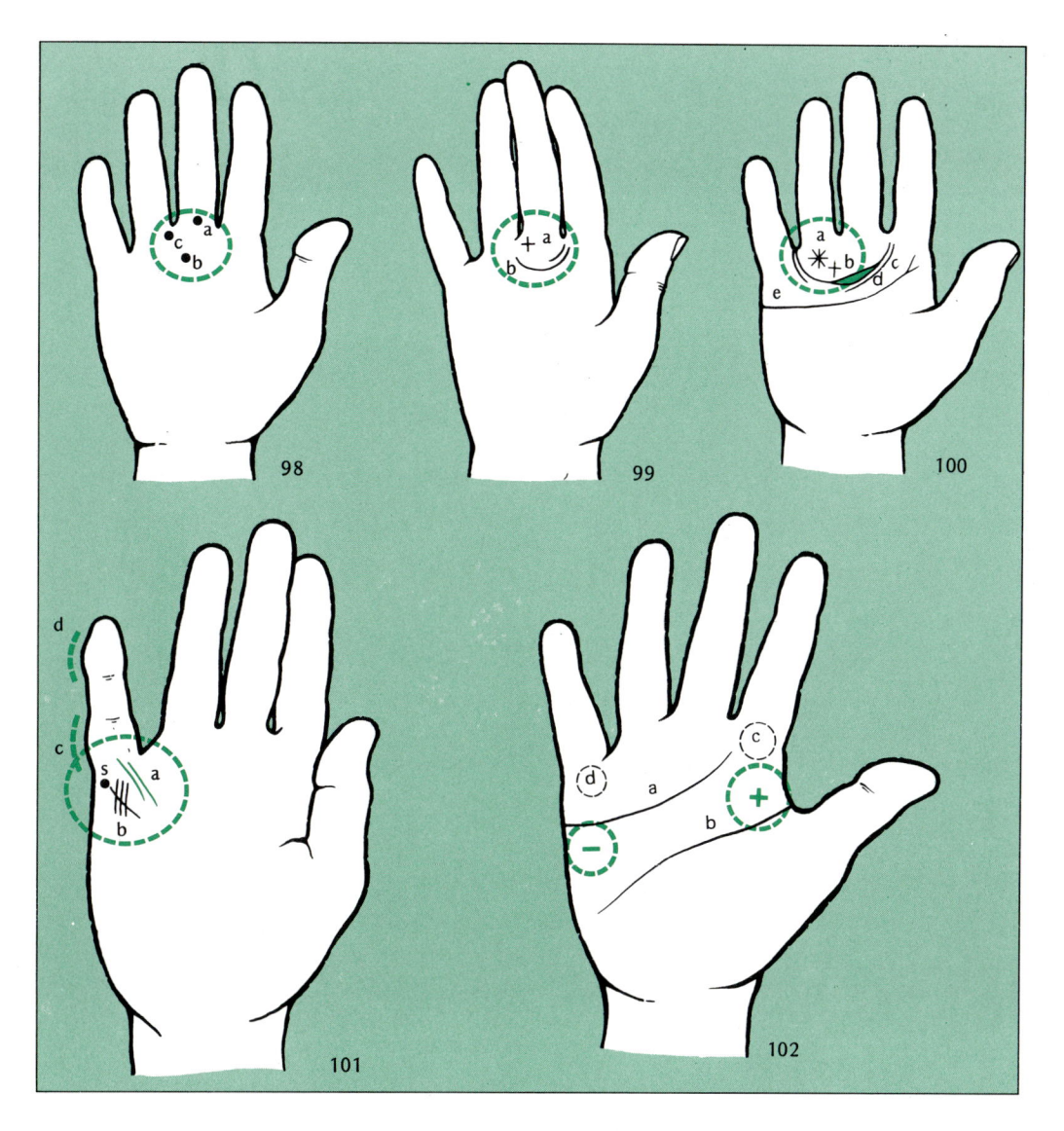

The mount of Saturn with its different summits (98): a *above,* b *below,* c *towards the mount of Apollo; and its special signs (99):* a *cross,* b *ring of Saturn.*
The mount of Apollo (100): a *star,* b *cross,* c *ring of Venus,* d *island on the ring of Venus;* e *is the heart line.*
The mount of Mercury (101): s *summit facing outward,* a *diagonal short line,* b *line of intuition,* c *and* d *signs of practical science.*
The mounts of Mars (102) active (+) and passive (−): a *is the heart line,* b *the head line,* c *the mount of Jupiter,* d *the mount of Mercury.*

A well-defined star (*100a*) signifies success, both in work and in life, especially if the profession has been chosen by following a natural inclination. A cross (*100b*) indicates the opposite situation, that is, difficulties in achieving goals even when the ability to succeed exists.

A typical sign of the mount of Apollo also involves the mount of Saturn. This is the ring or *girdle of Venus* (*100c*), a curved line that encircles the two mounts without touching the heart line. When well defined, this line signifies creative sensitivity in the artistic field combined with a practical sense that makes it possible to put the fruits of one's imagination into practice. It can also indicate a strong sexual drive.

Choosing between two interpretations depends on other information that emerges in the course of a reading. The ring or girdle of Venus can also be formed by many curved lines that together form a ring around the two mounts. The meaning does not change: achievements will be made even though there will be major difficulties. The girdle has a negative significance when composed of two semicircles. In this case an element of superficiality enters into the original picture, undermining artistic creativity with facile improvisation. If one of the two arcs of the girdle is broken by an *island* (*100d*), it means there is an anomaly of a fairly serious sexual nature to be substantiated elsewhere on the palm.

67

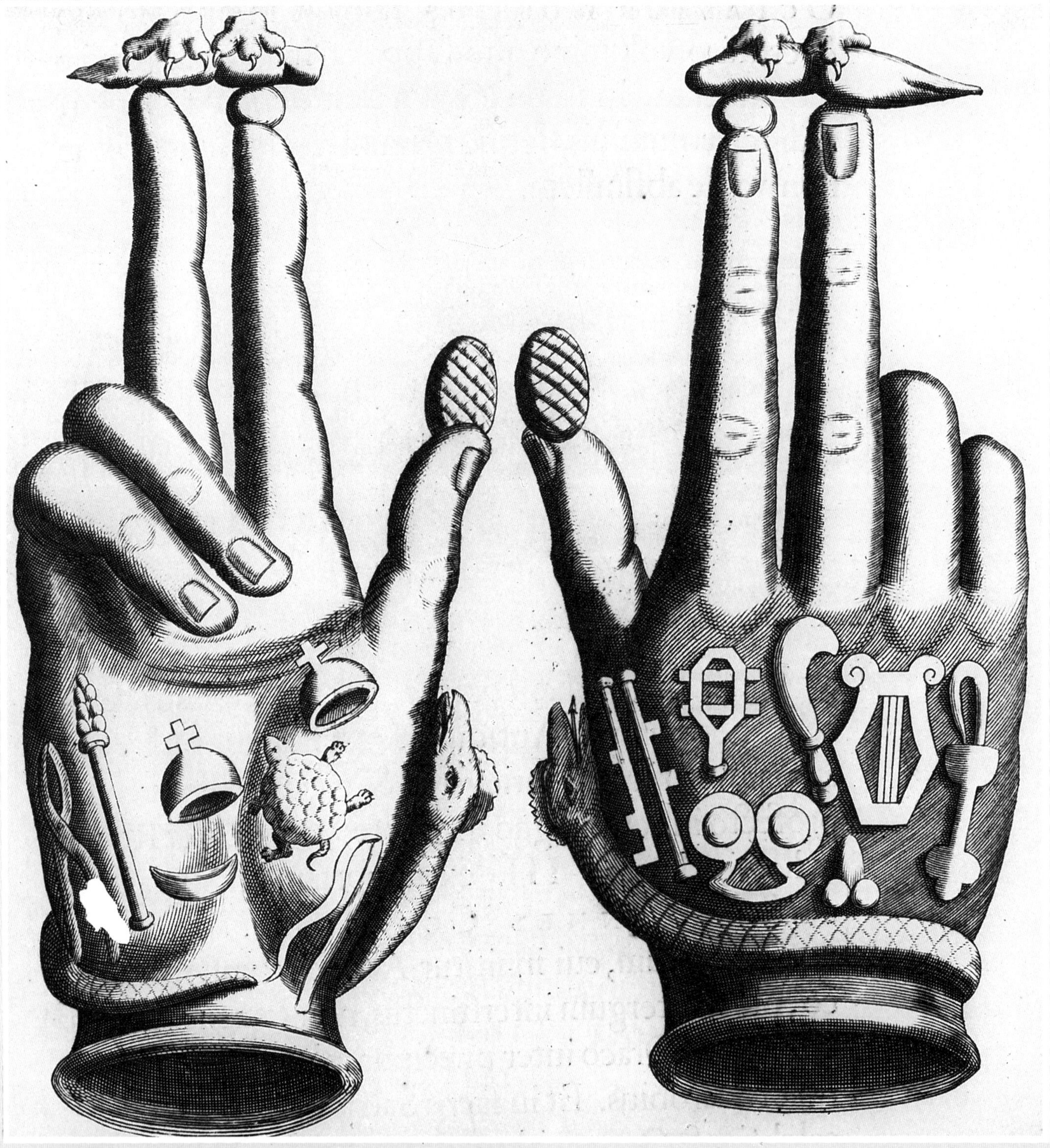

Egyptian magical hands (from Pignori, The Altar of Isis, *Amsterdam, 1669).*

The mount of Mercury

This mount lies below the little finger and reveals the individual tendencies missing in the mount of Apollo: a love of the scientific disciplines, business ability, eloquence, interest in money, and enterprise in practical matters. The last quality is particularly evident when the summit of the mount (*101*) is located near the outer edge of the palm.

Two *short lines,* (perhaps of different length), crossing the mount diagonally in the direction of the center of the palm, indicate the subject's scientific tendencies, especially regarding abstract subjects such as pure mathematics. If a knot appears between the nail and the joint of the first phalange of the little finger, then the interest in science is practical and directed towards chemistry, biology, or scientific research in general. Other interesting information comes from two or three vertical lines that cross the center of the mount of Mercury. They indicate remarkable insight into the handling of one's own affairs and in general denote a highly intuitive person.

The mounts of Mars

As stated earlier, there are two of these. The active mount of Mars is located between the thumb and the index finger between the head line and the heart line (*102*); the passive mount of Mars is located on the other side of the palm (*102*). The former gives the measure of the subject's physical courage; the more prominent the mount, the stronger this trait will be. The passive mount of Mars reveals the subject's moral courage, tenacity, and steadfastness. These two mounts have the same name because they are so closely related, for it is unusual to find physical courage without proportionate moral strength, and vice versa. Hence a weak and barely evident active mount of Mars may indicate a person still capable of a courageous deed, but out of logic not impulsiveness, if the passive mount of Mars is more prominent.

The mount of Venus

The mount of Venus (*103*) occupies the part of the palm called in medicine the "thenar eminence," covering the third phalange of the thumb that is inserted in the metacarpus. It reflects physical vitality and indicates the measure of one's sensuality and capacity to love, as well as one's attachment to family and children.

Owing to its position it is connected to a vast part of the active side of the individual's unconscious life. When it is large

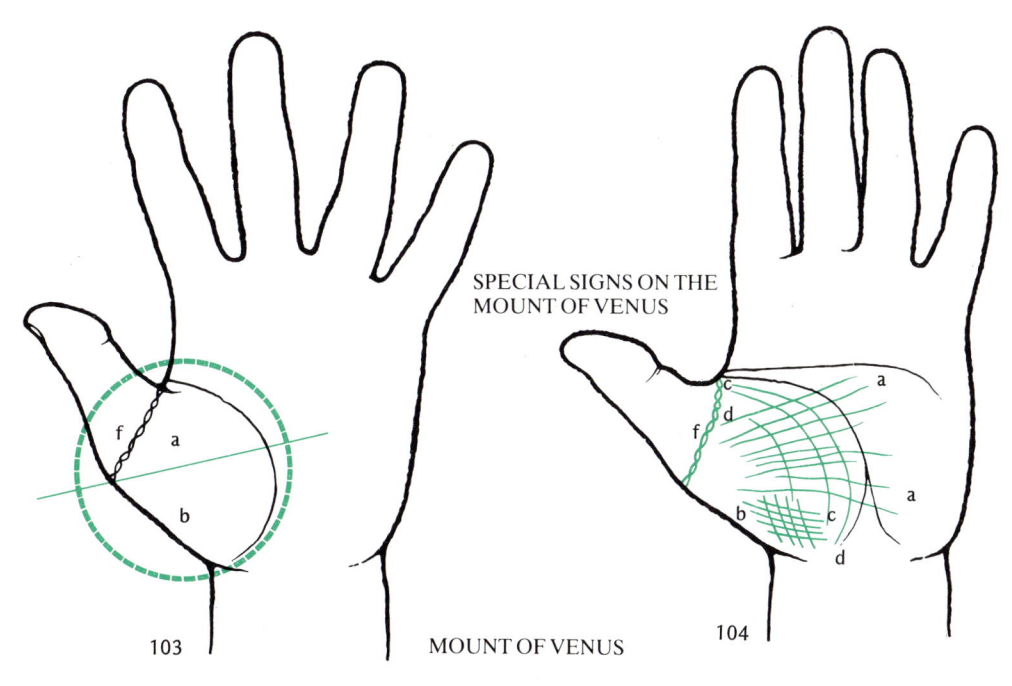

The mount of Venus (103): a *upper half,* b *lower half,* f *ring of family; and its special signs (104):* f *ring of the family,* a *lines running from the thumb to the palm,* b *grille,* c *and* d *lines of fate or of Mars.*

SPECIAL SIGNS ON THE MOUNT OF VENUS

103

MOUNT OF VENUS

104

and fleshy, it signifies a lively store of inner energy, sometimes excessive, which is continually in search of an outlet. This energy can take the form of brutality, which must be confirmed by the shape of the hand and the thumb. When the mount has little firmness or is flabby, it is a sure sign of a deficient sex drive, which may be temporary due to injury or illness. One must also take into account the age of the subject as lack of firmness may be a case of normal deterioration caused by old age. Some palmists, myself among them, divide the mount of Venus into two parts. The upper section, nearest the head line, refers to spiritual aspects; the lower section, particularly if it is well developed, indicates the subject's artistic abilities and sensuality. Because of this mount's size, it is often marked with lines and special signs. If the lines are numerous, then we are dealing with a vivacious personality with a busy social life. As the lines become fewer a progressive cooling is indicated, with an increasing indifference towards other people. Let us look at some of the most significant lines.

The *line of Mars* (*104c, 104d*) consists of a semicircle running parallel to the line of life. Some hands have two lines of Mars, others none at all. These lines are confirmation of the subject's vitality and his ability to recover from or react to illness. But there is another meaning as well: a person with these lines is protected from the dangers of magic and jealousy. These are usually people who may arouse feelings of envy because they are very gifted and have excellent career prospects. *Many small lines running from the thumb towards the center of the palm* (*104a*) indicate personal attachments of little depth. If these are accompanied by a grille on the lower part of the mount of Venus (*104b*), this means that along with superficiality of feeling there is a continual need for novelty and strong emotions, with a potential for danger.

Sometimes one comes across hands with many diagonal lines that cross the mount of Venus but without cutting into the life line. They can be of varying width, set close together or far apart. A person with these lines is engaged in work that brings him into contact with the public, but at a high level, and he has to work hard to stay on top. These are professional people, politicians, lecturers, and the like.

The *family ring* (*104f*). Almost always composed of two or three interwoven lines located at the base of the second phalange of the thumb, right on the joint. If it is well defined, it indicates a strong attachment to the family with a strong sense of responsibility toward it.

The mount of the Moon

This is the slight prominence (*105*) that doctors call the "hypothenar eminence." The mount of the Moon is opposite the mount of Venus and bounded above by the head line and below by the wrist. On the sides it is bounded by the outer edge of the hand and the line of Mercury. It expresses imagination and how much the subject can be influenced by his own fantasies. In contrast to the mount of Venus, which represents active energy, the mount of the Moon expresses sensitivity and sometimes, though indirectly, a form of creativity related to the subject's ability to put his imagination to practical use. This ability can be confirmed only by examining the shape of the hand in conjunction with the appearance of the mount. The theory only applies in the case of a large square hand of the practical positive type.

From the foregoing we can conclude that the mount of the Moon indicates how successfully the subject reconciles objective reality with his own perception of it vis-à-vis modifications and changes made by his imagination. This particularly complex study is worth pursuing because of the very important information that can be gathered regarding the different aspects of the personality.

A well-developed mount of the Moon signifies a love of nature. If the highest point faces downward, the subject has a strong feeling for music (especially for very rhythmical pieces), indicating a need for harmony and harmonious movements.

Special signs on the mount often have very precise meanings. Certain transverse lines on the upper part of the mount signify that the subject will have occasion to travel frequently. A grille on the lower half and

Opposite, detail from The Tributes *relief in the Palace of Sargon II at Khorsabad.*

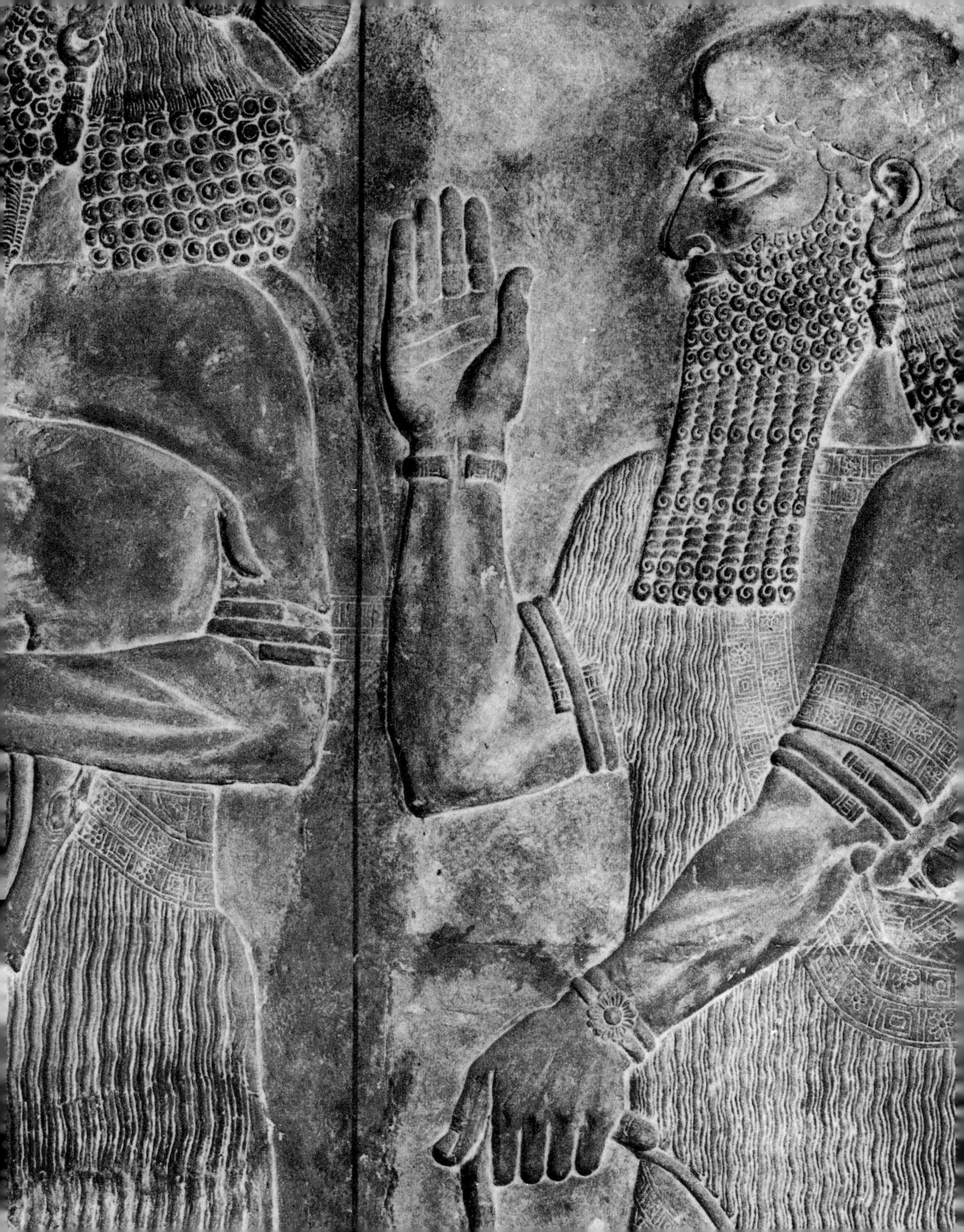

The mount of the Moon (105) and its special signs: s *summit facing downward,* a *diagonal lines,* b *grille,* c *cross,* m *line of materialism;* d *is the line of Mercury,* e *the head line* f *the life line,* g *the heart line.*
The Plain of Mars (106a) is the centre of the palm and is crossed by almost all of the principal and secondary lines; (106b) is the mount of the Moon.

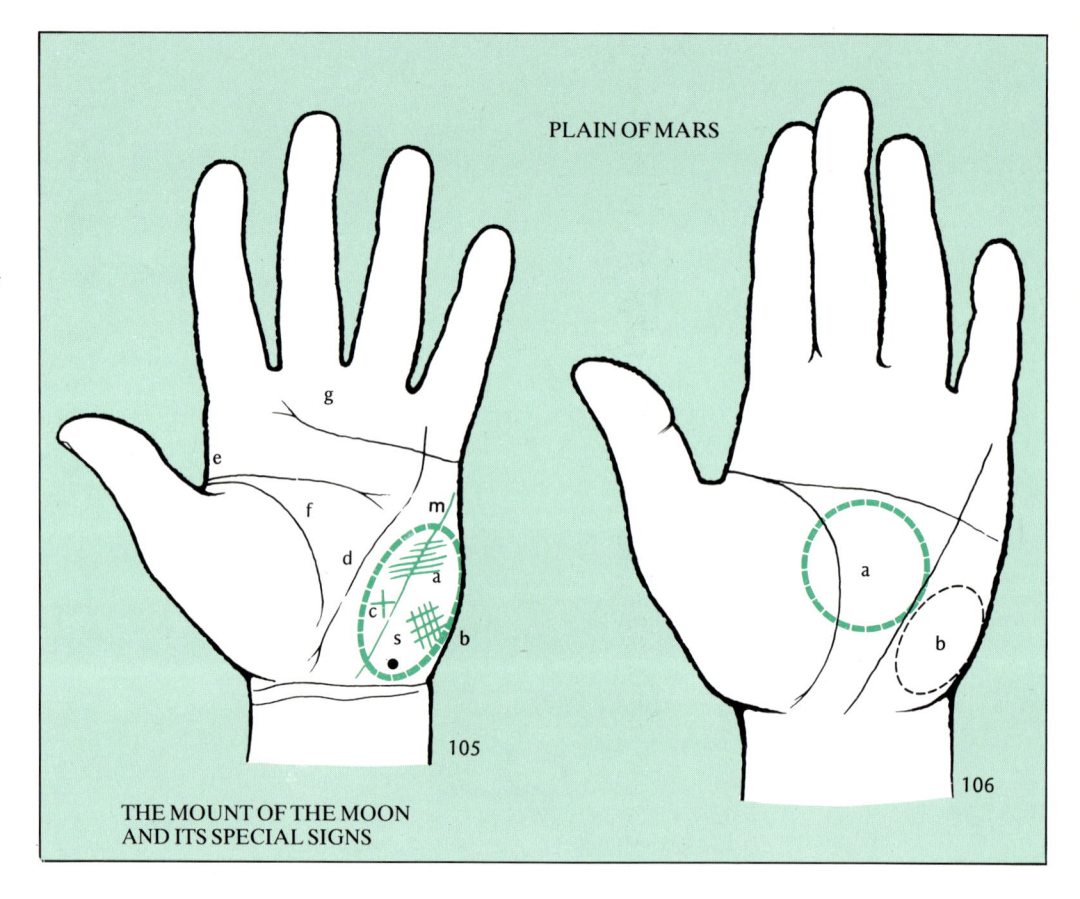

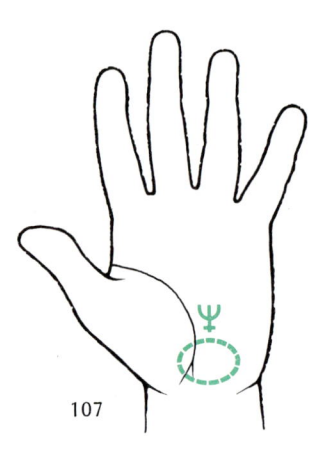

THE MOUNT OF THE MOON AND ITS SPECIAL SIGNS

PLAIN OF MARS

The plain of Neptune (107) indicates the degree to which the subject is able to influence people around him.

toward the back of the hand is a sign of difficulty in achieving success and being assertive. A well-defined cross anywhere on the mount signifies a lack of common sense or critical sense. A line that cuts across the mount of the Moon parallel to the line of Mercury indicates a strong attachment to material things. The colour, prominence, and consistency of the mount can provide useful information about the state of health of the spleen.

The plain of Mars

The plain of Mars lies in the center of the palm and is crossed by almost all of the principal lines and many secondary ones (*106*). Examination of this area using the same methods as for a general study of the palm will not yield more specialized information. Its significance needs to be ascertained through touch and the information obtained concerns the subject's character.

If the center of the plain of Mars feels soft when pressed firmly, it indicates that the character of the subject is weak and uncertain, easily influenced by those around him and the social circles he habitually frequents. When the center of the plain of Mars feels compact and hard, the subject has a stronger character and expresses his personality with greater confidence. He will sometimes consider suggestions from others, but only after subjecting them to thorough scrutiny.

The plain of Neptune

This plain consists of a small depression between the mount of Venus and the mount of the Moon (*107*). It has no particular importance unto itself but gains significance in relation to the lines that cross it, and its size. When the plain is rather large, marked by regular lines, and firm to the touch, the subject is able to influence people around him with his vital energy and powers of persuasion.

The lines and signs of the hand

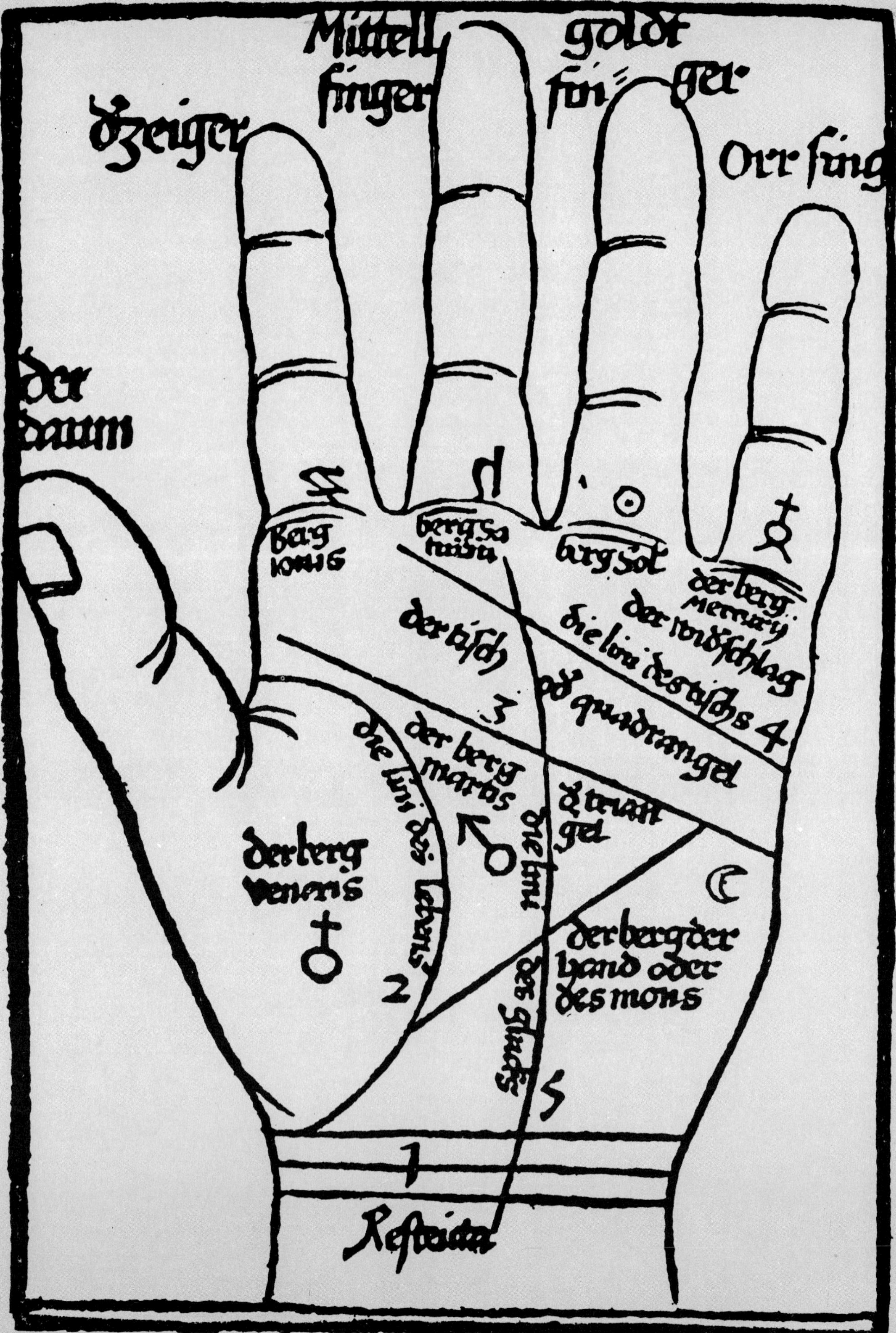
Mittell finger
goldt finger
d'zeiger
Orr fing
der daum
Berg Iovis
berg Saturni
berg Sol
der berg Mercury
der tisch
die lini des tischs 4
3
od' quadrangel
der berg martis
die lini des lebens
d' triangel
der berg veneris
2
die lini des glücks
der berg der hand oder des mons
5
1
Restricta

The four principal lines

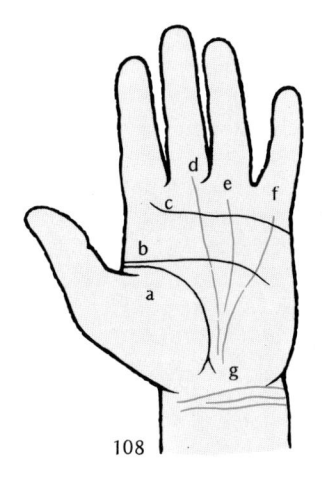

The principal lines of the hand (108): a life line, b head line, c heart line, d fate line, e line of the Sun, f line of Mercury, g wrist wrinkles. The life line (109) runs along almost all of the lower part of the mount of Venus; a is the mount of Jupiter, b the life line, c the wrist wrinkles.

Opposite, German print showing the lines, mounts, and their symbols (Trivulziana Library, Fondo Morando, Milan).

It is obvious to everyone that the palms of our hands are furrowed by marks, usually called lines. The most accurate possible interpretation of these lines is the task of palmistry. Why do we have these lines on our palms? What causes them to be there and what makes them different, despite a basic similarity, for each hand? These questions cannot be answered with absolute certainty, at least for the present.

We already have referred to currents of opinion that today enjoy the highest standing among men of learning dedicated to these studies. Many theories have been formulated over the centuries in an effort to explain what still today remains a mystery. When definitive answers are provided—and there is no doubt that one day they will be—palmistry will emerge from the shadows it has been relegated to for so long.

One theory highly regarded at the beginning of the nineteenth century maintained that the lines on our hands are the consequence of actions committed during our previous lives, in keeping with the principle that "the sins of the father will be visited on the son." However, in this case "father" is taken to mean our past incarnations. By the turn of the century this interesting but improbable idea had been supplanted by others, including a new theory expounded by Desbarolles in his book *Les mystères de la main*, published in Paris in 1859. "There is nothing more surprising than the electricity that passes through the nervous system from the hands to the brain and back again to the hands, leaving traces behind in its continual passage and conveying with it destiny from the stars and will and passions from the brain."

If we observe an open palm under good light, we immediately notice that there are two types of lines: larger ones that cross the palm horizontally and vertically, which are more accentuated and noticeable as a rule, and other more numerous short lines, often following a peculiar course and barely cutting into the firm surface of the palm. On the basis of this observation we can divide the palm lines into two principal types: main lines, and secondary lines (which again can be subdivided into two parts).

There are basically four main lines (*108*), designated as the life line, head line, heart line, and fate line. Practically every hand has them. The absence of one is considered extremely important, indicating an unusual destiny. The four main lines have been given their names because they describe a given subject's basic characteristics.

The life line, which is never absent, includes the thumb—the finger of the will—and thus reveals how the will is used in the most diverse situations. The head line practically divides the palm in half and represents one's understanding, intelligence, and memory. It retains memories and looks toward the future (represented by the plain of Mars) and it marks the boundary between one's ideals and their practical application. The heart line reveals sensitivity, emotionalism, and one's capacity to love. In these three lines alone there is enough to describe a person in general terms.

Along with these main lines are others that are less important because they are not found on everyone's palm, and their absence is not considered unusual: the *line of children*, the *marriage line*, the *widow's line*, the *hepatica* (or *health* or *Mercury*) *line*, the *line of Apollo* (or the *Sun*), and the *wrist wrinkles*.

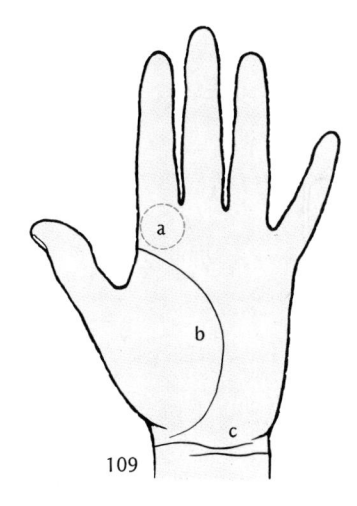

The life line

This line starts from the depression between the thumb and index finger and

The various starting points of the life line (110): a near the mount of Jupiter, b midway between the index finger and the thumb, c near the thumb.

The life line: the last section with descending branches (111), the last section directed toward the mount of the Moon (112), ending in two branches, one of which turns toward the mount of the Moon (113)—a is the life line, b the mount of the Moon.

continues along to the bottom of the mount of Venus, which one could say it outlines.

A perfect life line (*109*) begins below the mount of Jupiter and describes a symmetrical, well-proportioned curve as far as the wrist, where it blends in with the first wrist wrinkle. It should be a steady but shallow line with a slightly darker pink colour than the skin of the palm. The line should not be interrupted by special signs such as spots, islands, squares, stars, crosses, and the like, nor should it be cut across by other lines. Those rare people who have a perfect life line enjoy good health, are well balanced and full of vitality, and have normal sexual appetites.

Perfect life lines are few and far between. In reality it is the life line that almost always shows the greatest number of variations, and these must be studied very carefully as they are extremely important for our purposes.

The starting point of the life line
An appropriate place to begin is the starting point fairly near the mount of Jupiter.

1. *Starting point near the mount of Jupiter (110a).* The subject has a very remarkable personality that can sometimes lead to a too high opinion of himself and to overambitious aims often disproportionate to the circumstances (depending on the prominence of the mount of Jupiter).

2. *Starting point centered almost exactly between the index finger and thumb (110b).* The subject has a rather even temper but allows himself to be influenced by circumstances, which may consequently bring about sudden changes in behaviour.

3. *Starting point very near the thumb (110c).* The subject does not have a very strong personality. He often shuns the company of others and tends to prefer solitude. This trait has been observed in people who have taken up asceticism.

End of the life line
It is important to make careful note of how the life line ends. There are various possibilities.

1. *The life line completely encircles the mount of Venus, sometimes blending in with the first wrist wrinkle (111).* Without doubt this person has a great interest in home life; the house is seen as a refuge to return to as soon as social obligations allow. It is not a matter of wanting a hiding place so as to withdraw from sight, it represents a preference. If there are short, curved thin lines on the last section directed towards the mount of the Moon (*111*), this signifies that the love of domesticity is disturbed, sometimes by a desire for freedom and more open spaces, a desire that can be resolved by taking a trip. But this may also express the need for more radical changes, in which case a comparison of the two hands can be useful. If these signs appear only on the left hand, the subject is not able for various reasons to leave home

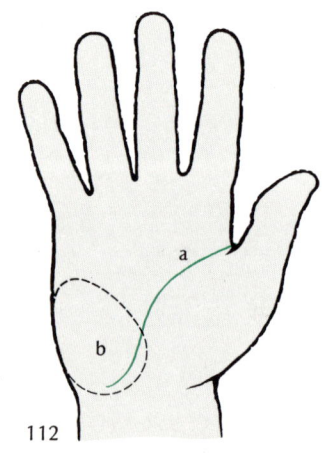

and takes refuge in daydreams. If the signs appear on both hands, this means that the subject leads a very busy life that includes travel which he does not enjoy but is unable to change.

2. *The last section of the life line is directed towards the mount of the Moon (112).* If the

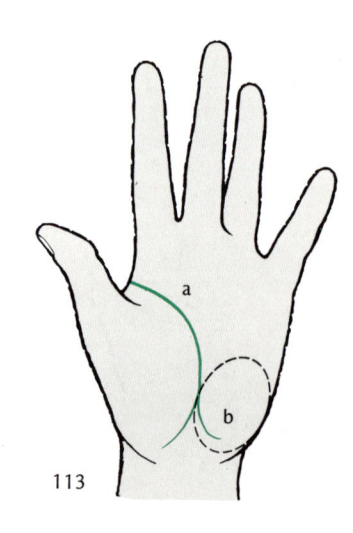

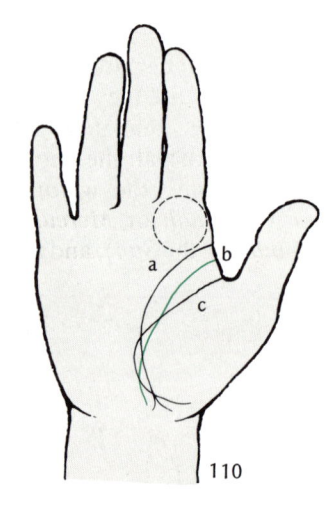

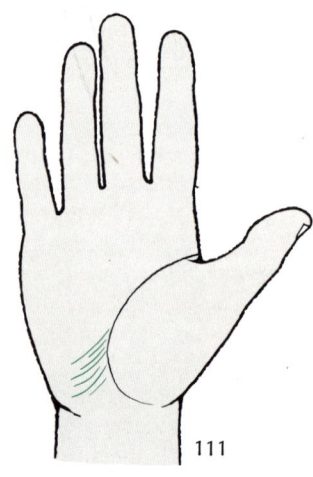

The life line can be long and thin (114a), poorly marked (114b), very deep (114c); it can have different kinds of breaks (115), have a square or rectangle on the break (116), or be broken by elongated islands (117).

line curves very decisively, then we have a person who loves travel and adventure, like the solitary yachtsman or the astronaut. It is very unlikely that circumstances will dampen this desire and these people will leave everything behind sooner or later to search for their "Northwest Passage."

3. *The life line divides into two branches which go in opposite directions, one of which shoots across to the mount of the Moon (113).* The subject allows himself some travel but soon wants to return.

The course of the life line

As we have seen the life line may describe a regular arc, or it may show deviations and interruptions of various kinds, including changes in colour and depth. Let us look at each case separately.

1. *The life line follows a regular course forming a well-shaped arc (109).* Denotes the ability to look at life very objectively, assessing the positive and negative aspects calmly and sensibly.

2. *A long, narrow life line (114a).* Here we have a person with an unusually nervous nature, which may cause serious nervous exhaustion especially when coinciding with the menopause.

3. *An indistinct life line that is uncertain and not at all deep (114b).* A person with this kind of line has little energy and is bothered by small disturbances, but nonetheless will have a long life.

4. *A very deep life line that is a dark pink colour (114c).* The character of this person is rather violent and aggressive. His nature is passionate in all its manifestations, including opinions, and he is unlikely to be stopped by reasonable advice.

5. *A broken life line (115).* The line must show a clean break. This indicates a serious illness or accident that may endanger the subject's life. Interruptions in the life line can appear at birth and become deeper or darker only when the event, serious illness, or accident is about to happen. With a dating system it is possible to determine roughly when this will occur and whether it will be illness or an accident. If both ends of the broken line are contained within a square or rectangle formed by four capillary lines intersecting at right angles (116), the illness or accident will occur but without endangering the life of the subject.

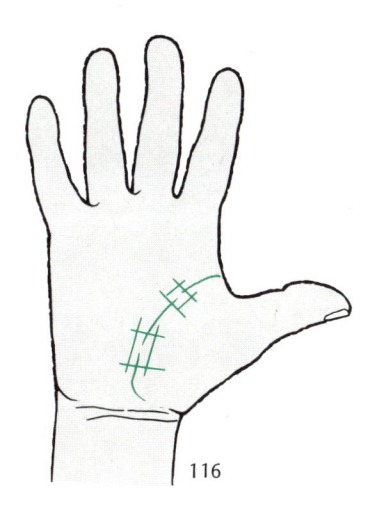

However, permanent marks, physical as well as psychological, may be left. The square, which rules out death in the case of a broken life line, often appears a few months before the illness or accident takes place and disappears some time after. This confirms that the will can be a vital factor in overcoming the obstacles of life.

6. *The life line is marked by one or more separate and distinct islands (117-119).*

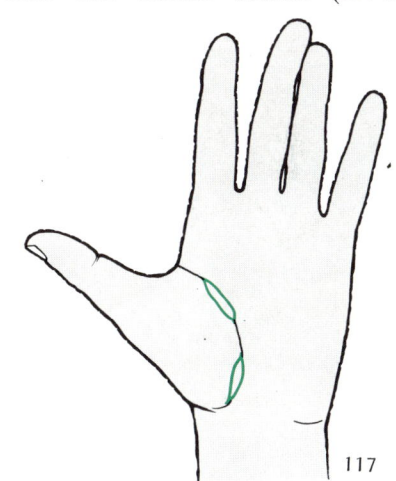

Often an indication of poor health: a fairly serious but not dangerous illness that tends to return periodically. These are not chronic infections but the frequent malfunctioning of a weak organ. The islands are symptomatic of exhaustion and a nervous condition.

If the island lies across the life line (118), its position or the angle that it forms with the line itself must be considered. In this case we are not dealing with the subject's health but instead with matters of an

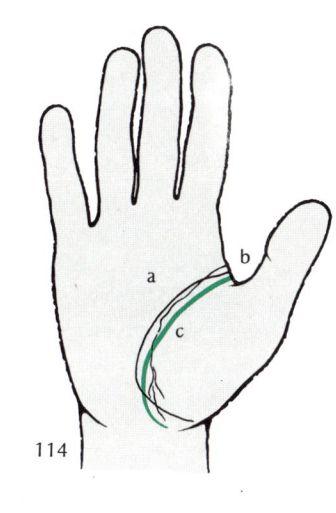

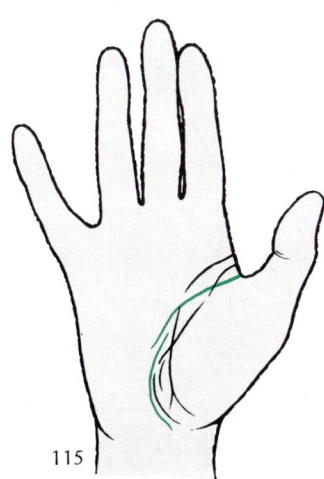

77

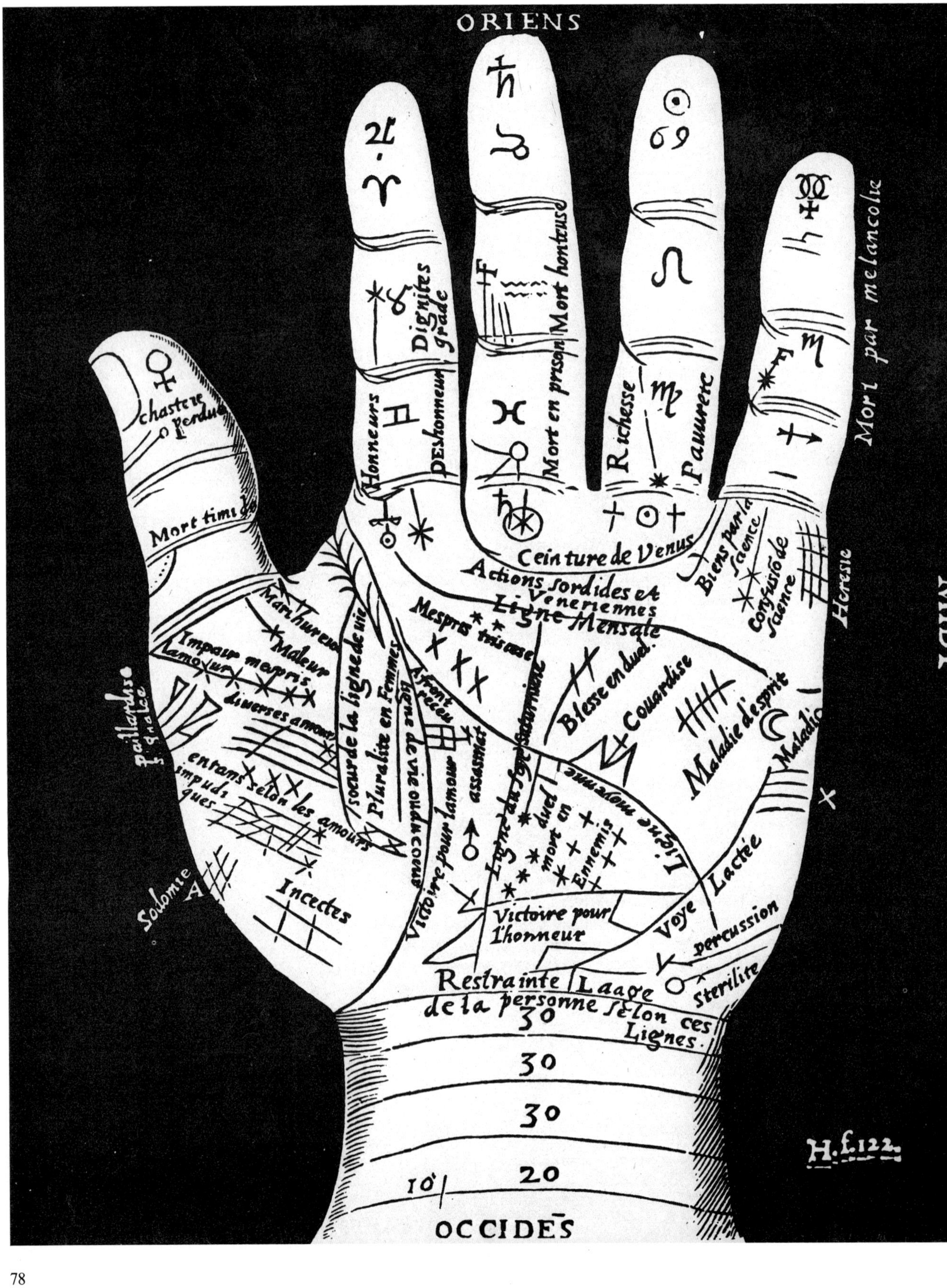
ORIENS
MIDY
OCCIDĒS
Mort par melancolie
chastete perdue
Mort timi de
Honneurs
Dignites grade
Deshonneur
Mort en prison
Mort honteuse
Richesse
Pauurete
Ceinture de Venus
Actions sordides et Veneriennes
Ligne Mensale
Biens par la science
Confusio de science
Heresie
Mespris triste
Malheureux
Maleur
Impair mespris
lamour
diverses amours
paillardise
entans impudiques
selon les amours
soeur de la ligne de vie
Pluralite en Femmes
Ligne de vie ou du coeur
Affront receu
assassinat
Victoire pour lamour
Ligne du foye Saturniene
Blesse en duel
Couardise
Maladie d'esprit
Maladie
Ligne moyenne
duel
mort en
Ennemis
Voye Lactee
Sodomie
Incectes
Victoire pour l'honneur
percussion
Sterilite
Restrainte Laage de la personne selon ces Lignes.
30
30
30
20
10
H.f.122.

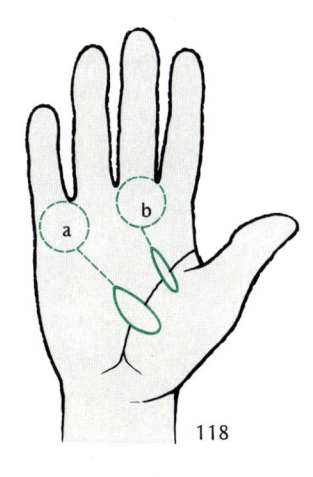

economic nature. When the island is pointing toward the mount of Mercury (*118a*), it indicates business problems or, depending on the period of life in which it is placed, worries about one's children. When it is pointing toward the mount of Saturn (*118b*), it indicates that during the period in the subject's life determined by the dating method there may be rather serious economic difficulties of the sort to change his life-style. If the island is pointing toward the mount of Apollo, that is, toward the base of the ring finger, the subject's problems are of a moral nature. Something has

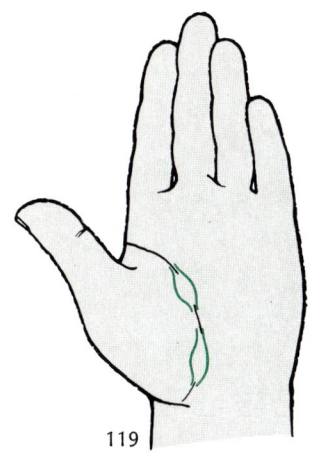

The life line may be broken by transverse islands facing the mounts of Mercury (118a) and Saturn (118b), by kidney-shaped islands (119), by spots and short diagonal lines (120), by a long island marked off by short diagonal lines (121), by grilles facing the plain of Mars (122a) or the wrist (122b).

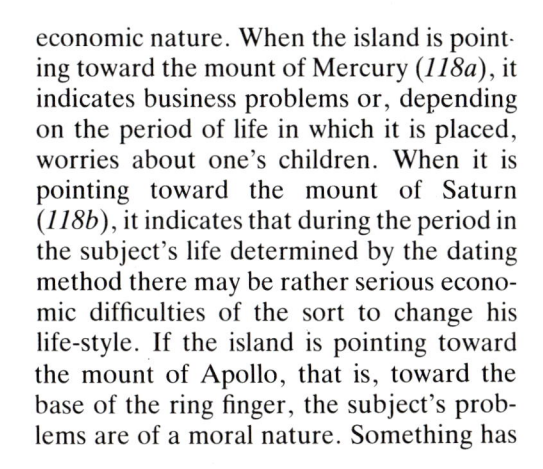

happened to him during that period that he wishes to hide from other people out of fear of criticism or gossip. It is something that can mar the image he wants to present to others.

7. *The presence of spots on the life line (120)* usually indicates short illnesses. Their seriousness is revealed by the appearance of the spot: the deeper and redder it is the more serious the illness.

8. *The life line is crossed by short lines (120).* While these may be single lines or groups of lines, the meaning is the same: they indicate moments of anxiety, apprehension, and uncertainty corresponding to the period established by the dating method.

9. *A long island appears on the life line (121)*: indicates problems and obstacles over a long period of time. If the island is crossed by lines, that can also signify an injury affecting the subject's personality. In this case even a slight disturbance tends to become chronic and during this long period

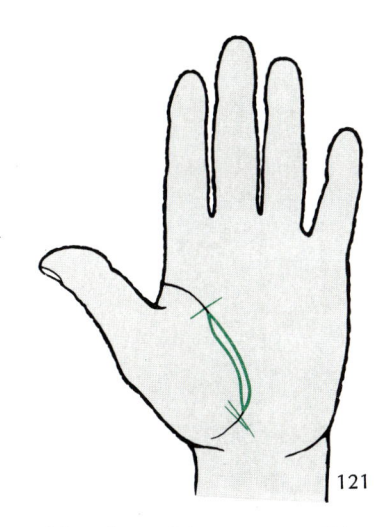

Opposite, lines and other signs of the hand with interpretations and with the position of the signs of the zodiac, a French etching of 1640, from the Works *of Jean-Baptiste Belot.*

the subject is unable to express himself well due to poor health. As a result there may be complications affecting his work, as every undertaking requires considerable effort and this can prolong the illness.

10. *A grille begins at the mount of Venus and extends across the life line (122).* Always indicates a slowing down of the subject's potential, a temporary reduction of vital energy, but with subtle differences according to the area in which the grille is located. If it appears midway on the life line, exactly opposite the plain of Mars (*122a*), it relates principally to work and only rarely to a temporary failing in the sex life. Should the grille be found on the bottom part of the line near the wrist (*122b*), its meaning changes considerably. The subject tends to withdraw from an active and productive life even though he may be in good health, creating an inner world in which he closes himself off as if in self-imposed exile.

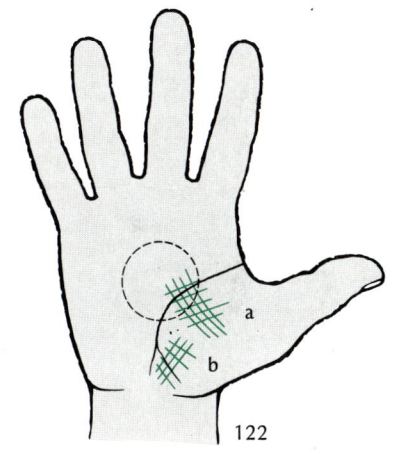

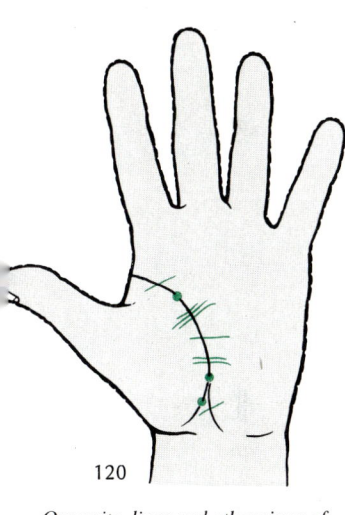

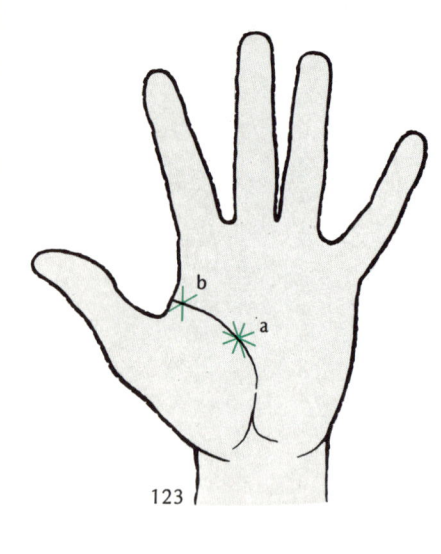

11. *A star or cross cuts across the life line (123).* Either is symptomatic of a sudden, unfavourable event for which the subject is only indirectly responsible. If the star or cross is very deep and red it may signify a heart attack.

Branches on the life line

Branches on the life line are rather fine, almost like capillary lines. Their significance depends on whether they point upward or down.

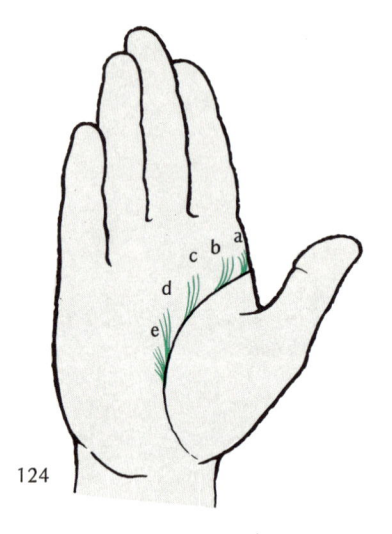

Branches on the first part of the life line, which would correspond to the first twenty years (*124a*), indicate problems occurring during the subject's youth. Branches pointing toward the base of the index finger (*124b*) indicate the subject's efforts to affirm his personality, often a difficult process. If they point toward the mount of Saturn (*124c*), the subject's problems and conflicts are or have been caused by the family; if accompanied by a cross, there has been a change in the subject's life as a result of the death of a parent. If the branches point toward the base of the ring finger (*124d*), the subject has had or could have had the kind of success that child prodigies enjoy.

If the branches point toward the head line (*125a*), they indicate successful enterprises, high earnings, or a government job. Branches pointing downward (*125b*) indicate problems in business, poor earnings, and sometimes hard times. When they point toward the thumb (*125c*), the mount of Venus, the meaning is negative: anxieties and problems are in store for the subject and progress toward goals will be retarded.

Special signs on the life line

If the life line rises from the depression between the thumb and index finger with a clearly marked cross (*126a*), the traditional interpretation is that life will not be without its difficulties, but the subject will nevertheless achieve his goals. When the cross is to be found at the end of the life line (*126b*), it signifies death at a time of happiness, or perhaps *because* of some great happiness.

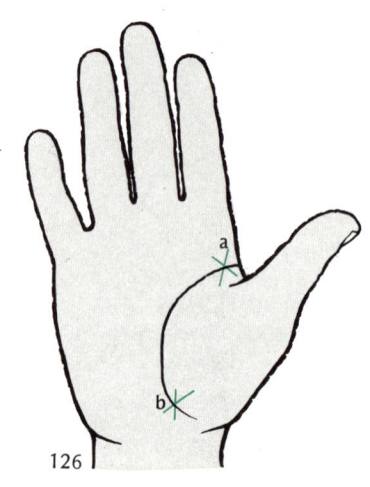

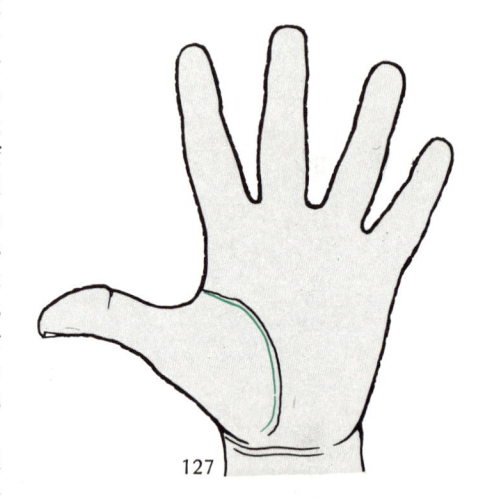

It sometimes happens that we see two life lines running parallel to each other (*127*). This quite unusual arrangement signifies physical and economic well being, but for greater accuracy one should compare the two hands. If they both show a double line

The life line can also be marked by a star (123a) or a cross (123b). It can have ascending branches (124), branches pointing toward the head line (125a), downward (125b), or toward the thumb (125c). The life line can begin and end with a cross (126); sometimes it may even be double (127).
Opposite, "a break in the heart line, simple sentiments but constant," a French postcard from the early 1900s.

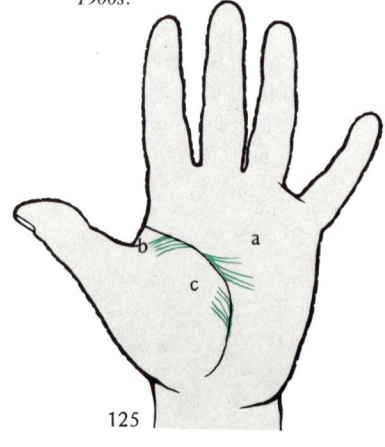

Ligne du Cœur

Interrompue

Sentiments Simples mais Constants

A perfect heart line (128) is very rare; its position can be calculated by using the method described on this page and illustrated in figure 130.

There can be breaks in the heart line (129a); b is the head line.

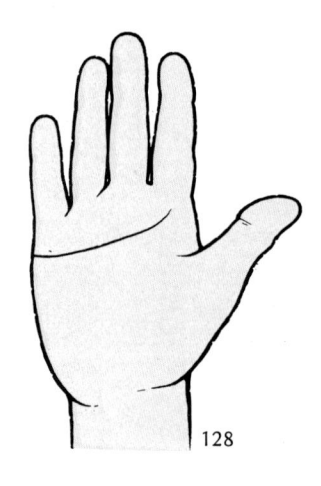

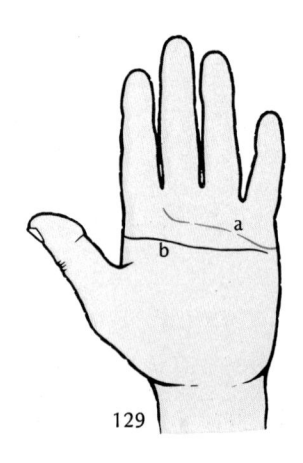

the prediction will be confirmed. If the double line appears only on the left hand, the prophecy holds true but in a modified form, and many obstacles will have to be negotiated before success is achieved. In any case it is an indication of a very pronounced sensuality that does not require any sentimental relationship.

The heart line

This line is located at the top of the palm just below the mounts of Mercury, the Sun, Saturn, and sometimes Jupiter (*128*). As its name suggests, it can provide very useful information about the heart in general, but also about the nature of the subject's feelings, sensitivity, moods (which are usually thought to be in some way connected with the heart), emotional life, and sex life.

We have already noted that this is one of the principal lines, but unlike the life line it is not always present. Sometimes we have instead some very vague, broken lines (*129a*) or the heart line may merge completely with the head line (*129b*). However, these are very rare instances which we shall discuss later.

The beginning of the heart line

Not that long ago there were palmists who placed the starting point of the heart line on the side of the mount of Jupiter, and thus it terminated below the mount of Mercury. This custom did not in any way affect the importance or significance of the heart line, but it was abandoned by more modern palmists for reasons of simplicity and coherence. The section of the heart line below the mount of Mercury shows little variation in a comparison of different hands; the greatest number of differences is found at the opposite end. Further, the system of dating used by many palmists places the *first* twenty years of life at the *initial* section of the heart line under the mount of Mercury.

The heart line, unlike the other principal lines, begins under the mount of Mercury at the outer edge of the hand and ends, when it follows a normal course, in the area of the mount of Jupiter.

To describe a perfect heart line we need to have a very good imprint of the palm.

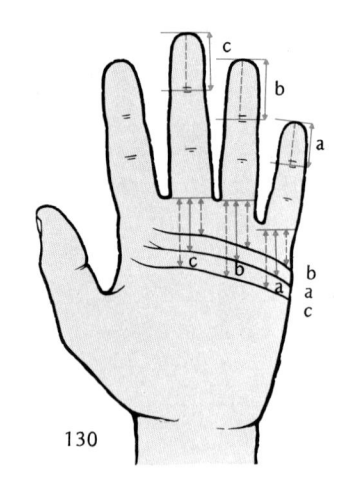

We then draw vertical lines from the center of the base of the middle finger, the ring finger, and the little finger to the heart line or an extension of it (*130*). If the length of the vertical lines we have drawn is the same as the length of the first phalange of the middle finger, ring finger, and little finger respectively, then the heart line is in a perfect position (*130a*). A person who has such a heart line—actually a rather rare circumstance—can be regarded as emotionally stable, well balanced, and as having normal sexual appetites.

When the lines we have drawn are clearly shorter than the first phalanges of the respective fingers, which means the heart line runs very close to the arc at the base of the fingers (*130b*), it indicates a person who is excessively emotional, tends to over react (which means poor self-control or lack of a sense of moderation), and who has unexpected passions or enthusiasms.

If the vertical lines are decidedly longer than the corresponding first phalanges, meaning that the heart line lies closer to the head line (*130c*), then the subject is the opposite of the previous type. Though not actually devoid of emotions, he is very much in control of them. He makes decisions carefully, acting with prudence and only after much reflection. In other words he never acts impulsively in any of his relationships, the result being that he almost never gives vent to his true feelings and thereby loses genuine opportunities.

Returning to our description of a perfect heart line, we should add that it must be clearly visible and curve slightly toward the

The heart line can be concave (131), straight (132), convex (133); a is the heart line and b the head line, in all three figures.

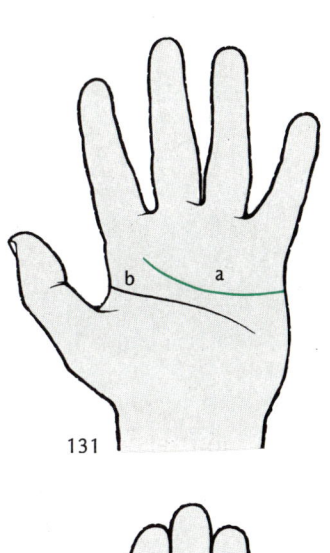

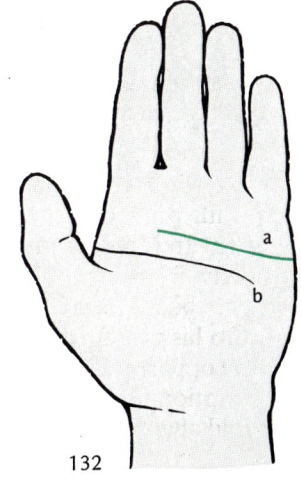

head line. The line must be continuous, not very deep, and pink in colour. Before continuing with a more detailed examination, however, we should make one point clear: whatever results we obtain from our study of the heart line, they must be seen in relation to and interpreted along with our findings about the head line (which we will discuss later). Bear in mind that the heart line represents a bridge, bringing energy from the unconscious side of the hand to the conscious. It further indicates how much emotion emanates from this mysterious world of the subconscious and what kind of emotion emerges in the subject's conscious self. Remembering that the head line moving in the opposite direction represents the subject's rational control over irrationality and instinct, by a thorough and comparative reading of these two lines we can solve this equation with four variables that give a complete picture of the subject's psychological nature. Other elements can be added to clarify certain points. For example, expert palmists look particularly at the structure and length of the little finger and sometimes at certain aspects of the mount of Venus. What emerges from a reading of these two main lines is more than adequate to give us a reliable picture of the basic personality.

The course of the heart line
The course of the heart line is very variable, but generally speaking there are three basic types.
1. *Concave heart line (131).* A more pronounced curve than that of the perfect heart line, this is the type most frequently encountered in palmistry. It can be lightly or heavily marked depending on the person's capacity to react and his sensitivity both in the amorous sense, and more generally in relation to family and friends.
2. *Straight heart line (132).* Runs parallel and fairly near the head line, but is always completely distinct. It denotes an element of coldness in the person's temperament. This type of line—quite common— indicates an understanding of love and friendship that departs from the average interpretation. The subject tries to satisfy psychic rather than physical needs. He introduces a large measure of intellectual-

ism, particularly in his romantic life, but that does not prevent a deep attachment.
3. *Convex heart line (133).* From its point of origin under the mount of Mercury, the heart line tends to rise slightly toward the mounts of the Sun and Saturn, curving abruptly downward until it joins (or almost joins) the head line under the mount of Jupiter. We can now add an interesting observation to what we have already learned: the subject has had or will have a mental or psychophysical shock that will profoundly affect his way of feeling, his particular sensibilities, and the way in which he shows them. A comparison of the studies made before and after the shock can give the impression that one is dealing with two different people. It is possible to determine the nature of the shock by examining all the lines together and applying the appropriate method of dating to say when this event took or will take place.

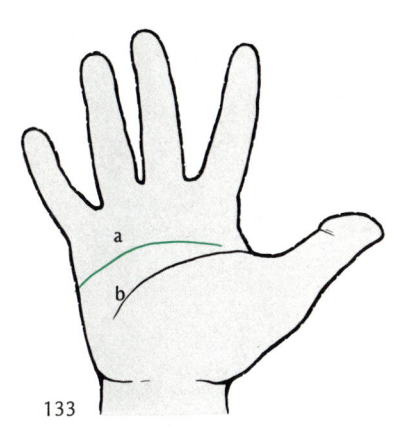

Ends of the heart line
The point at which the heart line originates rarely presents any irregularities; the ways in which it ends, however, are infinite. In the vast majority of cases it finishes under the mount of Jupiter one way or the other. The many variations can be grouped into several more typical categories (134).
1. *The heart line ends near the highest point of the mount of Jupiter (134b). The meaning is positive: the subject's emotional life is rich, varied, and well balanced.*
2. *The heart line tends to extend to the edge of the palm below the base of the index finger, crossing the mount of Jupiter (134a). The person tends to be jealous, possessive*

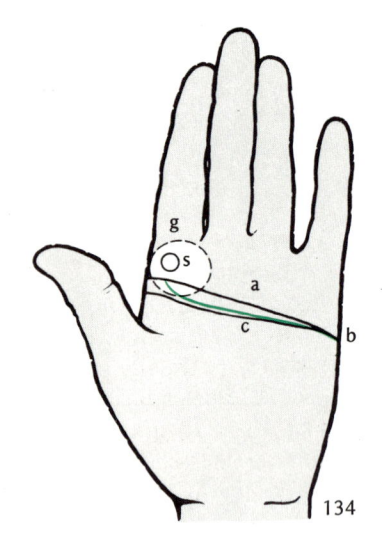

The heart line can cross the mount of Jupiter (134a), end by the summit (s) of the mount of Jupiter (g) (134b), pass under the mount of Jupiter (134c); it may end between the index and middle fingers (135a), under the mount of Saturn (135b), or under the mount of Apollo or the Sun (135c).
Branches of the heart line (136) can be a ascending or b descending; t is the head line.

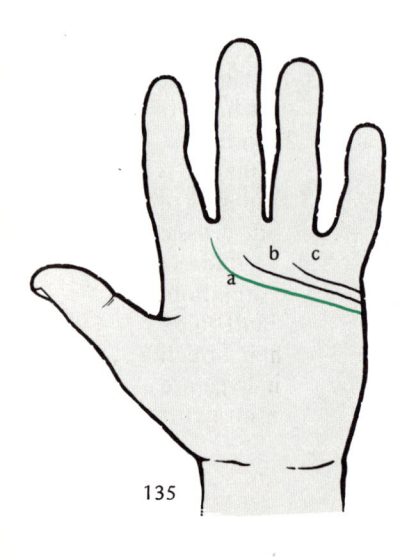

in love and has a strong attachment to material acquisitions—not avarice but a sharply defined sense of ownership.

3. *The heart line reaches the edge of the palm, passing under the mount of Jupiter (134c).* Here the subject's jealousy extends beyond the loved one to the group of people around him: family, friends, professional associates, club, political party. This attachment, more common than is believed, coincides with the person's need to defend in every possible way his own role in society, his only means of satisfaction and single opportunity to exercise power. Understandable behaviour, but without much stability because it lacks the counter-balancing effect of family affections or a loving relationship which clearly do not carry the weight they should for the subject. Evidence of this imbalance: it is almost always the subject who ruins everything by being overzealous.

4. *The heart line ends at the meeting point between the index and middle fingers between the mounts of Jupiter and Saturn (135a).* A person with this kind of termination is quick to show enthusiasm, but almost always without practical application. His goals in life are wholly self-oriented. Some experts in palmistry assign another meaning to this line, but it only appears to be different. They interpret it as indicating a great love for which the subject is prepared to sacrifice much of his own personality.

5. *The heart line ends under the mount of Saturn (135b).* Fairly common. It denotes considerable emotional disquiet accompanied by great uncertainty in making choices. This attitude bespeaks little depth in one's affections. The result is frequent disappointments in love and friendships, but the regret is usually short-lived. As a rule the real interest of this subject is concentrated on other problems, both of a personal nature (with obvious egocentrism), and those of others, who end up taking the place usually occupied by the loved one and to whom the subject devotes all his energies.

6. *The heart line ends under the mount of the Sun (135c).* Quite rare because the line is exceptionally short. Not a positive sign. It indicates an unusual poverty of spirit, an inability to establish satisfactory relationships with others and a consequent need to withdraw into oneself, with all of the attendant psychological harm that implies. This is a serious problem and should have the attention of a psychiatrist. Do not confuse this inability to communicate with another state of mind, which may appear similar but stems from great spiritual resources that induce a need for solitude and soul-searching. In the latter case signs must be sought elsewhere, especially in the head line and in the mount of Jupiter.

The heart line very rarely ends with a single line. Mostly it branches out in the final section and one can learn very interesting things about the subject's emotions from the type and number of *branches*. Given the importance of these branches, let us consider them in some detail, as we did for the life line.

Branches from the heart line
When branches appear on the heart line, that great link between the conscious and the unconscious, they are like an indicator board displaying the subject's choices, preferences, tendencies, and deviations. We shall limit ourselves to brief descriptions; a good interpretation requires a great deal of experience.

Branches (*136*) do not only appear at the end of the heart line. They may appear all along the line, referred to as *ascending* (*136a*) or *descending* (*136b*) depending on whether they point upward or down.

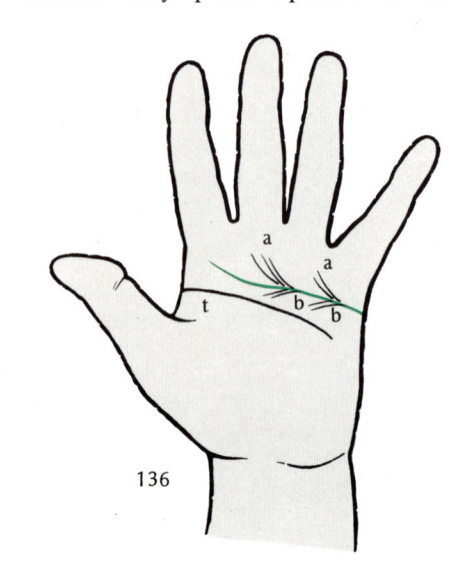

Ascending branches usually are regarded as positive; their orientation toward the mounts of the Sun, Saturn, or Jupiter influences the general reading of the heart line, affecting its interpretation. (The variations are too numerous for us to give examples here.)

In general we can say that ascending branches facing the meeting point between the index and middle fingers are the most positive for the emotional serenity of the subject. For example, if the branches form a trident (*137*), it is a sign of great success in love.

By ascending branches we not only mean the lines that point upwards from the heart line—from the mount of Mercury toward the mount of Jupiter—but also the lines pointing upward but facing in the opposite direction—starting from the mount of Jupiter and pointing toward the mount of Mercury (*138*). What they signify is of the greatest importance.

1. *If they face the mount of Apollo (138a)* the subject tends to idealize love affairs or the loved one. He may not be completely honest, but he likes to think he is.

2. *If they face the mount of Saturn (138b)* the emotional life of the subject is more turbulent, always full of doubts and uncertainties. But sooner or later he finds the right balance.

3. *When the branches face the mount of Jupiter*, the most common variation, the subject introduces into his love life (or, more generally speaking, his emotional life) a practical element—we could even call it ambition—that clouds the purity of his feelings but adds a down-to-earth quality with positive value in daily life.

4. Similar conclusions apply when these branches face the mount of Mercury. In this case the romantic feelings are weaker. The economic interest is more sharply defined, both in love and in friendship, to the extent that there is very often some form of close collaboration, usually profitable for both parties. Branches facing the mount of Mercury should be interpreted with great prudence because they can sometimes be a sign of a sexual conflict that may become an actual perversion, depending on how close they come to the beginning of the heart line.

Descending branches, the lines facing downward (*136b*) from the heart line point toward the head line and negatively influence the reading that emerges from the study of the heart line. In most cases they indicate a romantic relationship that begins with great problems and often ends badly, for reasons not connected with the subject's wishes. Often it is a relationship in which one or both of the parties are married, an affair that drags on for many years, providing little satisfaction and preventing other encounters and relationships.

In such cases a fine capillary line accompanies the branch for the whole of its course. Where a short perpendicular line crosses the branch, the romantic relationship will end with the sudden death of the partner. If the capillary line crosses the branch at an acute angle, it signifies a deep disappointment in ending the relationship. This kind of branch can be found on people who are very unselfish in their affections, which also tells us that their lives are not simply a succession of disappointments and failures.

Bear in mind when examining these branches that when the subject is about to begin a new relationship, he may not be in the best of health or perhaps a brief illness may temporarily have reduced his physical energy and ability to make decisions. In all cases considerable complications can develop and it will take great willpower for the person to extricate himself.

The heart line can end in a trident (137a) (b is the head line). Ascending branches of the head line can point in different directions (138): a shows ascending branches pointing toward the mount of Apollo and b toward the mount of Saturn; t is the head line.

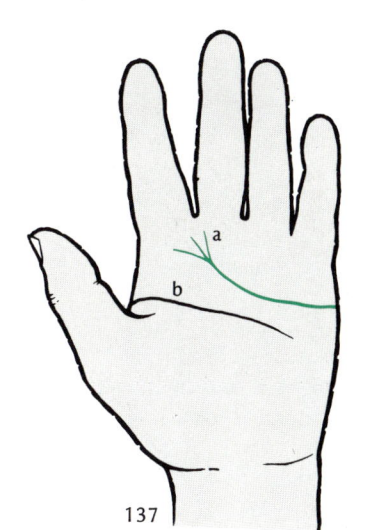

85

The heart line can be thin (139a), in which case it indicates the subject's shyness, or broad (139b), a sign of pathological brutality.

Emotional involvements are a prime illustration of situations in which free will plays a fundamental role in the destiny of the subject. Meeting someone who arouses a romantic interest means the beginning of a relationship only if the subject deliberately wishes it. The decision to begin a relationship despite obvious obstacles is a matter of free choice, and the inevitable misfortune that follows cannot be assigned to bad luck or fate. The subject cannot avoid meeting the person involved, but he can, by exercising his will, influence the length of the relationship. This is the kind of situation to which a palmist of many years' experience commonly refers in order to explain that free will exists and how it often plays a crucial part in the events of our lives.

Some palmists also ascribe another meaning to the descending branches of the heart line. They are said to signify a very intense relationship between the heart and head lines, a sort of drawing together of the two lines, as it were. In this case colour is a determinant of the interpretation. Sometimes this linking tendency takes concrete form. In very rare cases the two lines join and become one, cutting across the palm just below the four mounts. From what would otherwise be only a tendency to cruelty—that is, reason still prevails over impulsiveness—we move to a person who instinctively expresses his feelings with violence whatever the situation happens to be.

Short of certain extremes, the proximity of these two lines is always a symptom of intense conflicts that, in emotionally weaker subjects, explode in outbursts of violence or drive them to seek oblivion in artificially created paradises.

Colour, depth, and width of the heart line
The normal colour, as we said before, should be somewhat rosy. A deeper shade indicates poor circulation or heart trouble. One can note with periodic observation of the hands how the line changes colour in relation to the progress of the disease. Naturally this alone is not sufficient to establish whether there is heart disease or how serious it is. There are other signs to confirm the diagnosis and they must be carefully investigated.

The depth of the heart line can also reveal interesting information. If the line is regular and well defined, the subject has deep feelings and is faithful in love and in friendship. If the line is very deep, the preceding is skewed by an egotism that prevents the subject from talking to his partner with the necessary understanding. This sometimes makes it difficult to continue the relationship even though the subject may wish to do so. When the line is very fine (*139a*), it is a sure sign of shyness and sensitive but deep feelings. A very broad heart line (*139b*) indicates harshness and heedless brutality, which manifests itself only when the subject is undergoing a violent emotional crisis. This is considered a pathological trait; there is no element of a calculating use of brutality as an end in itself.

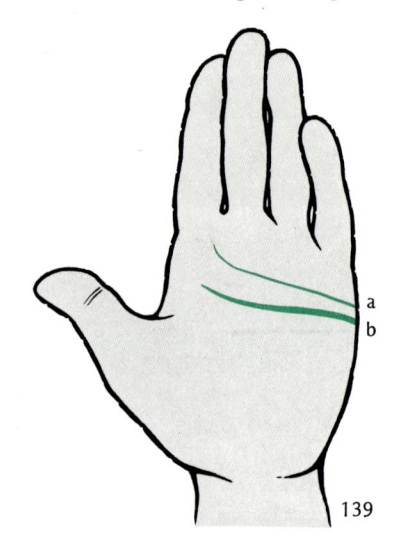

Special signs on the heart line
Now what about the modifications produced by the presence of special signs?
1. *One or more spots on the heart line (104a).* If the colour of the line remains unchanged, we are dealing with problems of a psychological nature—emotional or sentimental anxieties. If the colour around the spot is dark red, this is most probably a minor cardiac disorder, like tachycardia.
2. *The heart line is crossed by short lines (140b).* Small, diagonal capillary lines indicate romantic problems of short duration.
3. *One or more islands on the heart line*

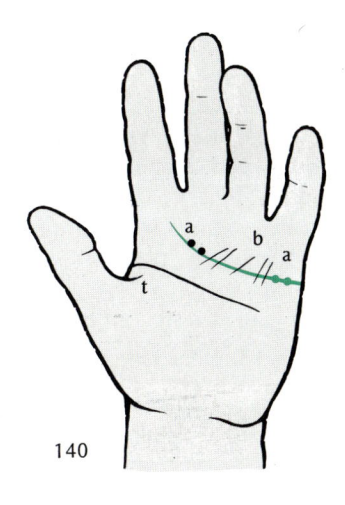

The heart line can be broken by special signs: spots (140a), short diagonal lines (140b); different kinds of islands (141), grilles (142a), stars (142b), crosses (142c), it can be plaited or chained (143); t in figures 140, 141, and 143 is the head line.

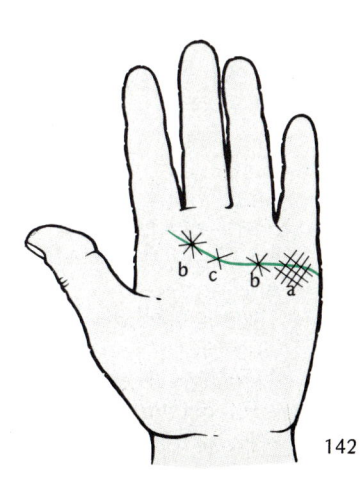

(*141*). A sure reference to the heart itself. Exactly what and how serious must be ascertained through further examination of other parts of the hand. If the island is long and narrow, and starts almost at the beginning of the heart line, this very likely indicates a congenital or childhood disorder. By way of exception, when the island is small and located near the mount of Jupiter, the meaning is different. This denotes romantic disappointments or unhappiness. It is often found on the hands of children of divorced parents who have experienced a trauma in infancy due to the break up of the family.

4. *A grille located on the first section of the heart line* (*142a*). The meaning is rather negative: almost always circulation problems in the lower limbs. The distinctness of this sign is related to the seriousness of the disorder; it tends to disappear as soon as the condition improves, as with the other signs described here.

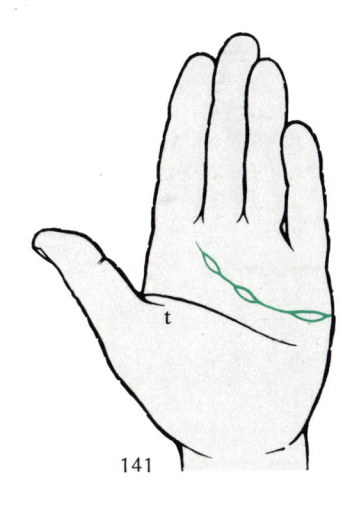

5. *A star located on the heart line* (*142b*). Always an inauspicious sign. It tells of disorders that can directly harm the heart or the circulatory system. The seriousness of the danger can be determined by a more complete examination, which will also indicate with some accuracy when it will happen. Foreknowledge allows the subject to take steps to reduce the danger to a minimum. In this instance too we can speak, though less directly, of exercising free will.

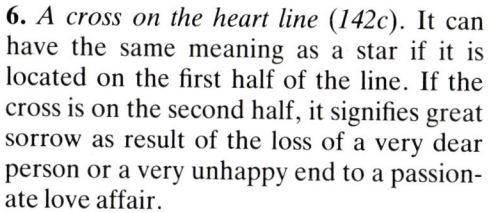

6. *A cross on the heart line* (*142c*). It can have the same meaning as a star if it is located on the first half of the line. If the cross is on the second half, it signifies great sorrow as result of the loss of a very dear person or a very unhappy end to a passionate love affair.

7. *The heart line is chained* (*143*). Many meanings here. We are dealing with a rather emotionally unstable person who is very susceptible to falling in love but whose feelings are shallow. Hence this person alternates between moments of great tenderness and of indifference. Heart lines of this sort often belong to people who, because of their prominent position, are the objects of great romantic interest they naturally cannot always or will not accept.

The head line

One of the main lines (*144*), located on the upper part of the palm below the heart line. It originates in the area between the mount of Jupiter and the insertion of the thumb, running across the palm toward the outer edge of the hand, which it very rarely reaches.

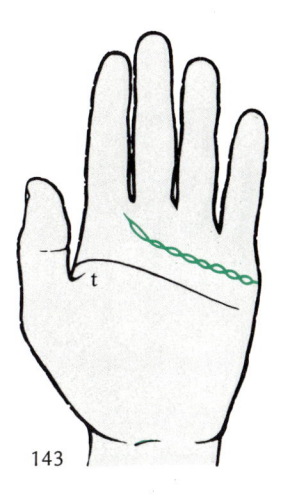

It is called the head line because, when properly interpreted, it can give important information about the extent and depth of the subject's reasoning powers—the method of reasoning he uses—what we can call his mentality beyond just the power of concentration. Other information that will emerge from studying this line concerns the subject's suggestibility, that is, how easily he can be influenced and to what extent he is able to resist blandishments from the people around him or the allures of his setting. Among the interesting indications that emerge from the head line is the subject's ability to empathize with the people he comes into contact with or to identify with the situations in which he might find himself. In other words, how well he understands the world in which he lives. Thus we can determine to what degree he feels that he belongs or, conversely, how much he withdraws into himself. Hence, from an examination of the head line, we can draw meaningful conclusions about the intelligence of the subject. We mean intelligence in the broadest sense of the word, similar to the Latin meaning, which is not confined to the ability to understand but embraces the ability to feel, to perceive something beyond a cold rational assessment. However, this does not include intuition, which as we have already noted is expressed by the heart line. This further confirms that we must study the head and heart line together.

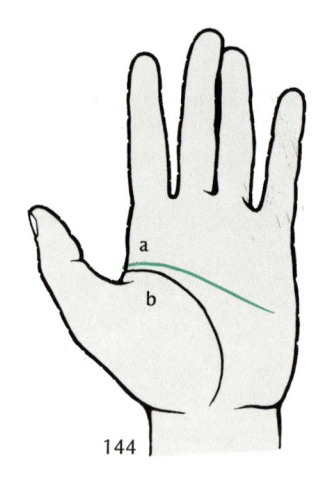

The beginning of the ideal head line must be separate from the life line and rise beneath the mount of Jupiter. It should stand out clearly but not be too deep; it should be pink in colour and without any special signs. It should curve gently downward and end without blurring just below the passive mount of Mars (*144a*). Of course it is very unusual to find a head line like this, just as it is unusual to find people with exceptional intellectual gifts, but on those rare occasions when we do come across a head line that approaches perfection, then we have a person with great stability, understanding, sensitivity, intelligence, etc.

Let us now try to establish the most common variations on this perfect head line and review the most reliable interpretations we can give them.

The beginning of the head line

As mentioned, it is located between the attachment point of the index finger and the joint of the second phalange of the thumb. The life line also rises in this area and as a consequence the two lines may start off either together or separately.

1. *The head line and life line originate as one line* (*145*). This beginning, very common, is always found on the hands of people who are highly sensitive but who have very little self-control. They are subject to outbursts, therefore, especially when faced with small, everyday obstacles. For important events they know how to draw on inner resources and show remarkable forebearance and powers of reflection. These people usually attach a great deal of importance to the impression they make on others. They want to be liked, so they dress carefully and never say anything that might offend, sometimes even to the extent of not telling the truth.

Despite these rather contradictory modes of behaviour, these persons are very sensitive and extremely kindhearted. They need to be appreciated, understood, and praised in order to give of their best, which is usually of the highest standards. Consequently they do nothing to show themselves to advantage, waiting for others to do it for them, which happens very seldom. Unscrupulous people will take advantage of this weakness and exploit them mercilessly.

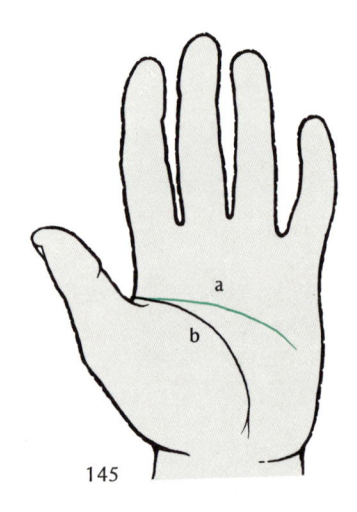

The longer the head and life lines remain intertwined, the easier it is to determine how much and in what way the emotions, dreams, plans, and disappointments of childhood have influenced the subject. With the dating method one can establish

A perfect head line (144a) must be clear and well-defined for the whole of its course, pink in colour, not too deep, and end beneath the passive mount of Mars; b is the life line. It sometimes originates together with the life line (145).
Opposite, the hands of the Virgin from the Annunciation *by Antonello da Messina (Galleria Regionale della Sicilia, Palermo).*

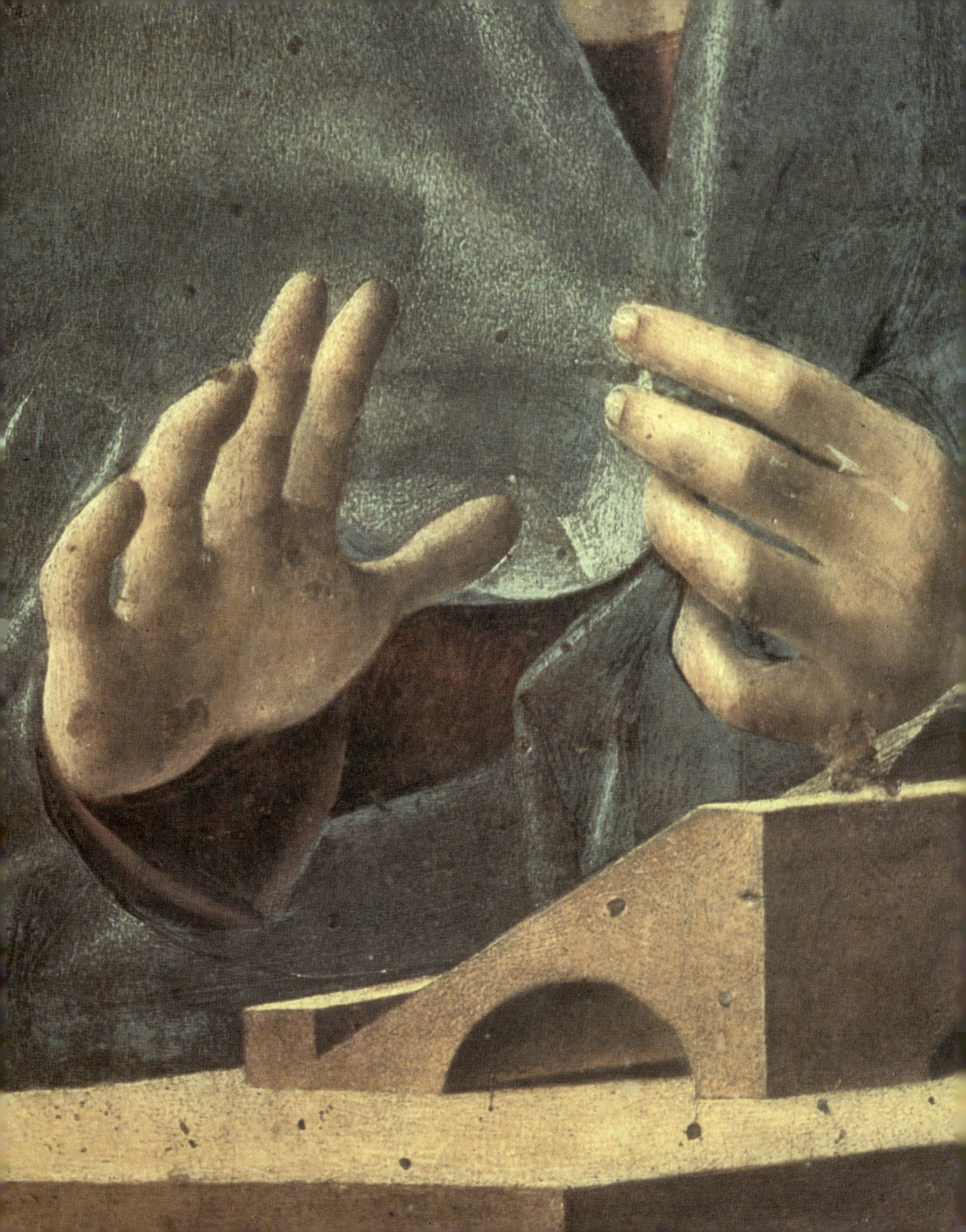

Opposite, reflections of love, hands from Arnolfini and His Wife *by Jan Van Eyck (National Gallery, London).*

until what age the subject was dominated by the family's influence, particularly that of the father. By extending the examination to the area around the mount of Jupiter, one can learn if and to what degree the subject has broken free of his upbringing through early childhood and puberty.

The information that emerges from studying this type of head line may have to be modified upon checking the shape and colour of the nails. If they tend to be square and coloured dark pink, the nervous outbursts characteristic of the subject may become more violent and his self-control subsequently less effective. However, this type of person does not hold ill feelings toward those who irritate him and soon forgets incidents, but the people he is involved with do not always forget. If the nails are conic in shape and a pale colour, the subject's reactions are less impulsive but more deeply felt. He harbours resentment.

2. The head line and life line originate near each other but at two distinct points (146). In this case we can say with certainty that the subject has some degree of sensitivity but assuredly less than the preceding personality type, so his reactions and susceptibility will not be as quick. The subject is better able to control his emotions and his behaviour toward others, showing more self-confidence and consistency. He enjoys praise, naturally, as well as esteem, but if they are missing he is not that unhappy. Their absence might even act as a stimulus to do more to oblige people to notice him and his gifts.

Sometimes one finds that these people hold too high of an opinion of themselves, with all of the dangers that can entail. It is in any case certain that people whose head line originates separately from their life line have a remarkable ability to judge situations rapidly and face them openly and frankly, almost always without bias. Their critical sense is highly developed, and sometimes they express themselves with such combined clarity and harshness as to be almost offensive. Such an offensive sort of person is indicated mainly when the beginning of the head line is very near the mount of Jupiter *(146b)*. The closer it is to the beginning of the life line *(146a)*, the softer and more attenuated the harshness. The person's behaviour, although still a bit rough, is more controlled.

The greater the distance between the starting points of the two lines the more pronounced the subject's selfishness will be in all relationships. In love, with family and friends, and even in work he will try to assert his own point of view in an aggressive way. He is the typical sort of person for the classic impulsive act, and his imagination can lead to rather dangerous choices.

Before drawing any fast conclusions about this type of head line, one should look at the shape and colour of the subject's nails, as they have a great deal to do with his capacity for forebearance. If the nails are square and a dark colour, the subject is frequently impatient and ill-disposed toward the deficiencies of others, especially those of young people. If the nails are conic and a pale colour, the subject's manner seems more reserved, but in reality there is a note of contempt in his attitude which sooner or later comes to the surface and may wound profoundly. Broadly speaking, such persons are brusque in their manner but not wicked. With tact and patience one can find a wealth of affection and friendship behind their gruffness.

While for the majority of people the beginning of the head line takes one or the other form, there are some rare exceptions. We shall look only at one, which although rare, we are more likely to meet.

The head line begins on the summit of the mount of Venus and crosses the life line before beginning its course (147). Shy and ashamed of being so out of a misguided sense of pride, the subject compensates with aggression against those around him and society as a whole. His behaviour seems prompted by a continual lack of trust in his relations with the outside world. In reality he subconsciously longs to express quite different ambitions, which seek more acceptable justification for revealing themselves. Not too long ago this was regarded as a typically masculine line; but over the past twenty years it has been appearing in the hands of women who have had to overcome their own shyness in order to go out and work. In taking on a traditionally male role in the family, with all the

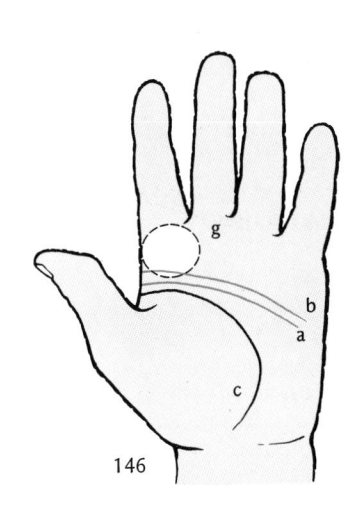

The head line can begin (146a) very distinctly but very close to the life line (c), (146b) very close to the mount of Jupiter (g), or actually cut through the lower part of the mount of Jupiter.

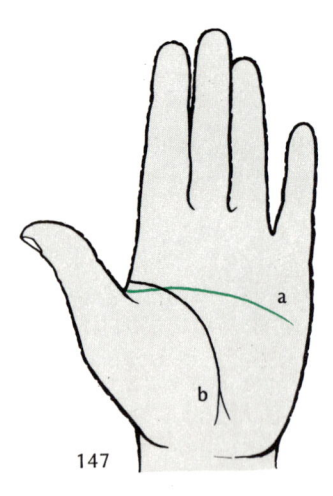

Here the head line (a) rises from the mount of Venus and crosses the life line (b) before beginning its course.

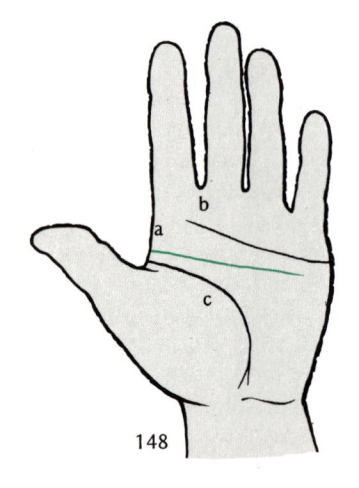

A straight head line (148a), in part running parallel to the heart line (b). The head line can also be curved (149a) or broken and uneven (149b). (In both drawings c is the life line.)

accompanying advantages and disadvantages, the result has been that their own personalities have been suppressed.

The course of the head line
Having established these few basic facts about the beginning of the head line, we can now look at the course it takes.

1. *A straight head line* (*148*), a line without any pronounced curving up or downward, running relatively straight across but with a very slight downward curve. Some palmists interpret this type of head line as a sign of harshness, little sensitivity, and no imagination. It almost always signifies persons in whom logic prevails over feeling and emotion. Actions are dictated by cold rational thought rather than impulse, even in sexual matters if they feel they could be overpowered by a partner. Hence the frequent accusation of being miserly both materially and spiritually, though in actuality they have an heightened sense of fairness, impartiality and justice.

All the foregoing may be modified in part by what emerges from the heart line. If both lines are straight and proceed in a parallel course for a certain distance, traits of coldness and miserliness become more consistent. They are not just outward impressions but fact.

2. *A curved head line* (*149a*). This is a very summary and general category and serves only to indicate those head lines whose courses are not straight but which maintain coherent and compact lines that cannot be described as unclear or broken.

This curve and its orientation will be examined in detail later. For now we shall simply say that a person with this type of head line is very sensitive, with a strong intuitive sense that allows him to perceive very accurately what is hidden beneath the image that each of us presents to other people. The subject merely takes note of what is perceived without saying anything to others because he is extremely reserved. His impressions of people, moreover, are primarily sensory and await confirmation or modification. Nevertheless he voluntarily takes them into consideration in his decisions.

3. *A broken head line* (*149b*), or one that follows a rather irregular course. It can be described as both fragmented and "sinusoidal." It is not very common but never fails to appear on the hands of subjects who place too much importance on the opinions others have or might have of them. Such subjects consequently modify their own behaviour according to the tastes and preferences of the people they are around and tend to follow the dictates of current fashion to the letter. They have little personality and have benefited very little from their studies. They are capable of making only superficial judgments and are limited to the small world of their own daily interests. If this line also displays darker coloured areas, it is often an indication of kleptomania.

The type and nature of the head line
1. *Very thin* (*150a*). The subject is intellectually gifted, his understanding of people and situations as a rule is profound, and his sensitivity somewhat greater than average. However, he lacks the physical energy that would allow him to apply himself to his work for long periods.

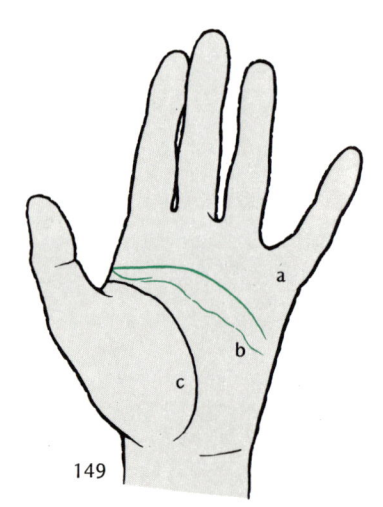

2. *Wide but not very deep* (*150b*). We have before us a very charming person with a winning manner and brilliant conversation, but someone who refuses to talk seriously about anything not strictly related to his own work, and even then tends to drift into digression. He is virtually incapable of keeping a promise or being punctual.

3. *Narrow and deep* (*150c*). Here the subject always seems to burn with an intellectual ardour, as though driven by an inex-

The head line can be: thin, (150a), wide and not very deep (150b), narrow and deep (150c), short and end by the mount of Saturn (e) (151a), average length and end by the mount of Apollo (f) (151b), long and end by the mount of Mercury (g) (151c); d is the mount of Jupiter.

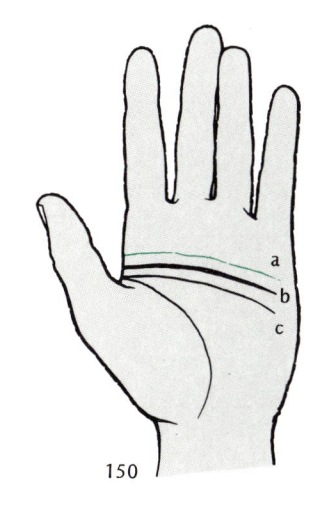

150

151

plicable haste to get to the bottom of things. It is almost as though he were in the grip of an intellectual fever, but more often than not, instead of leading to significant results it burns itself out. Very frequently this type of head line is accompanied by a similar heart line, narrow and deep, which adds a characteristic element of anxiety to the subject's behaviour.

The length of the head line
The length of the head line adds some interesting information to our reading.

Unlike the life line, whose length has no relation to how long we live, the head line indicates by its length the quality of our intelligence. Starting from where the line rises, between the index finger and the thumb, we would consider it *short* (*151a*) if it ends within the area that normally belongs to the mount of Saturn. In this case the subject's intelligence would be termed weak. With such a short head line the subjecty's intellect will undoubtedly be very limited. His interests will be confined to a very specific area in which he will nevertheless reach a high degree of understanding. Further, the subject has the possibility of widening his range of interests, but usually he has no motivation to do so and avoids taking up subjects that he considers pointless. Naturally we add to this information everything else that emerges from the other characteristics of the head line.

When the head line goes beyond the mount of Saturn and extends into the area below the mount of Apollo (this being the most common case), it is termed *medium* (*151b*). We must not expect an exceptional performance from this type of intellect, but this person is able to face up to and solve life's daily problems. Academically he is not very brilliant but with hard work he can reach university level. The obvious choice for a career is in the white collar section; rarely will the subject attempt the professional skills that require a stronger personality and more confidence in one's own abilities. Understanding other people's problems is always preceded by a selfish appraisal of situations and one rarely finds the kind of insight that will sacrifice a small advantage today for something more sub-

stantial tomorrow. When the medium head line is very straight one frequently finds the subject has an innate business sense, especially if this line is accompanied by a little finger with a very square nail.

When the head line extends beyond the mount of Apollo, then we can talk about above-average intelligence. The more the line extends toward the outer edge of the hand, the greater the intelligence. With regard to the head lines examined so far, this type (*151c*), besides a greater depth of understanding and intuition, presents elements of creativity that indicates an individual destined to stand out (or at least capable of doing so). If he is to succeed in reaching the goals to which he can aspire, it should be visible in other parts of the hand. The relationship between the length of the head line and intelligence is so direct and universally accepted that when a discrepancy arises, it should be investigated. Usually illness or the consequences of a serious accident will be the cause.

The course of the head line and intellectual ability
We must now examine the course of the head line, which will tell us about the subject's intellectual capabilities. The numerous types, of course, can be divided into the three main groups:

1. *The head line runs straight across* (*152a*). If a perfect extension were drawn, it would reach the outer edge of the hand at the spot where the heart line originates. The subject has an eminently practical intelligence and is inclined to consider worthless anything that is not intrinsically logical. Such persons are almost never sparkling or lively but cautious with money, conservative not only with things but in their habits and way of living. These are people on whom one can rely for their ideas, which are few but very clear and which they are loath to change. Very often they find themselves in conflict with the world around them because it has evolved, or at least changed, while they have remained solidly anchored to their original concepts. If they make the right choice in their work, they can derive great satisfaction from it. If, however, they have had to accept what circumstances happened to offer them, they will

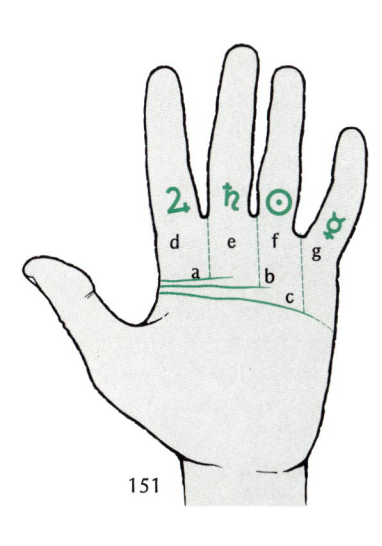

The course of the head line (152) can be: a *horizontal,* b *straight and pointing upward,* c *straight and pointing downward toward the mount of the Moon, or* d *curving downward until it touches the mount of the Moon.*

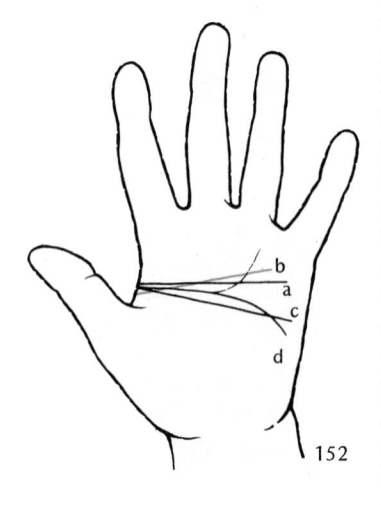

do their duty scrupulously but without enthusiasm because they will always feel like an outsider.

2. *The head line runs straight in an upward direction (152b).* It comes close to the heart line without actually reaching it. This is a sign of a cold, calculating person who never does anything without thinking it through first, and who is in complete control of his impulses, however limited. For him feelings have only a relative importance; they scarcely enter into his way of thinking and formulating ideas. He is capable of deliberately working out a plan that toys with the feelings of others without realizing the seriousness of what he is doing let alone the trouble it could cause. This is not sadism or even cruelty, for he does not take pleasure in causing pain to others. It is, rather, a form of selfishness—he is only aware of his own needs. These are people who are very perspicacious in their choices and they conduct their affairs with tenacity and self-assurance. It is as well to have them as friends in the hope of benefiting from their good points, but it is preferable not to have anything to do with them. In any case they are fortunately very rare.

3. *The head line runs downward toward the mount of the Moon (152c).* There are distinct types: if the head line is straight *(152c)*, the subject, although not lacking in imagination, maintains a practical and realistic attitude that represents a very effective rein on any tendency to escape into a world of fantasy. This practical turn of mind is particularly evident when the line tends to be decidedly straight. If the head line proceeds a little uncertainly, then the imagination may predominate.

If a section of the head line *curves and runs toward the mount of the Moon just touching the upper part (152d)*, then we must add an element of imagination that increases creativity and in some cases determines the ingeniousness of the subject, especially if a branch goes toward the mount of Apollo. Typically, these individuals can see in their minds a finished picture of their ideas, which they can then translate into practical terms without too much difficulty. They are also very versatile, but this can be a limitation: while able successfully to find a solution to every problem, for what it costs them in terms of time spent, the solution is not always economically practical.

This type of head line means that the subject is continually stimulated by new ideas that arise out of everyday circumstances. But very often he does not have time to complete projects that have been set aside to make way for fascinating new ones. However, this is never a cause for regret because this person takes pleasure principally in launching ideas, not in completing them—that is for other people to do. This haste and inconstancy, which does not prevent some few from pursuing their interests more thoroughly, creates an aura of incompleteness that is very disappointing for those close to the subject.

There are two other examples worth mentioning due to the unusual data they provide, even though they do not occur often enough to merit a separate section.

The first is a head line that curves downward well into the mount of the Moon *(153a)*. To the observations we have already made we can add another: this sign is found among people such as antique dealers, archaeologists, historians, and so on, whose studies and interests create a strong link with the past. In their work they combine a solid practical and creative ability with the vital element of imagination.

The second example is a head line with a very pronounced curve *(153b)* that runs parallel to the life line, entering well into the plain of Mars. This type of line indicates a very acute sense of observation that almost always produces a need to write about and report real events filtered through the imagination, or the reverse with elements of fantasy set in the real world. It is the mark of a writer or journalist, and is found on those who have great curiosity about life and everything around them that has to do with people and events. Naturally not all writers have this sign, and not everyone who has it is a writer or journalist, but we are now getting into that elusive area of free will where we have ventured before, albeit with great caution.

Another very distinctive head line worthy of mentioning here is one composed of two lines, usually very fine, that

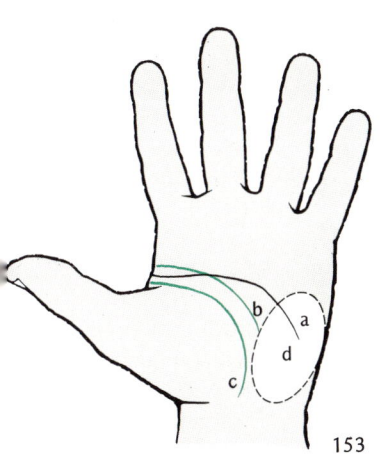

The head line can end in the mount of the Moon (d) (153a), run alongside the life line (153c), or end in the plain of Mars (153b).

A double head line (154), composed of two lines, generally thin and partially or wholly parallel. The head line can be broken (155a) or branch out (155b) in the direction of the mount of Mercury; c is the life line.

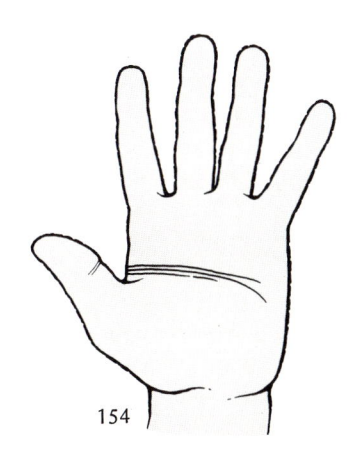

run parallel for the whole course or a good part of it (*154*). Unfortunately, it occurs rather often and does not signify, as one might suppose, a double personality. Rather it indicates poor powers of concentration, shallow reasoning ability, heedless decisions, and immaturity. We need other confirming signs, however, before we can establish that this type of head line signifies a tendency to psychic dissociation.

When only a part of the line is double, the above-mentioned disorders apply only to the corresponding time period, which can be established with the dating system. As to the intensity of the disorder, particularly with regard to dissociation or immaturity, it can be determined by examining the colour of the line. Dissociation will display a darker colour, whereas immaturity is only slightly darker than normal. The presence of dark spots on these sections of the head line signifies a need for protection.

Another type of head line deserves to be mentioned even thought it is not particularly common. Its course is broken, composed more or less of short, clearly distinct sections which neither overlap nor intertwine (*155a*). It is a very negative sign if found during early childhood because it can produce the same problems caused in an electrical system by disconnected wires. Conversation can be inconclusive and disconnected, and behaviour, in varying degrees, like that of a retarded child. The sooner a specialist is consulted the better the chances of recovery.

An unusual case, rare but of considerable interest, is the head line that is rather long and initially straight but which turns almost suddenly upward in the direction of the mount of Mercury (*155b*). The meaning is very precise, with a rate of confirmation in almost nine out of ten cases. The subject devotes most of his thought to economic problems, either because he is temporarily or chronically in difficulty or because his interests are mainly concerned with finances, all the way from how to procure more money in more or less legitimate ways to how best to invest one's capital. In any event the subject is engaged in making the most of his own situation in order to enjoy the greatest possible benefits. As we can easily see, this is a situation involving choice on the part of the subject. If it is not just the last part of the line that rises toward the mount of Mercury but a whole series of branches moving in the same direction, the meaning changes, although only slightly. It

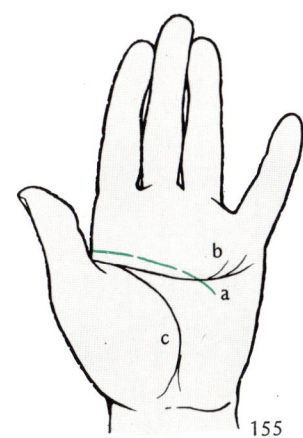

is circumstances that prompt the subject's choices, and these lines, little more than capillaries, disappear when the cause of a problem disappears. When these branches appear in well-off people (as sometimes happens), it denotes strong resentment by the subject toward his environment, almost always the family, which has placed restraints on his development in a direction considered incompatible with the family's position. Naturally this reading is not sufficient by itself and requires further study of the heart line.

Endings of the head line
Like all the other lines, the head line can end in many different ways, each with its own particular meaning. As some are more common than others, they have been categorized into four groups:

1. *The head line ends cleanly* (*156a*). An extremely positive sign for those whose work requires them to concentrate for long periods on a very exacting subject. It is found on people who keep to themselves and are very withdrawn, who persist in a task until they either reach their objective or realize that it is beyond their capabilities or the time at their disposal. Classifying a head line in this group requires that the last section be absolutely straight.

2. *The head line ends very vaguely* (*156b*). This line is also straight, but disappears into the palm like a brook in the sand. It is a sign

Opposite, an old hand of papier mâché with all of the lines and their meanings indicated.

of regret and dissatisfaction with past events (or future ones) that are almost always work-related. There are many and varied reasons for such failures: economic difficulties, adverse circumstances, sentimental reasons, accidents, illnesses, even war. Whatever the exact reason, whether or not among those listed, it can be discovered by studying the general shape of the hand.

3. *The head line ends in a fork (157).* A fairly widespread termination belonging to people with sparkling intelligence, who are not very profound but subtle, and are able to see the world as it is or to cloak it in the colours of their imagination. These persons rarely finish their studies. They do not need a thorough preparation for the work they usually do, because the talents they draw on they already possess naturally. In some cases, academic learning can upset their spontaneity—one of their best qualities. They pursue occupations in the arts or in some field related to art: interior decorators, costume and set designers, night club performers, certain categories of artisans, to mention only a few. To them we must add the many people who daily translate their imaginative ideas into practical terms in ways that are not always orthodox but new and different, which we can broadly describe as "the art of doing one's best." When one of the branches of the fork reaches the edge of the palm, the person has a good chance of achieving success and fame, but not necessarily financial success.

4. *The head line ends with a very large fork (158),* almost two branches, one ascending, the other descending. Not a favourable sign. The person is aware of the promptings of the imagination, but the message is too vague and he does not succeed in translating it into something concrete. It only serves to create a state of confusion which impedes decision-making so that in some cases the subject's life becomes uncertain and problematic. These are persons of normal intelligence, often with remarkable insight, but they do not know how to run their own lives in a coherent fashion. If the head line is very straight and horizontal before the fork, the practical sense at least predominates in some areas; if instead it curves downward in the direction of the mount of the Moon, the negative consequences are very evident.

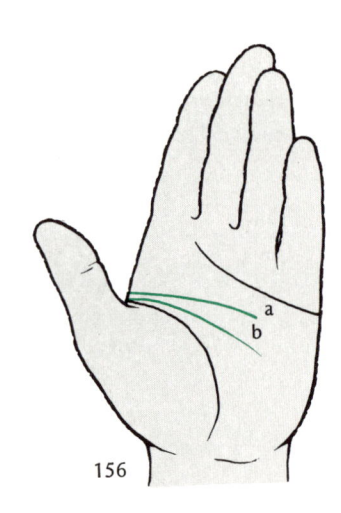

The head line can end: abruptly (156a), in a vague manner (156b), or with a fork (157).

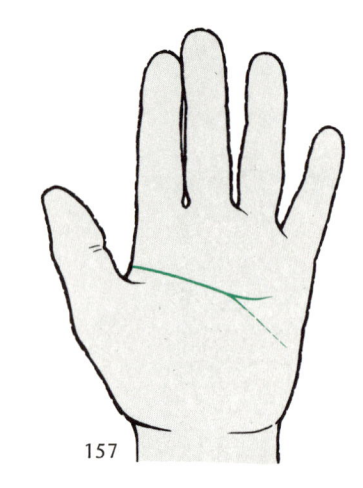

Branches from the head line

We must now look at the important subject of branches, even though they do not have the same significance here as they do for the heart line.

The branches of the head line can be either ascending or descending. If the former is the case, they rise toward the heart line moving from the mount of Jupiter to the mount of Mercury. These branches are just visible, little more than capillary lines, and can be seen clearly only with a magnifying glass. They are regarded as reasonably positive signs.

If the head line is straight, the most prominently marked ascending branches are those pointing toward the mount of Mercury. In this case the subject is usually an able speculator. If the ascending branches rise from a curved head line, the most interesting ones will be pointing in the direction of the mount of Apollo. Here the subject has a general artistic sensitivity that he will never manage to translate into an artistic profession but will retain at a good amateur level.

The only descending branches worthy of attention arise from straight head lines and run toward the mount of Mercury. Like all descending branches, they have negative significance and tell us that the subject is driven to speculate in business that proves mainly unsuccessful and therefore damaging. We find that these persons have a tendency very similar to that of gambling addicts. When the head line is curved the

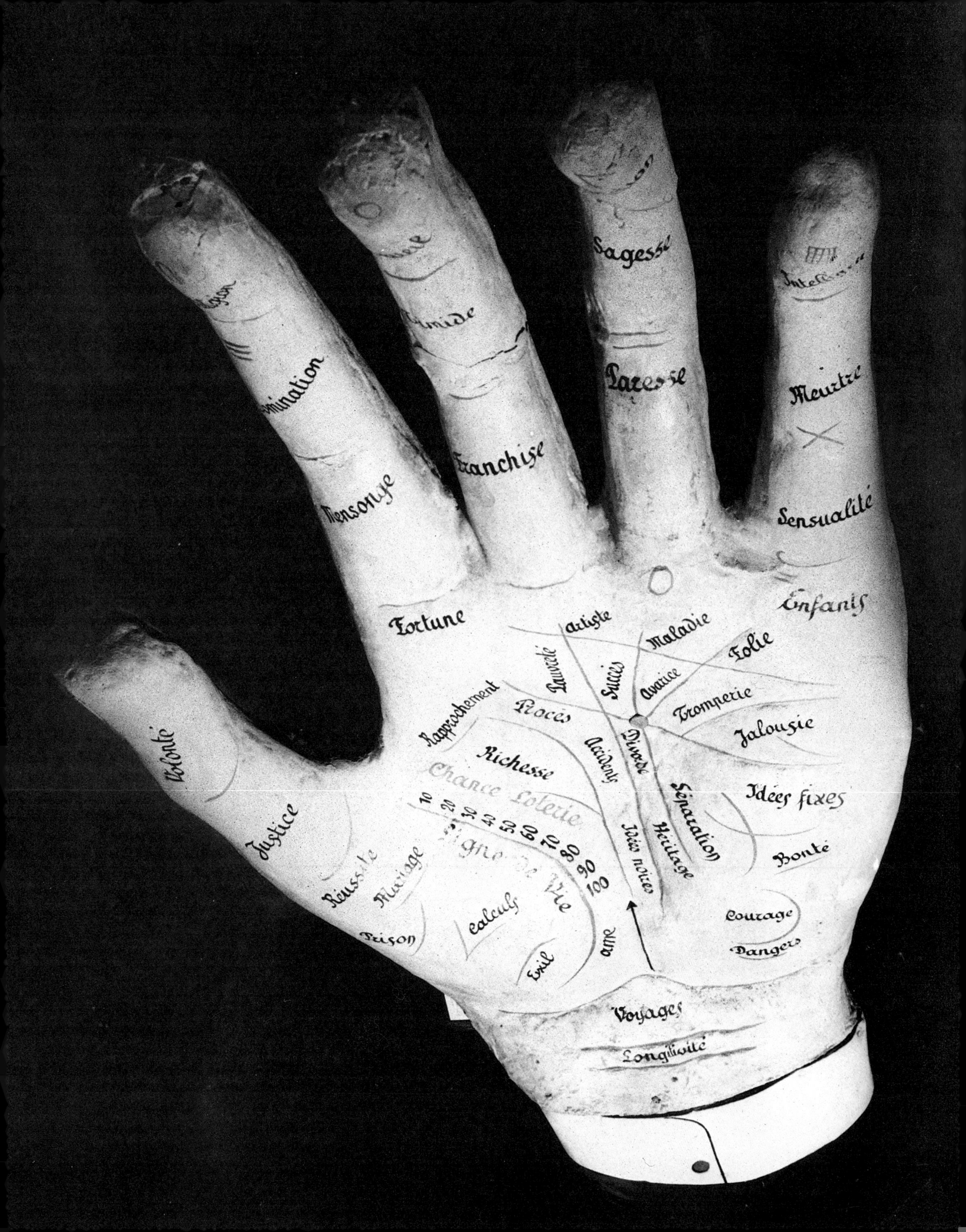
Sagesse
Paresse
Meurtre
Sensualité
Franchise
Mensonge
Fortune
Enfants
artiste
Maladie
Folie
Pauvreté
Succès
Avarice
Tromperie
Rapprochement
Procès
Jalousie
Richesse
Accidents
Divorce
Chance Loterie
Séparation
Idées fixes
Volonté
Justice
10 20 30 40 50 60 70 80 90 100
Ligne de Vie
Idées noires
Héritage
Bonté
Réussite
Mariage
Calculs
Courage
Prison
Exil
âme
Dangers
Voyages
Longévité

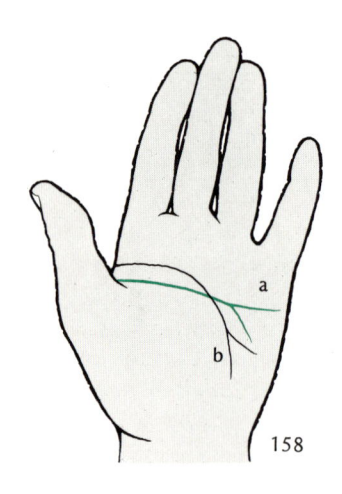

The head line can end with a large fork: straight (158a) or curved (158b).

Opposite, head line (160) with a grille, b spots, c short lines; merged head and heart lines (161a), b is the life line; short descending head line (162a) and short ascending heart line (162b), joined in one line in the center (c) called a "conjunction."

The head line (159) with: a islands and grilles, b near the heart line d, c in the plain of Mars; e is the life line.

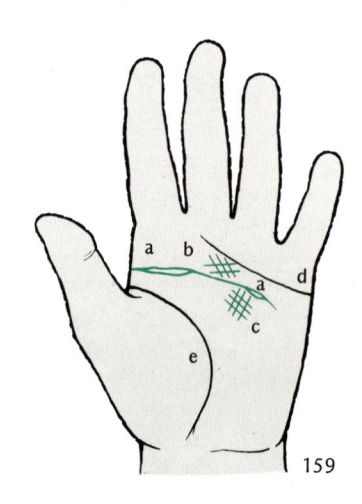

descending branches under the mount of Apollo indicate without a shadow of doubt that the subject has undertaken an artistic career with some success but has had to interrupt it prematurely for reasons beyond his control.

Special signs on the head line

We must now establish how the information we have about the head line is modified by the presence of special signs located along its course (*159*).

1. An island on the head line (*159a*) is a sign of exhaustion. A simple observation but without indication of cause, which must be sought elsewhere. It may derive from a bad fright or stressful work, a long period of concentrated effort or psychophysical trauma, or from incorrect food which hinders circulation and nourishment of brain cells. If the island is very long and thin, it may mean prolonged, almost chronic exhaustion whose consequences are similar to those of two parallel head lines.

2. A grille situated alongside the head line (*159b*). If it is above the line, between the head and heart lines, it means a lack of concentration, dispersion of energy, little interest in romantic problems. If the grille is under the head line (*159c*), approximately in the area of the plain of Mars, we have the same lack of interest, particularly with regard to work and initiative. The subject temporarily lacks will power and common sense.

3. A grille located right on the head line (*160a*). The lack of concentration or interest in everything around the subject is due to pathological causes that can be treated with the proper methods. Grilles can sometimes be caused by physical or psychological traumas.

4. One or more dark spots (*160b*) on the head line are a symptom of worry, the seriousness of which is in direct proportion to the intensity of the colour. Usually they appear and disappear with the problem causing them. They are mainly to do with worries about work.

5. Short lines (*160c*) at any point along the head line have a similar meaning to that of spots, but less serious. They change continually, as we might expect. If indicating something more serious (almost always to do with family problems) with a permanent impact, then the short line is more evident. It may of course refer to events in the past or future; this can be clarified with the dating system.

Head and heart lines merge

Now that we have reviewed both the head and heart lines we can discuss an aspect of these two lines that is neither common nor very rare: when they join together completely (or in part) and form one line. Some palmists call this the *simian line* (*161a*) because it is often found in certain primates.

As we have pointed out repeatedly, through palmistry one can roughly establish how well balanced the subject is, what kind of relationship exists between his intellect and emotions, and how they help him to adjust to the world around him. Given that the heart line goes from the unconscious to the conscious, with the head line running in the opposite direction, it is inevitable that by merging completely or in part a significant imbalance is created. If the head and heart lines, whose customary separation bespeaks the classic conflict between logic and emotion, are joined together, how should they be interpreted? What direction will the energy charge produced by this anomalous juncture take? The easiest and commonest energy release is violence. Indeed, until very recently, the merging of these two lines was automatically considered a sign of great violence and mindless cruelty, not least of reasons being that it often appears on the hands of dangerous criminals.

However, its presence on the hands of people with no criminal tendencies has caused this valid but inconclusive opinion to be revised. It has been noted that this sign appears regularly on persons who have obsessively channelled all their intellectual and spiritual energies in a single direction. This is true of a certain type of criminal, but equally true of deeply religious persons who want to give concrete form to their faith or to artists who need to create in order to give form to the tumultuous sensations within. In each of these examples—and there are many others—the subject experiences the same need for sublimation, but it defies the control achieved by most people through common sense and reasonableness.

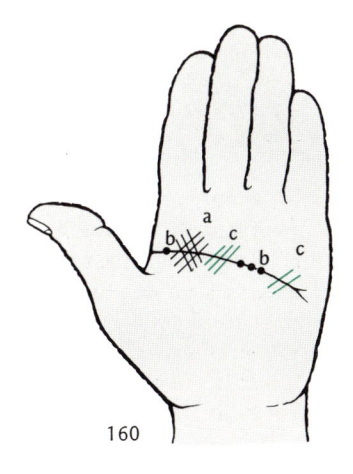

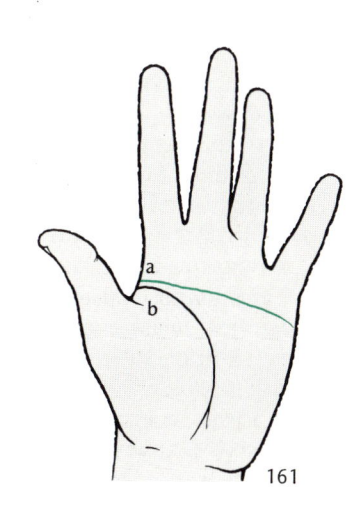

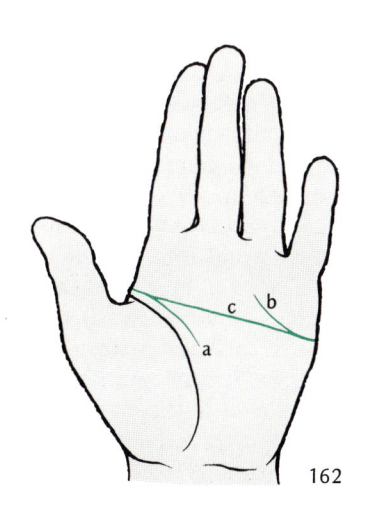

To determine where the conflict will move and which forces will carry it along toward good or evil we must consult all of the data at our disposal: hand shape, the shape of the little finger and thumb, the distance between thumb and index finger, the development of the mount of the Moon, and other considerations that can yield conclusive information, positive or negative, about the potential force expressed in the complete merger of the head and heart lines.

When the merger is only partial (*162*), its significance is much more limited. Only a mild form remains of the violence mentioned above. The subject has an uncommon ability to abstract himself from his surroundings and pursue his own thoughts. In a certain sense it is the quality of the absentminded professor, a source of many an anecdote and joke. Incidentally, if this type of joined line is accompanied by a pair of diagonal short lines on the mount of Mercury, the subject has a particular talent for scientific research.

Today palmists generally ascribe to the partially merged line some of the attributes of the situation in which the head and heart lines are both present but separate. Even if short the joined lines are seen as two branches, one ascending, the other descending, of the line joining them. In the example in the illustration, a rather common one, the subject shows remarkable perspicacity, a fine imagination, and a good measure of clairvoyance.

In examining the head line, one should not stop at first impressions. It is not enough to say "it is straight" or "it is unclear." A comparison of both hands is always advisable and not just for the head line alone, even when there is no doubt about the interpretation. As we have said, in most cases the left hand reveals *what* nature has put there and the right hand reveals *how* the subject has changed it through his own efforts. For example, when the head line originates by cutting across the life line and this appears only on the left hand, the subject does not feel aggressive towards society but rather deep admiration for the courage displayed by others. If this appears only on the right hand, then it is the subject himself who is courageous.

The fate line

This is the fourth main line and the most unstable (*163*). It does not always appear, and when it does it can be extremely variable in appearance to the extent of being difficult to identify. To begin with, this line forms fairly late in life and it changes very little after the age of twenty, because the ability of people to adapt to their environment begins to crystallize around that time. The line is rather unpredictable and probably owes its name to this very characteristic. Actually, palmists have different names for it depending on the importance and exact significance it has for them. It is called the line of success, the Saturnian line, the line of fate, fortune, or direction, or the longitudinal axis. This last designation is possibly the best way to define it, even though very often all that remains of this longitudinal axis, which should divide the whole palm from the wrist to the base of the middle finger, is a small section in the plain of Mars.

Let's think in terms that take into account the many meanings of this line. It divides the hand in half, separating the conscious from the unconscious, the rational from the irrational, the material from the spiritual. It therefore seems the most suitable means for determining what practical use the subject has made of the gifts nature has bestowed upon him.

This line can also be regarded as an equation with many unknowns: given a certain number of natural qualities, a certain type of sensibility, a particular character, and a set number of occasions, we can determine what an individual can make of himself. Fate, as we see, scarcely comes into it; this line expresses primarily the subject's ability to adapt to situations, to benefit from them, and to choose his own course. We could easily call it the line of freedom of action, of choices, or simply of adaptability.

Naturally for a sound interpretation we must include the information that emerges

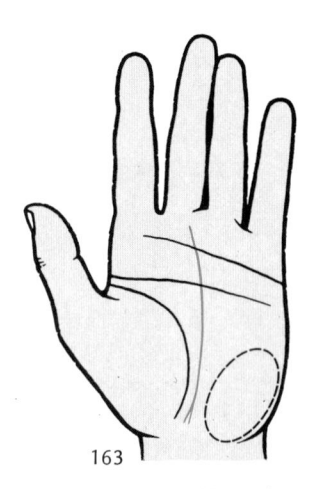

A perfect fate line (163) runs from below the mount of Saturn and crosses the whole palm, reaching almost to the wrist between the mount of Venus and the mount of the Moon.

from a careful examination of the other main lines. Indeed, one had best not review the fate line until last, as it may prove useful in confirming or modifying some of the theories formulated in the course of the reading, especially in discovering what interpretive approach to take.

The fate line does *not* refer to the subject's social condition but rather to the type of relationship that exists between him and his surroundings. Moreover, it serves particularly to determine whether the subject, assuming he has the necessary qualities to succeed and maintain his achievements, can attain the success or goals he has set for himself. In addition, we can see which is the best course, the quickest and least tiring, for achieving his aims.

Some people have an innate ability when it comes to solving life's problems. For others—the majority—an opportune reading of their hands, carefully and conscientiously done, can represent a wholly valid means of acquiring the basic understanding indispensible for solving certain problems or making fundamental choices, based not on personal desires but on intrinsic capabilities.

The fate line does not appear on every hand, only on about half. However, people who do not have it are not destined for failure in life. If they want success they can achieve it, perhaps by making a greater effort than others. As a rule a person who does not have this line is less prone to set ambitious goals. His ambitions are more modest and the road to their fulfilment easier to travel.

The perfect fate line (*163*) originates in the lower half of the palm just between the mount of Venus and the mount of the Moon, the area normally called the plain of Neptune. Its course, which tends to be vertical, proceeds as far as the mount of Saturn, cutting across the head and heart lines. The line must be clear, fine, continuous, pink in colour, and have small ascending capillary branches to the right and left vaguely suggesting a spike of wheat.

A perfect fate line of this kind is practically nonexistent, but sometimes we find nearly perfect ones on individuals who are not only self-made in the usual sense of this word, but who have actually developed talents that nature has barely roughed out, practically inventing themselves and their own lives. These are very unusual people. They have known how to find their way toward the achievement of an ambitious goal, like success, by using their own efforts intelligently and giving up many of life's pleasures in order to achieve their aims. They have made difficult sacrifices to reach an important target, as confirmed every day in the experience of palmistry.

The beginning of the fate line
Let us now see what the fate line actually looks like and how much it can differ from the ideal. Its beginning is rarely located exactly in the plain of Neptune.

1. *The fate line originates in the lower part of the mount of Venus (164) and runs toward the mount of Saturn.* Relatively positive. The subject evidently desires or needs to lean on the family because, even if able, he is afraid to stand on his own two feet. Very often this inability to be independent is due to a misguided protectiveness on the part of the family, which has never allowed the subject sufficient freedom. There is also another theory: circumstances or family backing have procured a safe job at an early stage in the subject's life and this "prolongation of the cradle" for an obviously weak character has led to a total renunciation of all independent aspirations. This is also the case when a young person steps into a thriving family business, because he is too lazy to do otherwise or has no strong desire to make his own way in life.

We have begun with this first example of the fate line because it is the most common and can be found at all levels of society, especially in families with an only child or only one male child. Reading the hand of one of these children from adolescence could be very useful for clarifying certain aspects of personality and to point out to the family members their often unwitting contributory mistakes. If one comes across this same situation on the hand of an adult, it would not be helpful to insist on the same counselling since obviously the desire for independence is not strong enough to carry the subject very far.

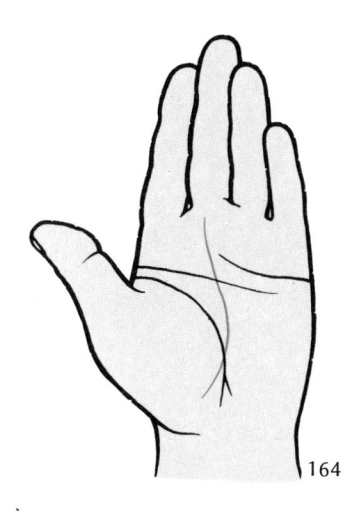

2. *The fate line rises from the life line (165).* Similar in many respects to the preceding example: the subject would have liked support from the family but circumstances prevented it and he has had to learn how to make his own way with some difficulty. He nevertheless remains very nostalgic over the years about what might have been and often recounts fantasies on that subject, which eventually he begins to believe himself. A fate line that originates in this fashion can be interpreted in another way subject to confirmation by the head line. The subject, being particularly enterprising, begins with a small family firm, develops it, and achieves a high level of prosperity, or he rises from a subordinate position in a small business to one of importance.

As we can see, the fate line lends itself to various interpretations. That is why it is advisable to leave it until last, when the basic view of the subject has been fairly well defined.

3. *The fate line rises independently and during its course runs into the life line (166).* Here again the family-career relationship comes into play, but the interpretation is less favourable. For reasons that can be established very clearly, the family interferes negatively in the subject's career, which is possibly well established. It may be that economic problems demand great sacrifices, or that a moral question involving a family member has an unfavourable effect on the subject's career. In any case a specific period is involved in both of these examples, and it can be calculated by the dating system. When moral blackmail is applied by certain members of the family, the problem is more difficult to resolve and may drag on for many years.

4. *The fate line rises from the mount of the Moon (167).* Here too the family plays an important role in the subject's career, but an indirect one. The family home represents a cage preventing the subject from trying his wings and he must therefore escape from it. This results in the subject choosing to move as far away as possible from the family, however much they try to prevent him. Oddly enough the umbilical cord tying the subject to his old home is never completely severed and wherever he may be, he often recreates a home resembling as much as possible the one abandoned so many years ago.

As the fate line rises from the lower part of the palm and moves toward the plain of Mars, the relationship between family and career grows weaker. The break occurs at the right moment without trauma, as it should. One interpretation that can be made for certain is that the subject has a balanced approach in his understanding of the laws of life. The farther away the starting point is from the plain of Neptune, the later success will be in coming. Moreover, the subject must overcome difficult and trying situations, which will nevertheless give him great satisfaction for having succeeded against the odds.

Endings of the fate line

If the starting point of the fate line is unclear, its ending will be even more so. Ideally it ends in the mount of Saturn, but in reality it can range from the mount of Jupiter to the mount of Apollo—but not the mount of Mercury, in whose direction for some strange unexplained reason the fate line never runs. Sometimes a branch will go there, but more on that later.

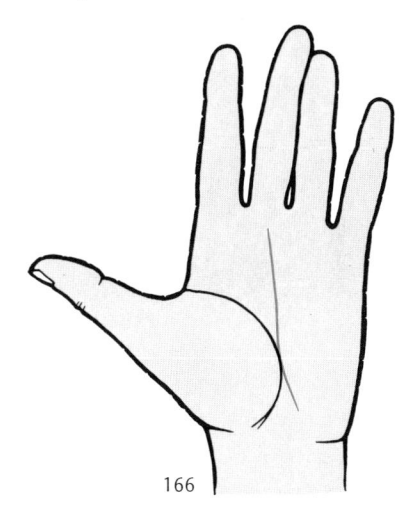

There are basically four types of endings:
1. *The final section of the fate line runs toward the mount of Jupiter (168a).* The subject is extremely ambitious and prepared to sacrifice everything and everyone to achieve power. If necessary he will trample on his family and friends and their feelings, because the only thing he truly

The fate line can rise from the mount of Venus (164), be joined to the life line (165), or brush against the life line (166).

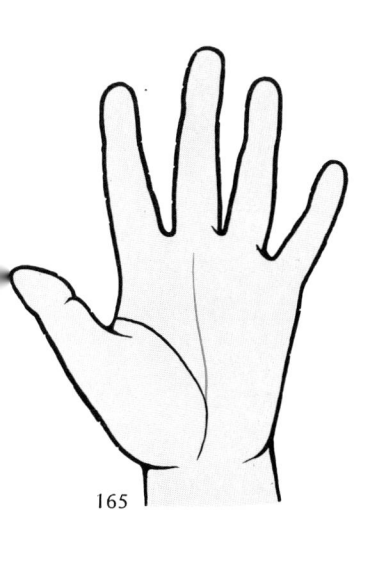

A fate line that rises from the mount of the Moon (167).

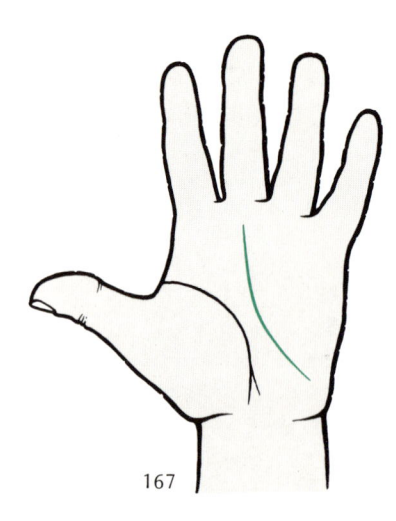

The fate line (168) can run in the direction of: a *the mount of Jupiter,* b *the mount of Saturn,* c *the mount of Apollo; it can also be short and deep (169).*

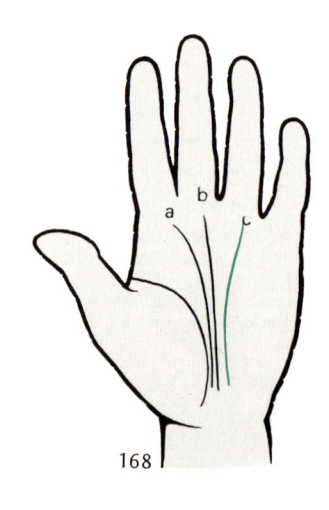

loves is outdoing others. In this case the fate line forms during puberty, for this is when the incentive is established that will lead to the subject's first contacts and subsequently to his first important career choices, which are very often political.

2. *The fate line ends in the mount of Saturn (168b).* The most common example. With this kind of person, the usual hope of a brilliant career does not overshadow the normal desire to have other interests in life. Quite often the most favourable result of a fate line like this is a sound balance between the inner and outer life, between the personality of the subject and his environment. The measure of success here is revealed by the intensity of the line's colour and by its length and depth.

3. *The fate line ascends toward the mount of Apollo (168c).* Here again it is ambition that drives the subject to achieve a brilliant career as quickly as possible, but his interests are in the art world. This interest is determined by the fact that the person possesses natural gifts which will improve with study and sacrifice. A brief examination of the mount of Apollo, the heart line, and the mount of Venus will reveal the kind of romantic relationships experienced by this kind of subject, who falls in love suddenly but only briefly.

4. *The fate line is very short but deep (169).* It usually originates in the plain of Mars and ends just under the head line. This is a special but fairly common case. It means that the beginning of the subject's career has been (or will be) very brilliant and helped by circumstances. Here we almost always observe very precocious careers of the infant prodigy type, especially in the fields of music and mathematics. With this kind of fate line the career usually ends in adolescence, having run its course, almost as though the maturing of the sex drive has diverted the energy that produced such brilliant displays of creativity.

Branches from the fate line
In describing the perfect fate line, we referred to capillary branches like spikes of wheat, but there are other much more clearly visible branches that sometimes obscure the real origin of the line. There are two significant examples of this (*170*).

The fate line rises from the mount of the Moon and has an important branch descending from the plain of Mars to the mount of Venus and crossing the life line (170a). It looks like a fork and some regard it as such. It is fairly rare but warrants looking at because the subject finds himself in a very delicate situation which a serious reading could help to resolve. Indeed, the subject will be faced with a dilemma and will have to make a crucial decision: his career takes him far away from his family home and family or romantic events stand in the way. The conflict can be resolved only by making a clean break—one of the two branches must be eliminated. The decision the subject will make is revealed by the upper part of the fate line. If it is directed toward the mount of Apollo, the choice will be in favour of family or sentimental needs; if it decisively enters the mount of Saturn, the choice will favour career for financial reasons; and if it is directed toward the mount of Jupiter, the subject will follow his own aspirations out of pure ambition.

In the second special case, *the fate line rises from the mount of Venus and the branch descends toward the mount of the Moon (170b).* The meaning is quite different from that of the previous example. At a certain point in the subject's life, which can be dated with remarkable preci-

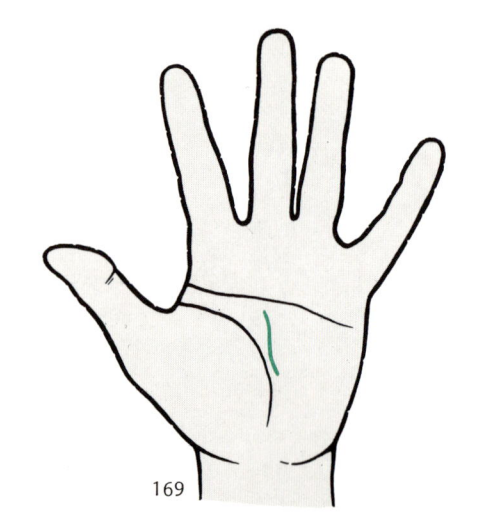

sion, he will meet someone who will be all important to his career. This person or group of persons can significantly influence both his decisions about the future and his career positively or negatively—positively if the branch merges into the fate line, negatively if the branch cuts right across the fate line. Some palmists believe that in the branch with positive meaning they can see a love that begins at school and continues for a lifetime.

Other important branches are found at the end of the fate line. These usually stop as soon as they have passed the head line. The direction of the branches provides the same information as that of the fate line itself when it is directed toward the mounts of Jupiter, Saturn, and Apollo. In this case we can also include the mount of Mercury (*171*). A fate line branch directed there indicates an excellent chance of success in the scientific or commercial worlds, in research or business. When the fate line branches toward the mount of Apollo, the meaning is quite interesting. Having achieved financial success by whatever means possible, the subject can finally display his love of art, either indirectly by collecting, establishing prizes for artists or study grants for promising young artists, or by opening his art collections to the public. He becomes a patron, which also satisfies his own exhibitionism.

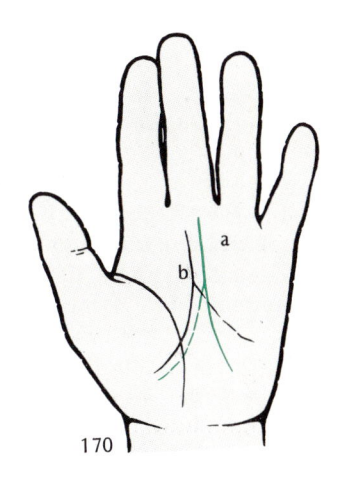

Islands and breaks on the fate line
In contrast to all the other main lines one rarely finds spots, grilles, islands, and the like on the fate line. Owing to its unpredictable course, a long list of special cases could be drawn up, but it is not difficult to interpolate the data the line provides with the meaning normally accorded a particular sign. In any event, breaks and the islands that do appear require some interpretation.

Breaks in the fate line (*172*) are always negative. They can appear in different ways and at any point along the line.

1. *There is a clean break in the fate line which resumes a little farther on (172a).* Signifies a serious obstacle in one's career, or a long suspension and thus a change in one's life-style, with all of the problems entailed in readapting. These breaks are not always unfavourable; if the subject has the ability and the necessary will power, he can regain, however laboriously, any lost ground and achieve greater understanding. He may even embark on a completely new career. There have been cases of people experiencing this kind of multiple interruption and having the resourcefulness and will to begin again from scratch within a short time.

2. *The fate line is broken but the two lines proceed in a parallel course for a short stretch (172b).* The meaning does not change: a change in career but not due to adverse events. The subject decides to change, thereby allowing an easy and untroubled passage from one job to another. Signs of confirmation of such events can be found on the head line.

3. *A break in the fate line is closed up by an island (172c).* In this case there is no actual change in the subject's career but there is a danger that can derive from the person himself and his personality: a moral scruple, a wrong move, annoying gossip. These are situations of limited duration and when they cease, things will return to normal or almost and the sign will disappear.

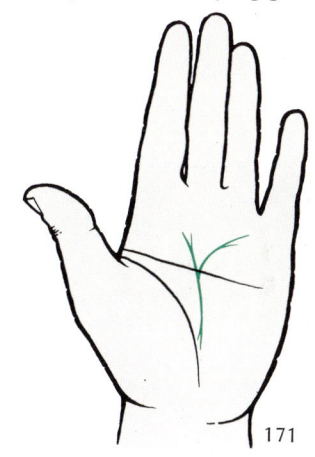

4. *A break in the fate line due to the head line (173a).* The meaning is always negative. A brief interruption in the subject's career is caused by a problem of an intellectual nature. The conflict arises when his rational self no longer wants to accept the reality of facts. This situation manifests itself in persons with strong personalities who, because of pride or too high an opinion of themselves and their own strength, are not prepared to accept compromises or even advice. This almost never happens at the beginning of a career. A

A fate line rising from the mount of the Moon with a branch running toward the mount of Venus (170a) and a fate line rising from the mount of Venus with a branch running toward the mount of the Moon (170b).
In figure 171, a fate line with a branch running toward the mount of Mercury.

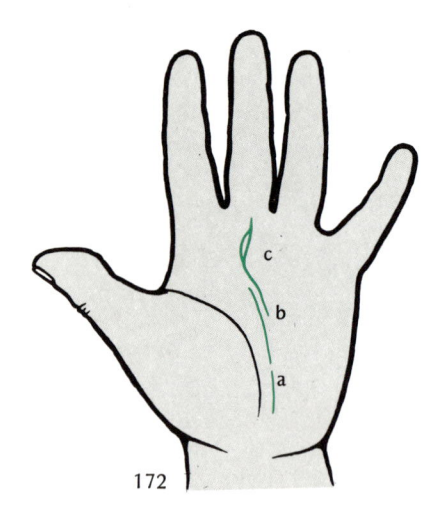

A broken fate line (172): a clean break that resumes immediately, b a break with the ends running parallel for a short stretch, c an island.
A fate line stopped by the head line (173a) and a fate line stopped by the heart line (173b).

drastic solution is always needed and economic factors are often brought in disguised as ideological problems.

5. *The break is due to the heart line* (*173b*). The results are the same but the motivation is different. The cause of incompatibility between the subject and his career is emotional: sudden qualms, or a new romantic relationship, too much faith in a partner, or the misdeeds of a family member. The signs will be clearly visible on the heart line. We are dealing here with a change of relationship between the subject and his surroundings that was probably never very sound, but nevertheless able to resist in its unstable state, until the cause that provoked (or will provoke) the break is established.

A very useful device for interpreting the signs of the fate line more precisely is a comparison of the left and right palms. Should there be but one fate line, on the left palm, which is rather common, the subject will not exercise much will power in the development of the events predicted by fate. If the fate line is present only on the right palm, it will be the subject who chooses to exploit and sometimes create opportunities in his race to success. When the line is present on both hands but with small differences between the two, it will require the sensitivity of an expert palmist drawing on acquired knowledge to interpret the double presence.

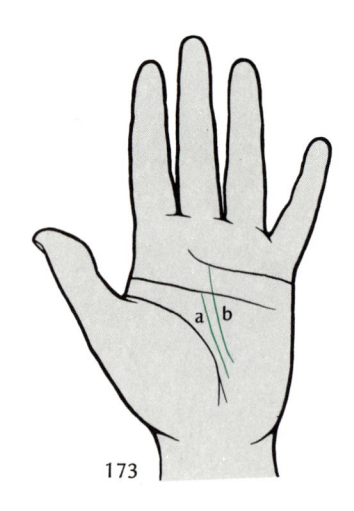

Secondary lines

On the palms of some hands one can sometimes make out lines other than the four principal ones we have studied. Tradition and the need to understand have led practitioners of palmistry to separately name and describe the character of these lines, which should be considered independently with each one examined as a special case. Their presence is relatively uncommon and in a certain sense superfluous to a thorough reading. Moreover, their appearance is always fairly vague; they are often barely visible.

It is advisable first to carry out the most scrupulous reading possible of the principal lines and then to see if there are other lines or line segments. Their location will indicate to the palmist what part they play in the scope of things.

The sun line

The most common of the secondary lines is the Sun line, so named because of its characteristic inclination toward the mount of Apollo.

Over the centuries it has assumed different names, which shows how much uncertainty there has been in defining it. It has been called the Apollo or Phoebus line, the line of intuition, the line of creativity, the line of riches. We shall abide by current terminology and call it the Sun line because it reflects the degree of brilliance inherent in the particularly creative temperaments who usually have this line—people full of spontaneity and intuition. Owning to its position and direction the Sun line confirms certain information that has emerged from the fate line.

From whatever part it originates, the Sun line always converges on the mount of Apollo. Having reached this mount, it may turn in the direction of Saturn or Mercury. In the first example (*174a*), apart from his abilities the subject owes his success to a serious approach in facing up to obstacles and performing his duties. With the second (*174b*) the subject has always been guided by financial considerations in assessing situations and things.

Very rarely the Sun line rises from the plain of Neptune. When this happens, and especially if its course runs directly to the mount of Apollo, we have a perfect Sun

The line of the Sun most commonly terminates in the mount of Apollo area but in some cases to the side just touching the mount of Saturn (174a) or to the side just touching the mount of Mercury (174b); it may start from the mount of Venus (175a), from the life line (175b), or sometimes from the mount of the Moon (176).

line. As we have said this is very rare and its significance is highly favourable. The subject will achieve success and without too much difficulty. Throughout his life he will be blessed with the gifts that fortune dispenses to its favourites: popularity, great love affairs, no financial problems, satisfaction in every field. The subject is well aware of his personal charm. Given the eccentric nature of this line, it can appear on the hands of people who are already internationally famous or on those touched by a more modest form of success.

If the Sun line originates from the mount of Venus (*175a*) or from the life line (*175b*), success will come mainly from the arts and entertainment, particularly in those areas requiring great application and training. We are speaking of ballet dancers, concert performers, acrobats, conjurers etc. Very often the Sun line crosses the fate line, in which case the subject's intuition and sensitivity are very pronounced. His success will be hard won and fully deserved, considering the effort involved. When the Sun line originates from the mount of the Moon (*176*), it means that success, mainly in the artistic world, has come quite easily and is helped by an element of physical attraction. It is a typical sign of actors who engage the attention of the audience by their likeable manner or good looks. Some palmists believe that when the Sun line rises just by the mount of the Moon it signifies a secure inheritance.

Lastly, if the Sun line is short and begins higher up (*177*), success will come late and with difficulty. Late success will allow for eventual achievement of very high goals, because obstacles encountered and the harshness of the climb will have sharpened the subject's intelligence and sensitivity. This is the case when the Sun line begins in the plain of Mars.

A Sun line that rises in the passive mount of Mars indicates that the subject will not only achieve success, though it comes rather late, but in many cases will prove a leader or, in any event, a figure of considerable importance in his field.

Special marks are found fairly commonly on the Sun line and their presence is usually negative in nature. A square (*178a*) signifies a serious danger to the subject's work, luckily a danger that will be avoided. When everything returns to normal, the square will of course disappear. If there is an island (*178b*) on the Sun line, it signifies a loss of esteem due to gossip, slander, or the events that they cause. This results in a lull in the subject's career, which will pick up again only many years later. If there are several small islands very close together toward the end of the Sun line or above the head line, the fame enjoyed by the subject will have resulted from a scandal that will be revived as a topic of discussion at regular intervals.

Chains (*179*), crosses, stars, and short lines indicate, as always, conflicts, whose seriousness depends on their colour. They will slow up the subject's career but never be serious enough to jeopardize his success.

A Sun line that ends in a plait, a decidedly unusual case, is a negative sign: in spite of the subject's abilities and determination, circumstances will prevent him from attaining the recognition vital to those who aspire to success and believe it to be their due. His work or art will be respected, but he will never achieve celebrity status, unlike others whose work is perhaps less important than his. He is by no means a failure, but it is certain that he will have to settle for modest rewards.

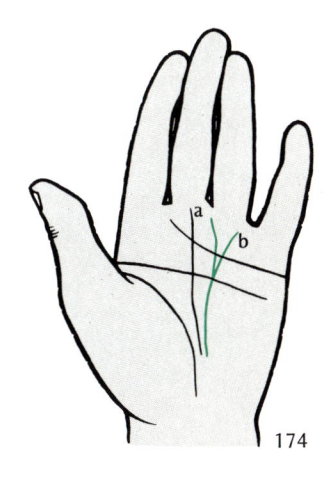

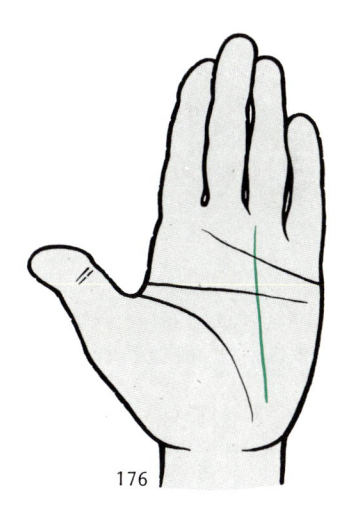

The line of Mercury

Here too we have chosen the name for this line from the mount toward which it is mainly directed. During the long, slow

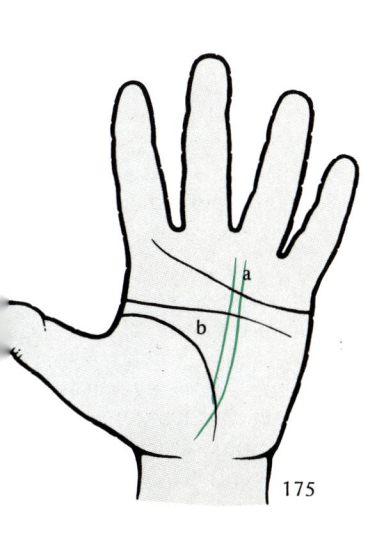

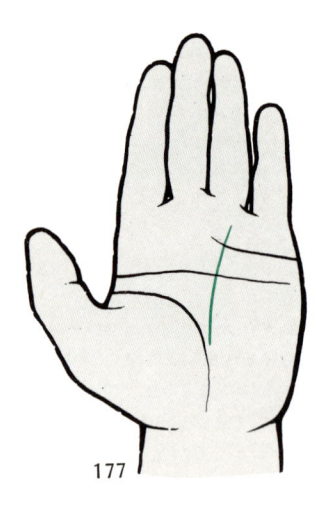

A short line of the Sun with a high beginning (177). A line of the Sun with a square (178a) and islands (178b). A line of the Sun with chains (179). A "perfect" line of Mercury (180).
Opposite, the hand of Buddha the Healer (Yakushi Nyorai) with some of the palm lines, and a wheel with spokes symbolizing the paths to Nirvana. (Detail from the bronze statue in the main hall of the temple dedicated to Buddha at Nara, Japan.)

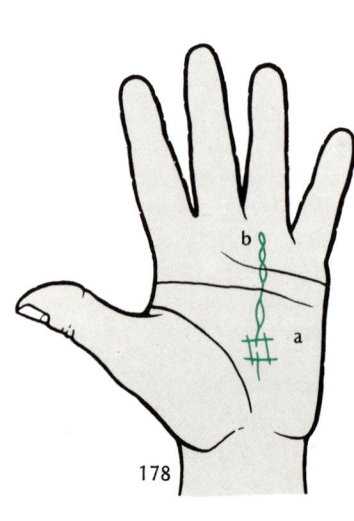

development of palmistry the line of Mercury (*180*) has had various names, but it has always been regarded as an index of the general state of the subject's health. It has been called the Hepatica or liver line, the line of temperament, intuition, or business, or the line of Mercury. (Every epoch has followed its own fashions in palmistry. Whereas the principal lines representing the subject's fundamental character cannot be subject to the whims of fashion, this is not the case with secondary lines, which by their nature lend themselves better to interpretations that reflect the state of mind of a particular moment.)

In old treatises on palmistry, importance was assigned to a line formed by many fine capillaries running parallel to the Mercury line. Now it is very rarely encountered, but considering the importance attributed to it, it was very likely much more common in the past. At one time it was called *soror hepaticae*, sister of the Hepatica, another way of referring to the line of Mercury. Today it is called the Milky Way or Via Lasciva in memory of its former meaning—that the bearer's primary interest in life was pleasure ranging from the carnal to the culinary. We tend to evaluate it differently. According to some, it signifies an idiosyncratic reaction to certain substances, so that it could be called the "allergic line." When it is found along with certain signs on the head line and the mount of Venus, its meaning can again involve the subject's sexuality, revealing instances of nymphomania and priapism. Be that as it may, the presence of the soror hepaticae (or whatever one wishes to call it) helps to reinforce the information that emerges from the line of Mercury.

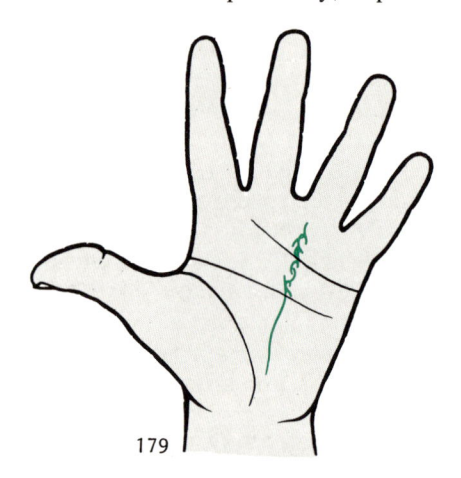

We have chosen the name line of Mercury because its significance is not just confined to an evaluation of the subject's physical health, but extends to the qualities usually revealed by the mount and finger of Mercury: intelligence, readiness, intuition, organizing ability. Furthermore the line of Mercury can give us fairly accurate information about the functioning of the liver, which as medical science tells us is basic to the body's proper balance and thereby to the subject's effective use of his intelligence and temperament.

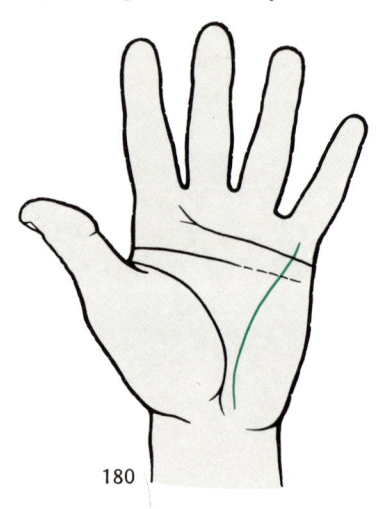

In the same way that the fate line represents the degree of balance between the subject and his surroundings, the line of Mercury represents his psychophysical balance, informing us whether or not he is able to express himself to the best of his ability. The line of Mercury is not so much an indication of the subject's health, which can be obtained more accurately from other lines or mounts, as it is a revelation of the degree to which the subject's health influences the quality of his performance in all sectors.

As we observed, the line of Mercury appears on very few hands, usually on a palm that is crisscrossed by a great many lines. Hence much attention is needed to locate it, for its presence can lead one to modify certain conclusions already drawn.

The perfect line of Mercury (*180*) originates primarily in the plain of Neptune and

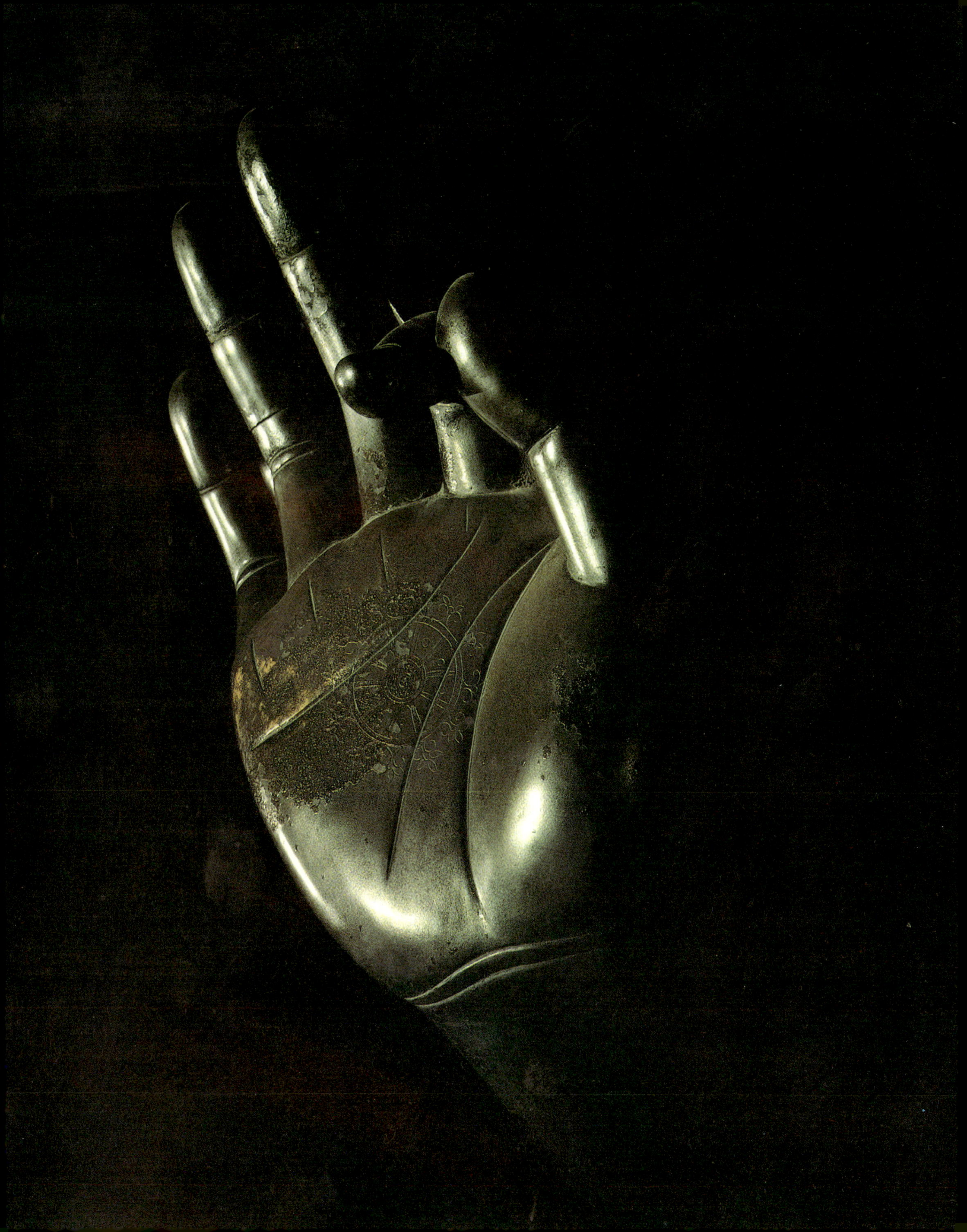

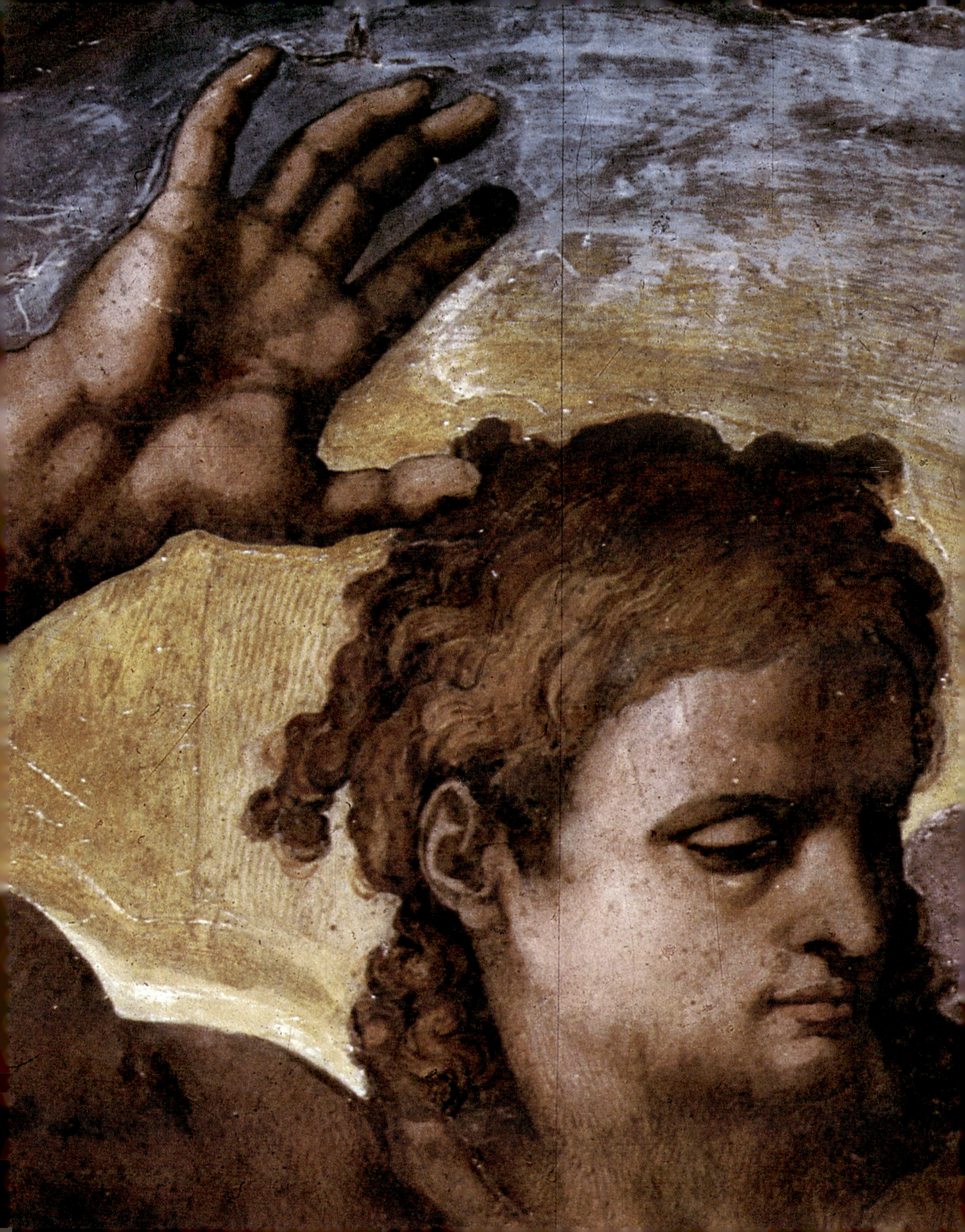

Opposite, the hand of Christ from the Last Judgement *by Michelangelo (Sistine Chapel, The Vatican).*

runs in a clear line toward the mount of Mercury, just skimming the mount of the Moon and the passive mount of Mars. It cuts across the head line (or its extension) and the heart line. It should be straight, not too deep, and rose coloured. Specifically, it should be on the light side and without any special marks.

A line of Mercury like this—a rarity—indicates a fortunate subject with a perfect balance between intellectual and physical abilities, a balance that allows him to involve himself with equal interest and satisfaction in the intellectual, cultural, and practical aspects of his work, whatever that may be. It signifies the ability to attribute spiritual values to eminently practical activities.

Appearance of the line of Mercury
Let us now look at the more common appearance of the line of Mercury and at its different meanings.
1. *The line of mercury rises from the mount of Venus, crosses the life line, and shoots up toward the mount of Mercury (181a).* As so often happens when the life line is involved, the family weighs on the subject, obliging him to take on roles that do not really belong to him. This often creates difficulties with his health. As this type of line is not very common and the interpretation is very special, look for confirmation in other areas of the hand.
2. *The line of Mercury originates from the life line without crossing it (181b).* Here we have the same situation as described above, except that it is the subject who feels morally obliged, without pressure from others, to take on family roles that have been left vacant for some reason. It is usually for a specific period of time, which can represent an interesting experience for the subject. Moreover, people with this type of Mercury line have high moral standards, intuitive intelligence, and eloquent use of language. It is common among celebrated criminal lawyers (together with a very curved thumb and a pointed little finger), judges, and lecturers.

When the line of Mercury begins very high up, toward the center of the plain of Mars, it refers mainly to health in the general sense described above.

3. *The line of Mercury rises from the mount of the Moon (181c).* In this case the subject has a talent for communicating, exceptional insight, extraordinary powers of organization, and a broad overview of things. Hence he is very logical and coherent. Persons with this kind of line of Mercury know how to write (particularly non-fiction), give lectures, and they are fascinating conversationalists. They have a total respect for the truth and are therefore completely lacking in any diplomatic sense—it is very unlikely they will choose a career in politics. The quality and extent of the related accomplishments are indicated by the length of the line. If it is short, ending before the head line or its imagined extension, the exceptional insight mentioned remains latent: the subject has only a vague premonition that something either good or bad is about to happen to him. If the line of Mercury extends further, crossing the heart line, the subject's insight is so exceptional that it enhances his intelligence. In addition, if the person in question has square fingers, then his advice may be highly prized, especially in business matters. In general an examination of this particular aspect of the line of Mercury is accompanied by a very careful study of the head line. Through interpolation it will be possible to ascertain with certainty whether the person is capable of operating shrewdly on the stock market, or instead if he can aspire to an important position in high finance or teach economics or finance at university level.

Special signs on the line of Mercury
It is common to find special signs on the line of Mercury (*182*, *183*); their significance concerns mainly health rather than abilities.
1. *There is an island on the line of Mercury (182a).* An old tradition says this denotes a serious liver disease and at the same time dishonesty. Today we tend to interpret it as the threat of an illness or a fear of falling ill—not always a well-founded fear, but in itself always a symptom of disorder. However, when the island is located right at the beginning of the line of Mercury, the meaning changes considerably: the subject sleeps very little. It is not that he suffers

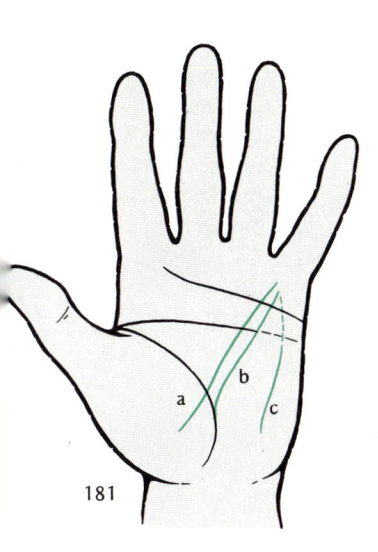

The line of Mercury can rise (181): a from the mount of Venus, b from the life line, c from the mount of the Moon.

109

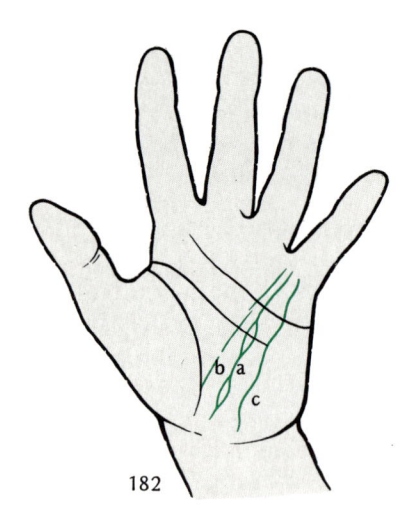

from insomnia, but that he needs only a little sleep to feel refreshed. He compensates for not having a long sleep by taking short naps at the most improbable times and places. In some very special cases, confirmed by the head line, the subject sleepwalks.

2. *There are breaks along the line of Mercury (182b).* This means that the subject's health, which is poor at times, does not allow him to carry out his work satisfactorily. There are periods of inactivity when the subject must reduce efforts to the minimum so as not to risk making a bad decision.

3. *The line of Mercury is wavy (182c).* The meaning is the same as for the preceding example, but the period of ill-health may be very long and due to a nervous disorder in the gastro-intestinal tract, with serious consequences to personality and hence work.

4. *The line of Mercury is crossed by well-marked short lines (183a).* On whatever part of the line these short lines appear they indicate difficulties of an intellectual nature for the subject, such as the inability to understand a situation or the refusal to face it. This attitude causes temporary indispositions that the subject uses to justify to himself his own refusal, which is logically indefensible.

5. *Any or all of a star, cross and spots occur on the line of Mercury (183b).* The usual interpretation of these signs is sterility for both men and women, but it is necessary to find confirmation elsewhere, such as the mount of Mercury or the wrist wrinkles, from which it may be deduced that fertility can be restored with the appropriate cure.

The line of marriage

Marriage is not quite the right word; it would be more logical to speak of cohabitation, but as the most common form of this in our society is marriage, we shall use this more generally accepted term. This line—or rather group of lines (184)—is located on the outer edge of the hand between the heart line and the base of the finger of Mercury. The meaning ascribed to this grouping is justified on the basis of what has been said about the finger of Mercury. It tells us not only about the subject's ability to express himself but also what kind of relations he has with those closest to him. These include sexual relations, and by extension family and marital relations. That is why these lines, rising from the edge of the hand and becoming visible when the fingers are bent toward the palm, can tell us so much about the subject's relations in cohabitation, usually with a person of the opposite sex.

We say lines plural because in the area defined above, which practically corresponds to the mount of Mercury, one almost never sees a single line. Two or three of different lengths are more usual. The marriage or cohabitation line to which we are chiefly referring is the one most in evidence (*184a*). The other, smaller lines represent any pre- (*184b*) or extra- (*184c*) marital relationships which, even when not casual, did not involve living under the same roof, but nevertheless left their mark. It is useful to compare the marriage lines found on both hands, because if the lesser ones appear only on the left hand, they may denote romantic infatuations which, even if long in duration, have never gone beyond a platonic level.

Details of the marriage line
Of course there is a perfect marriage line, but it is as rare as a perfect marriage itself. It would be a single, well-marked line entering deep into the mount of Mercury, ending gently, and with no special signs. What we actually find usually differs considerably. Let us examine the two most typical features.

1. *There are two marriage lines, almost parallel and of equal length.* The meaning is obvious: an extra-marital relationship, often previously initiated, has been at least as important as the legal marriage, possibly producing children, and it should be given the regard that it deserves. It may even end in a second marriage.

2. *The distance between the marriage line and the heart line (184d).* This allows us to find out at what age the subject married or will marry. If the line is near the heart line, the subject has or will marry at a very young age; if it is nearer to the base of the little finger, marriage has or will take place at a later age.

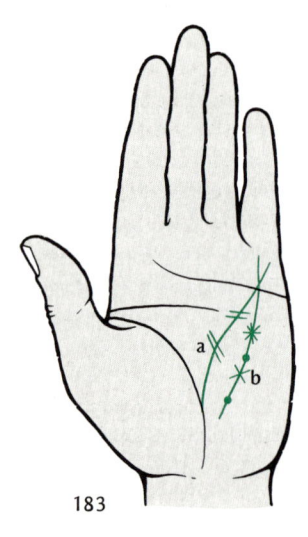

The line of Mercury, with islands (182a), with breaks (182b), wavy (182c), with short lines (183a), with crosses, stars, and spots (183b).

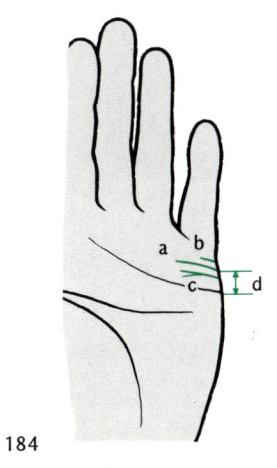

The marriage line (184a): b represents one or more encounters before marriage, c relations after marriage, d distance from the heart line. The marriage line directed toward the base of the little finger (185a), with a fork (185b), with a fork that reaches the life line (186), with a short line (187).

The beginning of the marriage line
There are three main ways in which the line can begin.

1. *The line starts straight and does not wander (184a).* From the start there will be a real understanding between the husband and wife that can guarantee a long and happy union.

2. *It begins as a double line, then becomes a single line and proceeds straight (185b).* We could say it begins like an open island. The union is in danger and a separation on grounds of incompatibility is probable. If after the two lines are joined they continue as a long and well-marked single line, the prediction is more favourable: after a period of separation, the relationship will become fairly stable. The prediction is the same if a fork marks the beginning of the line, like a triangle minus one side. If, however, the lower branch of the fork extends as far as the life line (186), then in the case of a separation there will be legal complications: struggles over the custody of children and the division of property.

3. *The marriage line is flanked by another finer line, often longer, rather irregular, and almost always wavy.* Indicates an extramarital love affair so strong that it destroys the marriage and takes its place. It can be a second marriage or simple cohabitation. In any event with the passage of time, if there is the possibility of checking, you will see that the fine, wavy line has achieved the consistency of a proper marriage line.

Special signs on the marriage line
1. *A short line crosses the marriage line (187).* There are obstacles to the union; they may come from the family or they may be economic in nature. If the short line is thicker than the marriage line, family obstacles will either prevent the marriage from taking place or cause it to be postponed for some years. If the short line is lighter than the marriage line then the economic or family obstacles will be removed sooner or later and the marriage celebrated. In the first instance the short line tends to disappear after a period of time, but not the marriage line if the subject is destined to marry.

2. *The marriage line runs toward the base of the little finger (185a).* Also signifies obstacles to marriage, but here they come from the subject, who cannot make up his mind to face the responsibilities of married life and wants to delay committing himself to the new arrangement. Such persons usually do not want to give up the life-style to which they have become accustomed over the years. If the reasons are different and of a sexual nature, the head and heart lines and the mount of Venus can supply useful information. Marriage lines of this sort usually denote rather fragile relationships which, if they last a long time, do so to the detriment of one of the partners who submits to the will of the other.

3. *There is an island in the center of the marriage line.* The cohabitation arrangement is threatened. The colour of the island can help us to establish how real the danger is. If there are no differences in the coloration, this very likely means a temporary separation or a serious disagreement between the couple, with a suspension of physical relations. If the island is located at the end of the marriage line, then the threat of separation or divorce becomes real.

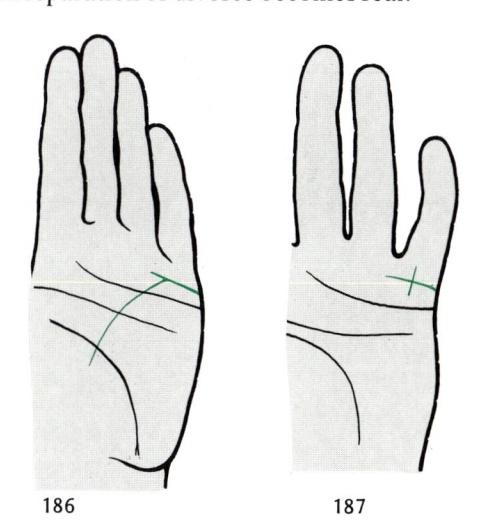

4. *The marriage line ends in a fork (188).* One must be very careful in interpreting this sign, making absolutely certain that it is a fork and not just a capillary line that happens to be on that spot and gives a very different meaning. The fork means that the subject will suffer much because of his partner.

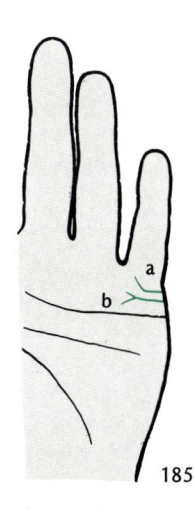

5. *The marriage line is interrupted in one or several places.* The subject will be separated from his spouse for rather long periods owing to trips to distant places, during which time there is no opportunity for physical contact. If very prolonged, the separation may cause the subject psychological problems. It will involve a considerable sacrifice in any case.

Branches on the marriage line
There can be disappointments even when there is great understanding between the marriage partners. These are indicated by branches that run from the marriage line.

1. *Capillary branches descending toward the heart line* (*189a*). Signs of displeasure caused by the other partner, a long separation due to work or other reasons, or a long illness that indirectly influences the subject's life. Only rarely is this a sign of bereavement, of which we shall speak further on and which would also be found on the heart line.

2. *Capillary branches ascending toward the base of the little finger* (*189b*). There are two schools of thought with regard to these branches. The oldest believes that this indicates love for the children that is stronger than marital love. This view also maintains that the number of branches represents the number of children. The other interpretation, which I consider more valid, is that these branches are not just a clear sign of love for one's children but for young people in general. They indicate an understanding of youngsters' problems and a genuine desire to help them in life. If this interest is not shared by the partner, it may cause discord and in time a progressive cooling of the couple's relationship.

The line(s) indicating children

This is perhaps the best time to bring up the subject of children and the relevant lines. We are still in the same area of the palm, the mount of Mercury. Let us look at the lines that descend vertically from the base of the little finger toward the heart line, which they almost never reach. Each line corresponds to a child of the subject; there will be in the area indicated one or more lines of different lengths and intensity of colour, indicating the number and sex of the children born or to be born.

The heavier lines represent male chil-

A marriage line that ends with an open island (188a) or a triangle without one side (188b). A marriage line with branches (189): a descending, b ascending.

dren, the fainter ones female children. However, it can easily happen that a female child of strong character is indicated by a heavy line and a male child of weak character by a line less clearly defined. Thus it is easier to read the character of an unborn child than its sex.

Between these lines can sometimes be seen lines that begin normally but quickly disappear. These are natural abortions and obviously found only on the hands of females.

These lines can also provide information about any birth traumas the child may suffer. If the line does not begin with a clean, straight course but instead curves slightly (*190c*), the length of this curve indicates how long the trauma will affect the child. As for traumas affecting the mother at the time of the birth, we have to look at the life line or the wrist wrinkles.

While the lines denoting children can be found on both male and female hands, they are less clearly marked on men. In the case of women it is possible to extract very precise information about the health, character, and certain basic events in the life of the child. This may seem a surprising statement, but we need only think of the importance to a woman of pregnancy and giving birth. Much of her life may be conditioned by the responsibilities of bringing up a child. It is therefore understandable why events like these should leave important marks.

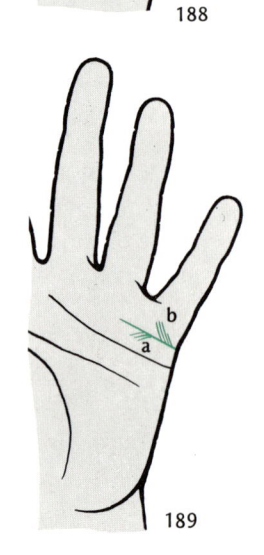

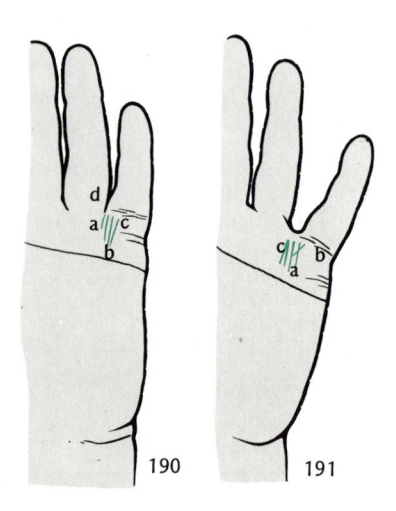

The problems children occasion can affect a long period of time, often a whole lifetime. Ideas that emerge from a thorough reading by a palmist will undoubtedly be extremely useful in deciding how to bring up a child—how it should be treated as a baby and as an adolescent—and be helpful in showing how to prompt a successful adaptation to life.

Let us see what is the most helpful information that can be had from examining these lines. As they are all contained within a fairly limited area, the lines we shall be looking at will be small and fine. It is best to use a magnifying glass in order to see them clearly and thus make more reliable predictions.

Different types of lines that indicate children

1. *The line is straight and well marked (190a).* This is probably a boy with a strong personality and exceptional intelligence, but who is rather stubborn. The way to deal with him during the whole of his formative years is to talk little but intelligently, especially to set for him an example of good behaviour, with as much freedom of choice as possible and responsibilities to develop his self-assurance.

2. *The line is straight but thin (190b).* If it is a girl, she will have a normal personality and enjoy good health. If instead it is a boy, it means that he will be a very sensitive child, easily influenced, and insecure. If the line becomes heavier as it proceeds toward the heart line, the same prediction applies to the male child, who will become more stable during puberty.

3. *The line is clearly defined at first and then becomes thin and indistinct.* The opposite of the previous example. An event immediately after puberty—very often a nervous breakdown—will bring about a change in the child's character, frequently taking the form of a new direction in studies and in life as well. If the thin section of the line curves slightly towards the mount of Apollo, it means that later in life the child will be a disappointment or a worry, often due to a bad marriage.

4. *The line is crossed diagonally by a thin, short capillary line (191b).* The subject will bear a scar from an operation, perhaps as a result of an accident. This holds true provided the capillary line does not undergo changes after it crosses the children's line. If it does change and proceeds indecisively, it means that the injury or accident will leave a more complex and permanent mark. The point at which the two lines meet will tell us the location of the scar, somewhere between the head and feet, proceeding from the top to the bottom of the children's line.

5. *The line is somewhat wavy (192a).* Not a good sign for the health of the baby. It indicates a weakness, especially in the nervous system, which will need observation until puberty.

6. *Two parallel lines.* Denotes twins. If the two lines are joined at the beginning, the twins will be of the same sex (*191c*). If one of the lines is usually darker than the other, they will be of different sex, or if the same sex, the difference will lie in personality. If one of the two lines is perfectly straight and the other somewhat irregular, the difference will be very marked. One of the twins will create problems for whoever is bringing him up. As a rule the darker of the two lines refers to the second-born.

7. *The line meets the heart line (192b).* The subject has a special fondness for this particular child, who will not fail to take advantage. There is a risk of spoiling the child and changing his personality as a consequence of giving him too much. In order to establish how the child will react to his upbringing, one must take into account the type and colour of the line. If it is pink and straight, the relationship between parent and child will be excellent in every respect; if dark pink and a bit winding, the child will rebel against discipline and be intolerant of the excessive affection shown by the parent.

We have explained how miscarriages are indicated on the palm, but there are also lines to show children who were not wanted (that is, induced abortions), which the female hand shows very clearly. They are located on the life line (*193*) and consist of fairly well-defined lines that rise from the life line and run toward the plain of Mars, like descending branches. The length of the line indicates the seriousness of the trauma suffered. If the spiritual trauma is accompanied by a physical one, then a rather clearly marked grille forms on the plain of Mars indicating the presence of a thyroid

Lines indicating children (190): a *strong,* b *fine,* c *child with birth trauma,* d *line of spontaneous abortion.*
Children's lines with special aspects (191): a *child with trauma during puberty,* b *child with scars from an accident or operation,* c *line indicating identical twins.*

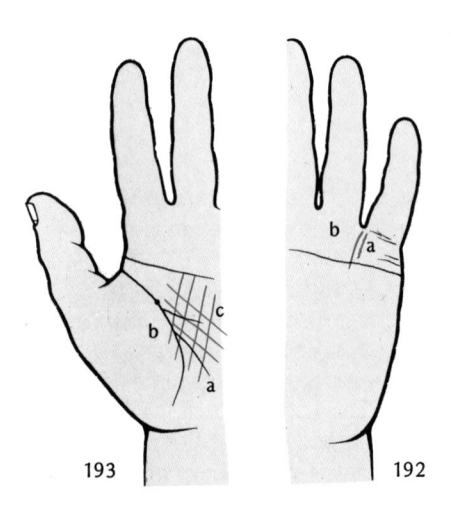

disorder brought about by the abortion. Naturally, this grille is only temporary, but it should be realized that while it is present the subject is troubled by nerves, irritability, and insomnia, and is therefore unable to make responsible decisions.

While on this subject and in connection with a similar type of line, we want to point out a children's line that denotes a difficult delivery, possibly one that endangers the mother's life. This line is located on the life line and appears like a descending branch, like that for an induced abortion, but it is preceded by a brief interruption or a very well-defined spot on the life line, indicating the risk run by the subject.

The line of widow(er)hood

To conclude the brief cycle that begins with the marriage line and is followed by the children's line, we shall briefly discuss the line of widow(er)hood.

There are two types, owing to the fact that the surviving spouse reacts with different emotions when faced with the death of the companion of a lifetime. Long experience allows us to state that only occasionally is the death of a spouse reason for deep sadness. In most cases one finds almost a feeling of liberation. Naturally there are two different kinds of lines corresponding to these two kinds of reactions.

1. *Death of the marriage partner causes profound sadness (194).* The line indicating this type of bereavement is a capillary line that descends from the marriage line with a slight curve and, having crossed the heart line, proceeds toward the head line, where it ends in a well-defined and deep spot, a sign of the seriousness of the shock experienced. A further confirmation of this state of mind is represented (especially if the bereavement has brought about changes of habit or economic position) by an island on the life line. Its darkness or lightness depends on the seriousness and extent of the changes. If there are other islands on the life line, it is possible to determine the relevant one through the dating system. The fate line, of course, is also involved and indicates very clearly how long the period of pain and upset will last.

2. *Death of the marriage partner does not cause sadness (195).* One can identify this type of reaction by carefully examining the marriage line. It terminates with a capillary line that runs in the direction of the heart line for just a few millimeters. The only other conclusion that can be drawn from the subject's hand is that as a consequence of the partner's death the course of both the life line and the fate line becomes more certain (which can be established with the dating system) providing clear signs of psychological adjustment. If this type of bereavement occurs after a break in marital relations, the capillary line is preceded by a break in the marriage line due to the separation.

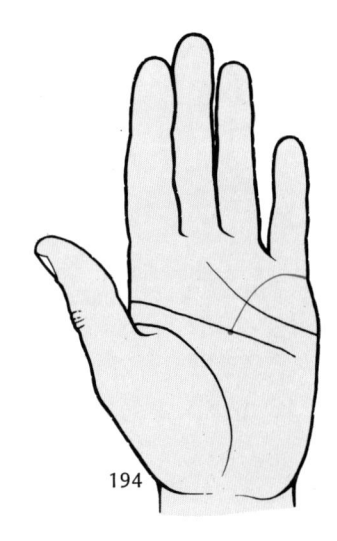

Wrist wrinkles

To conclude this brief study of the palm there remain only the wrist wrinkles (*196*) to consider. These are the lines, usually two or three in number, found at the folds of the wrist. By bending the wrist slightly forwards, one can see them clearly.

Every hand has at least one wrinkle. The first, nearest to the wrist, is regarded by palmists as the most important. The others are accessory lines—sometimes they are lacking altogether—and serve to emphasize or confirm what emerges from the first one. When this first line is slightly curved and clearly defined, it is a sign of good physical health. In addition this type of wrinkle is an indication that the subject keeps fit and avoids activities and habits that might damage his health.

The meaning changes when there are

Children's lines (192): a broken off, b touching the heart line. Lines can rise from the life line and run toward the plain of Mars (193): a is the line of procured abortions, b is the line of difficult births with a risk to life; a grille (c), sign of a thyroid malfunction, may form temporarily between the life and head lines, toward the plain of Mars.
The line of widow(er)hood (194) that crosses the heart line and touches the head line can cause the subject deep sorrow.

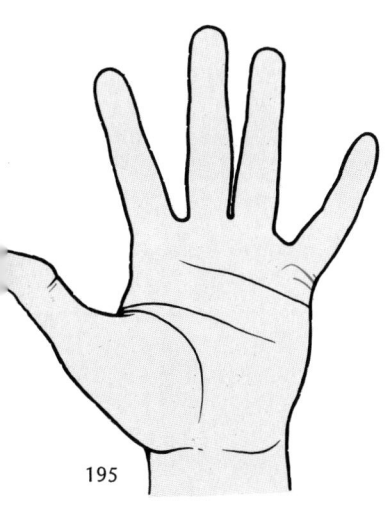

Examples of lines of widow(er)hood that do not involve sorrow (195).

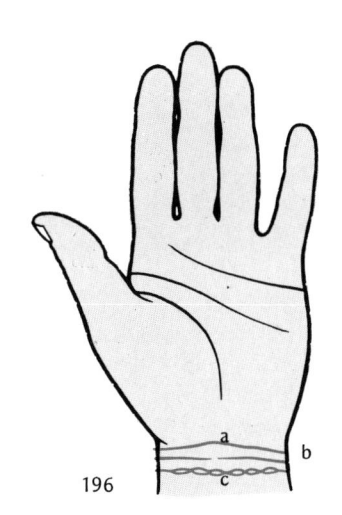

There generally are three wrist wrinkles (196): a first wrist wrinkle, b second wrist wrinkle, c third wrist wrinkle with chained or plaited formations.
The ring of Solomon (197) can be formed by: a two lines that do not meet, b two lines that overlap, c a single line.

breaks in the first wrinkle: the subject has an impulsive streak, is original, and fun-loving. He does not take good care of himself and overtaxes his strength—as we can easily ascertain from other lines—for the sole purpose of enjoying himself. He tends to lead the life of what was once called a libertine.

If the first wrinkle is well marked and the others (if any) have islands or are chained, it denotes a middle course. There will be problems but the subject is resilient and has the will to regain his former stability.

Some indications in the wrist wrinkles have to do exclusively with women. If the first wrinkle twists and turns, even though the line is unbroken, according to some palmists this signifies sterility or difficulty in carrying a pregnancy full term. This is actually a somewhat risky prediction and needs confirmation from other lines, especially the head and Mercury lines.

The wrinkles are usually the last item to be considered when a palm is being read, but we will devote a few pages to some other lines that, though less conspicuous than those discussed so far, are nevertheless significant. They are called *rings*.

Rings

We mentioned rings briefly in the chapter on mounts but considered it preferable to deal with them at the end of the section on palm lines. In this way they can be considered in the light of what emerges from a comprehensive reading of the hand. Rings are not main lines and normally serve only to modify or add to the reading of the more important lines. They are interesting because they are there and because they do add a special finishing touch.

The *ring of Solomon* (*197*). A semicircular line, located on the mount of Jupiter, that almost completely surrounds the base of the index finger. It sometimes appears in the form of two semicircles which try to join together and in some cases overlap. When this occurs, however, it partly disrupts the original meaning of the ring.

It is a sign of great wisdom and its location is totally logical if we take into account the fact that the finger of Jupiter and its mount reveal the subject's ability to adapt to life. After all, that is one way of defining wisdom—an amalgam of culture, common sense, intuition, objectivity, and prudence. Often a wise person, someone who has the ring of Solomon, is able to turn these qualities to his own advantage by choosing a lifestyle suited to his potential. When the ring of Solomon makes up one of the sides of the square of teaching (see mount of Jupiter), the wise man will also be an incomparable master of life. Very often the ring of Solomon expresses a need for solitude, which may be inferred from what has been said. This need is not dictated by a desire to get away from one's neighbour, but to reflect and improve one's spiritual life through silence and meditation.

The *ring of Saturn* (*198*). Just as the middle finger acts as a divide between the conscious and unconscious aims of the hand, so the ring of Saturn encircling its base can be a sign of emotional imbalance, which results from a continual compromise between the inner and outer self. It provides us with information not so much about the subject's stability, but about his instability: how unbalanced he is and what difficulties have to be overcome to achieve serenity. It represents existential anxiety, interior solitude, the difficulty of communicating, the degree of one's limitations; all judged with great objectivity.

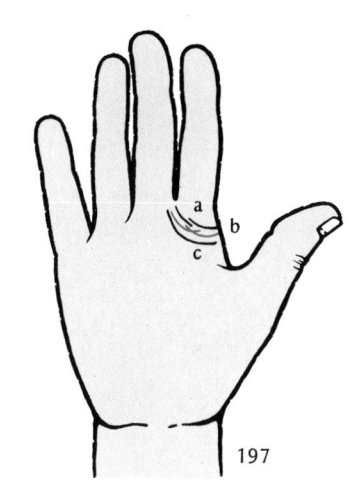

The ring of Saturn is rarely a stable sign. As a rule it becomes consistent and visible as the problems mentioned become more serious in the mind of the subject. It tends to disappear when a satisfactory state of

The ring of Saturn (198) can be formed by: a *single line or* b *two lines that do not meet;* c *is the heart line. The ring of Venus (199) or girdle of Venus can be represented by:* a *two lines that overlap,* b *a single continuous line,* c *a single line broken by an island;* d *is the heart line.*

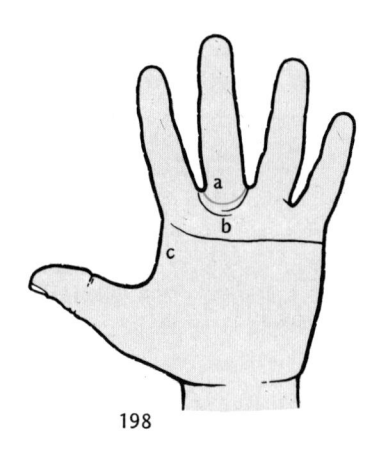

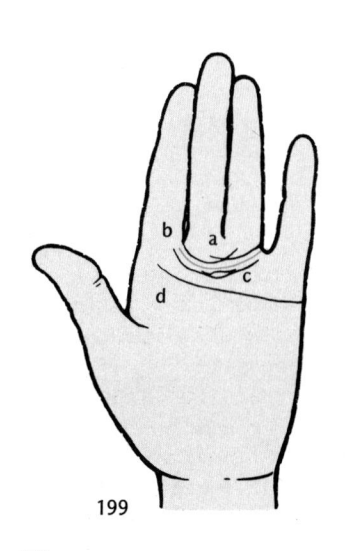

equilibrium begins to prevail.

Bear in mind that the presence of the ring of Saturn serves only to indicate the existence of problems. It does not specify their nature, which has to be sought on other mounts or lines of the hand, e.g., the head, heart, and fate lines.

The *ring of Venus (199)*. Some palmists call it the *girdle of Venus,* but the meaning is the same. It is a curved line that comes into contact with two mounts, Saturn and Apollo, and hence two fingers, the middle and the ring. It starts where the base of the middle finger adjoins the index finger and ends where the base of the ring finger meets the little finger. It always remains above the heart line.

It is traditionally assigned positive attributes to do with emotionality and creativity, plus is said to indicate a very active sexual life. This is why it was given the name of Venus. But modern science sees this ring in quite a different light. The ring of Venus is now regarded as a link between the ring of Saturn, which allays uncertainties and anxieties and promotes insights, and the conscious creativity of the mount of Apollo, which embodies as well as enhances the subtle gifts of sensitivity expressed by the finger of Saturn. Perhaps it does not provide the definitive solution, a stable balance between the subject and his environment, but it at least denotes an acceptable compromise allowing him to develop properly his own creative and imaginative talents. With respect to sexual activity, that too is balanced in appearance only and needs continual monitoring.

The limitations implicit in this sign, which by and large is positive, involve little ability for self-criticism and self-control in creative areas and in sexual relations. Nevertheless the mere presence of a ring of Venus should be regarded as an advantage in terms of vitality and energy.

Special signs on this ring have very precise meanings that are worth noting.

An island signifies a sexual disorder that may cause much embarrassment and problems, including homosexuality.

The ring of Venus takes on a negative meaning when it is composed of two intersecting semicircles. Then the subject's personality and creativity are marred by a streak of superficiality and amateurishness that vulgarize the beauty of artistic creativity.

The *ring of Mars (200)*, more commonly the line of Mars. It is a true ring and delineates the mount of Venus with a line running parallel to the life line. It can sometimes be double, in which case it reinforces the positive meaning of this line, healthy vitality, especially if the life line is not well-defined, is broken, or has special signs with a negative significance. There will be obstacles but the subject can overcome them. A ring of Mars denotes strong powers of recovery: periods of convalescence are fairly short and resistance to disease better than average. By extension one can apply this same trait to the subject's ability to defend himself from the dangers of other people's envy. People who have the ring or line of Mars are dynamic, keen, and determined to make the sacrifices needed for good results in their field of work which may arouse envy in others.

The *family ring (201)*. This ring is found on the joint between the second and third phalange of the thumb, where the mount of Venus is formed. It is very common and consists of two or three lines that form a chain. It is called the family ring because those who have it show a strong attachment to their families. The family is seen not just as a group of people united by affection but as a basic structure of society, a place for moral and material education and an environment from which to draw comfort and security. Moreover, a subject who has this line feels a strong sense of responsibility toward the other members of his family.

The contrary is true, however, if the family ring is entangled with other capillary lines. The structure of the thumb and the relationship between the first two phalanges will influence the final interpretation of this ring of course, but experience invariably shows that a subject with this ring has great respect for the nuclear family, an attitude compatible with his own tendencies and temperament.

The *celibacy ring (202)*. It is also called the *line of celibacy* or the *Mercury ring*. This is a curved line originating from the base of the finger of Mercury at the point where it meets the finger of Apollo. It crosses the mount of Mercury but rarely reaches the outer edge of the hand. People with this ring have not taken a vow of chastity. On the contrary, they are very interested in the opposite sex and perhaps for this reason do not favour living with someone for a prolonged period, as in a marriage. These people feel the need to change partners whenever they like and without a lot of difficulty. It is possible they will marry, but special conditions would be set concerning personal freedom, similar to what occurs in certain cases of the marriage line.

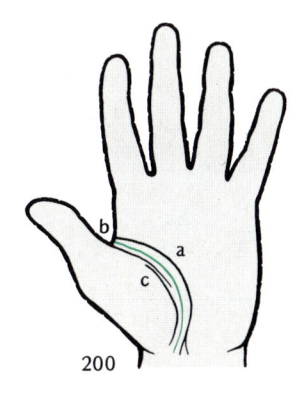

Capillary lines

These are truly the most distinctive and personal of all the lines on the human palm and for this reason we have left them till last. These fine surface lines, which are often indistinct but very important for a complete picture, are taken into consideration at the end of a palmist's reading.

Having constructed as precise a picture as possible of the subject's past and future from the principal lines, mounts, and other elements studied so far, we can now look at the present through the capillary lines. They tell us about important events that have just occurred or are about to so that one can intervene, if possible, to the advantage of the subject who has put his trust in our reading. With the information supplied by the capillary lines, the subject can exercise free will by offering resistance, within certain limits, to obstacles and thereby softening their impact and possible consequences.

One might infer from this that there is not much we can say in general terms about capillary lines. More than the other lines, they are linked to the person and change their meaning within the context in which they are found. Furthermore they appear and disappear with remarkable ease, for they are particularly connected with the recurrent phases of the moon. They also come under the influence of other fast-moving planets. By observing the same hand over a period of a few months, therefore, we are able to note perceptible changes in the capillary lines. They give advance warning—six months in more sensitive subjects—of approaching events, good and bad, that will have an effect on the subject. Very often these so-called fated events, about which we can do very little, have already emerged in reading the main lines. In other instances a capillary indicates an approaching event of minor importance, one less crucial in the general picture of the subject's life. In this case there is a much better chance of intervening. With a good knowledge of the situation and the character of the subject, it is possible to study ways of minimizing a looming impediment, or taking full advantage of a favourable event.

What about the subject's character? It is a good idea to dwell on this, as we can easily see how a suggestion by the palmist that does not produce the right reaction will not bring about the desired results. The weaker the subject is, the more he will be dominated by events; his reactions will be slower and less daring. The very opposite will be true when it is a matter of restraining the subject's impetuosity and violence. Here lies one of the most delicate and difficult tasks facing someone who intends to devote himself to palmistry in a constructive way.

The only information of a general nature that we can give about capillary lines is that they are located on different parts of the hand depending on their significance. As a rule they appear near a special sign indicating the nature of the event responsible for their appearance. The experienced palmist will be able to judge by their colour how long the event will last. If one closely follows how the situation develops, as seen on the hand, it is always possible to predict the outcome by the colour of the capillary line and to establish the validity of decisions taken to overcome the problem. Of course, the problems can vary a great deal, but they are mainly concerned with work, health, and love—the three pillars on which every individual's life is based.

Let us see how the capillary lines appear in these three main areas of life. To give a sound opinion one must have a strong magnifying glass large enough to view a large part of the palm.

Obstacles at work or in business. In this case capillary lines are found on the plain of

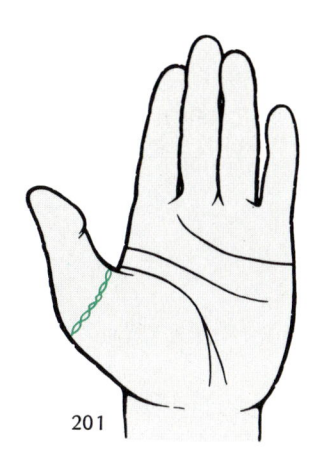

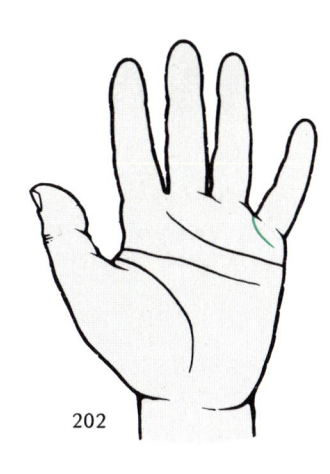

The ring of Mars or line of Mars (200) can be: b unbroken or c in part two parallel lines; a is the life line. The family ring (201) is a chained line at the base of the thumb. The line of Mercury (202) is also called the celibacy line.

117

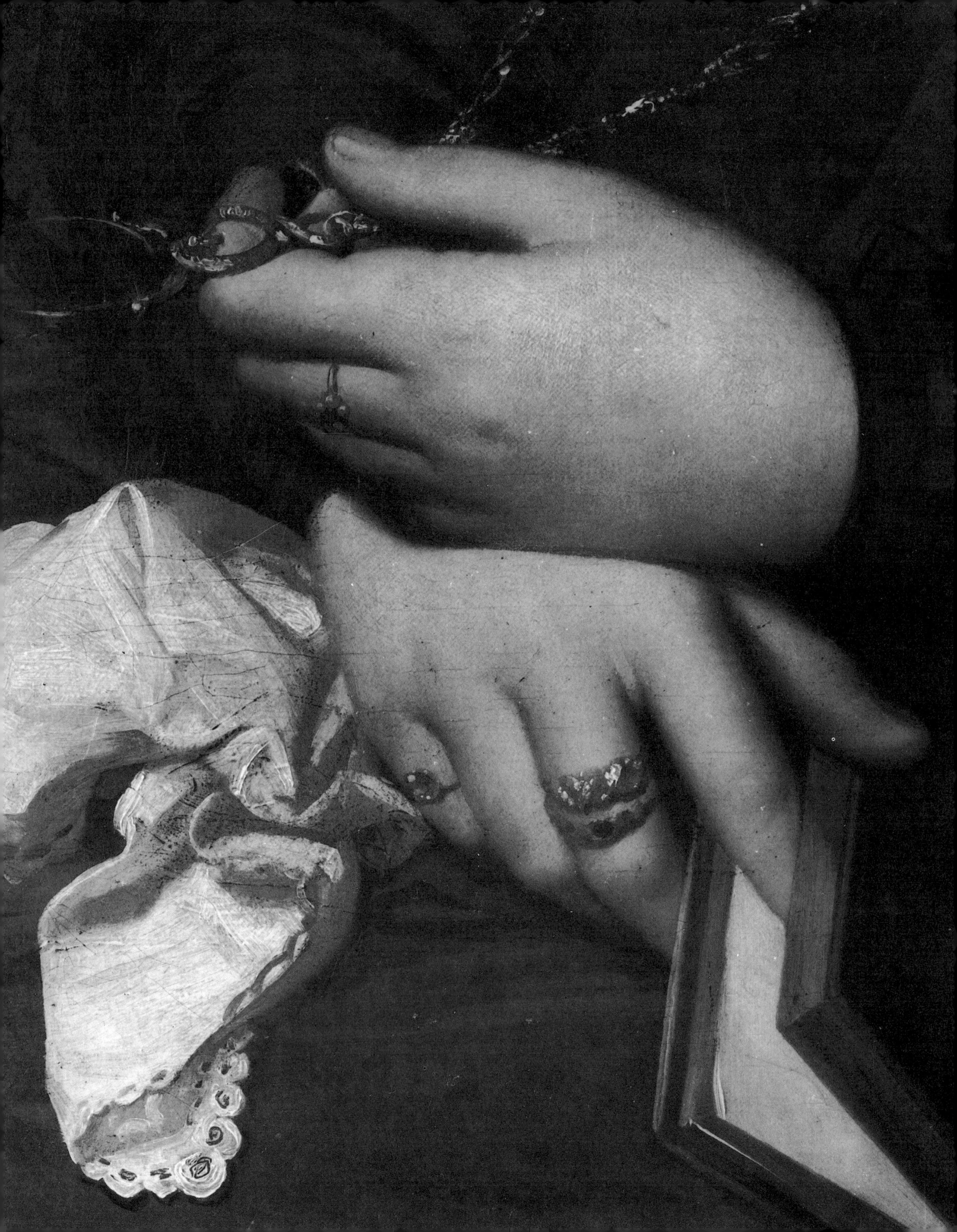

Mars and appear as a very fine grille between the head and life lines. Other capillary lines in the form of very fine short lines appear in the area of the line denoting the problem and its nature. Depending on whether it is an economic, artistic or work problem, the grille will face the mount of Mercury, Apollo, or Saturn, respectively.

Obstacles of a romantic nature. These can come from strangers who threaten the happiness of the couple. Capillary lines are found on the mount of Venus, parallel to the life line, virtually a faint grille located where the dating system indicates the danger. The capillary lines have a similar appearance when there is opposition from the partner's family or gossip from so-called friends. If the capillary lines are very fine, the danger is slight and when the obstacle is removed they disappear. If they are somewhat heavier and have a darker pink colour, then the conflict will last longer and it will be necessary to take initiatives of a more complex sort, sometimes involving an appreciable change in the subject's ways and attitudes.

In other circumstances a threat to a romantic relationship involving cohabitation is expressed by a capillary line that very lightly cuts across the marriage line and is visible through a magnifying glass. Its length depends on the duration of the threat.

There is another location where capillary lines may be found signalling danger to love and affection such as a parent feels for a child. These lines are found between the heart and head lines, which represent this kind of emotion. When heart and head lines are crossed diagonally by a very fine capillary line, it signifies a possible upset, an obstacle, often a separation. When the danger is over and the new situation has been accepted, the line disappears and everything returns to normal.

Danger of an illness arising. Here we are dealing with a fairly serious illness that cannot be avoided completely, but once treated properly will have no permanent aftereffects. More damaging illnesses are indicated by other signs that are evaluated differently. As a crisis point in those illnesses approaches, extremely dark capillaries appear in the area of the relevant line, giving a few months advance warning of the danger. This allows us to take the necessary precautions. Similar behaviour on the part of the capillaries occurs when they signal an approaching danger of a less serious sort for the subject's health, but one that nevertheless should not be underestimated. The duration of the physical disorder can be determined by the intensity of the lines' colour, whereas the nature of the illness is indicated by the area in which the lines appear. As soon as the disorder manifests itself, the lines lose their colour. The subject is given a time margin for taking necessary measures. Hence the course of the illness depends in part on decisions freely taken by the subject.

The "other" rings

We have concluded our observations on the rings that appear on the palm. We shall now look at other rings, those customarily worn on our fingers. This is not as frivolous a subject as may appear, if only because of the respect due a custom that goes back to the beginnings of civilization.

For many thousands of years rings have been a symbol of power: political, military, religious if worn by men, economic if worn by women, usually as a reflection of their husband's power. Indeed, an unmarried woman was not allowed to wear rings whatever her social position. Today this custom no longer exists, with the exception of the upper echelons of the clergy.

When we decide to wear a ring, it is still a matter of great interest to us. Placing a ring on a finger means calling attention to that finger. It is a way, often unconscious, of singling out or isolating that finger from the others, almost as though attributing special qualities to it according to the meanings palmistry gives to each. The choice also indicates some lack (almost always unconscious), in the attributes pertaining to that finger. Of itself this is certainly not enough to determine what the particular imbalance may be. It is an invitation to inquire further with the other means available to palmistry.

The popular custom today among young people, especially among very young girls, of wearing many rings on their fingers

Rings on the hands of Madame Marcotte de Sainte-Marie, *oil on panel by Daniel Tenois Ingres (The Louvre, Paris).*

including the thumb undoubtedly has to do with fashion. But what kind of emotional conflict produced such a fashion? Apart from the need for regimentation, to declare oneself part of a group and to herd together, which in itself reveals a lack of affection in the family group, this wearing of one or more rings on each finger is an obvious symptom of insecurity. This insecurity is due to too rapid a development of social customs to which the younger generations have not had time to adapt. It is a symptom of the embarrassment children feel about having too much freedom, including sexual freedom, which subconsciously makes them feel guilty. This is how they actually feel, despite their defiant attitude.

The fingers most frequently used for wearing rings are the little finger, or finger of Mercury, and the ring finger, the finger of Apollo.

The finger of Mercury, as we have said before, represents the subject's intimate relationships and therefore includes sexual matters. The desire to buttress insecurity in this area with a ring is an indirect statement of inadequacy, a need to compensate. In some this expresses itself in a desire to accumulate money beyond what is necessary. In others the insecurity takes on a more or less evident form of a sexual difference. It is very common among Western homosexuals to wear a ring on the little finger of the left hand as a sign of recognition. It is not difficult to guess the significance of a ring worn on the little finger.

In the West it is customary to wear the wedding ring on the fourth finger, or finger of Apollo. Chirology explains the significance of this choice, which is that we get our sensitivity and emotionality from the finger of Apollo. Marriage, representing a certain change in the subject's habits and relationships, brings about a modification in the emotional life and an inevitable (but temporary) disruption, which the ring indicates. To this one could add the positive action induced by the metal, in the particular case of gold, which is believed to create a more balanced distribution of the subject's electrostatic charges.

There are always some, though very few, who like to wear a ring on their index finger. It is interesting to compare this habit with what we know from history about famous people who used to wear a huge ring on the finger of Jupiter. They were known for their ambition and desire for success and power. Similar sentiments, though seen in terms of the epoch and the person's importance, can be discerned in people who display a ring on their index finger today.

A ring worn on the middle finger, the finger of Saturn, is quite rare. It is usually done by women whose hands are very tapered, of the sensitive type, on which the placing of a huge ring right in the center can achieve a very striking effect. The underlying reason for this choice is the emotional instability of the subject, who in this way tries to hide fears and uncertainties behind a display of confidence.

Reading palms

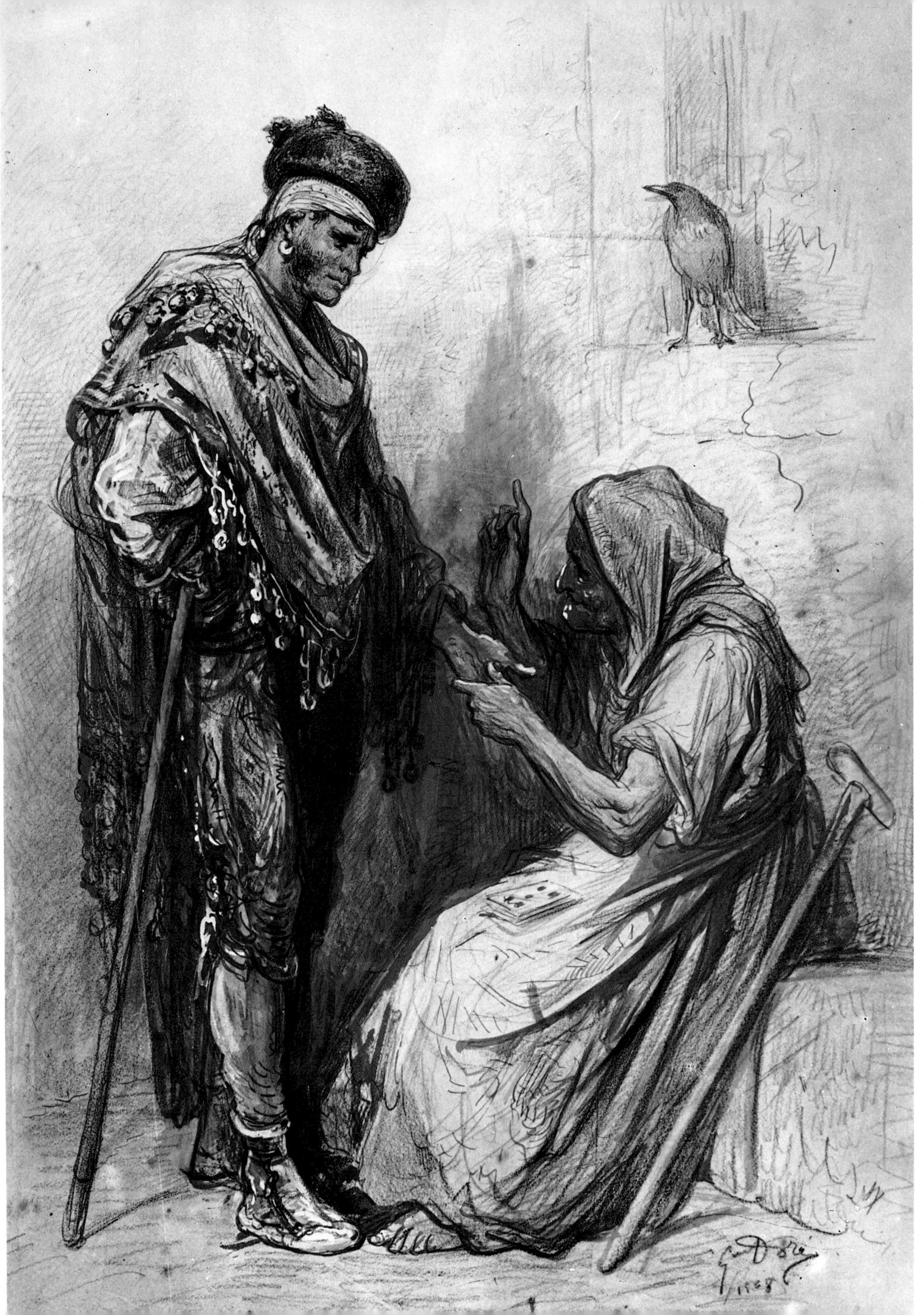

General advice

Those who have followed us this far and learned many of the rudiments already explained are now ready to turn their attention to reading palms, despite the shyness that accompanies all such debuts.

Here it may serve us well to repeat once more the principle expressed several times in the preceding pages concerning one's responsibilities when reading a palm. Not only do we literally hold the past and present of a human being in our hands, in some respects we also hold that person's future. This trust must not be taken lightly; particularly when one is just beginning and tempted to show off one's talents, blurting out things that a more thorough examination can and will reveal to be very different, or to touch on matters that will upset the subject's peace of mind.

Caution is a rule that palmists have repeated in their writings throughout the ages. The impetuous novice may regard such care as unjustified, but as he becomes more experienced and aware he will grasp how fragile the mood is of one who comes, perhaps with skepticism or even arrogance, to have his palm read, and how exact the science of palmistry can be when practiced with the necessary precision.

In keeping with this admonition, here is a passage from the renowned work of Tricasso de Cerasari, *Epytoma chyromantico*, published in 1635:

> This excellent rule of evidence should be followed: do not be precipitous in the observation of any one thing. ...And do not go by first impressions, but always try to consider and scrutinize every reason, probable though it appears....And in this way one will become aware of the truth of this principle of palmistry, which will find approval being entirely true and seriously reasoned.

This call for caution comes to us from but one great palmist. We could quote many others. But we shall simply counsel novices in this art to avoid the serious mistake of refusing to read a palm because there is some indication that in the course of the reading they might have to say something disagreeable. Deal with the situation sensibly, remembering that a half-truth is preferred to a refusal that might lead the person in question to imagine any number of threats to his future.

Someone who is about to embark on the reading of a palm regards the two open palms before him like the pages of a book—less a literary image than it seems—and is certain to experience unique and very personal feelings. Generally he will feel caught in a web of impressions, some of which will emerge more strongly than others. It is an extremely delicate moment and one must avoid becoming overwhelmed by these impressions so as not to form (often incorrectly) too emotional a picture of the subject's personality.

Abstain from personal feelings. Firmly reject any such reactions in this preliminary stage of the reading. We cannot allow ourselves to be caught up in emotions if the reading is to proceed as it should by stages. We must avoid drawing hasty conclusions before having collected and pondered over all the elements necessary to express a serious opinion.

Naturally the reason that has brought the subject to the palmist will emerge very clearly. But it would be a serious mistake to take that reason as the starting point. It may in fact be the final stage, unleashed by a number of events, states of mind, errors, delusions, etc., that have accumulated and contributed to the formation of the subject's personality. That is why we must create a protective barrier between our perceptions and the emotional flow from the subject, to undertake with detachment and objectivity as scientific an analysis of the hand as possible.

There are of course various ways and procedures for palm reading, each one with its own advantages and disadvantages. In all cases it is a very complex operation. I will confine myself here to describing the method I have used for many years and explain the reasons for this choice.

The first phase of the reading focuses exclusively on chirognomy. This is necessary not only because of the interesting information that it can provide but more importantly it allows us to narrow our field of inquiry and obtain some clear definitions of certain aspects of the subject's personality. Then the consistency of the hand is assessed through pressure. The colour and

A Palm Reading *(drawing by Gustave Doré)*.

transparency of the skin, suppleness of the joints, rigidity of the thumb, liveliness of movements, and the shape and colour of the nails are evaluated. At this point in the reading an expert palmist would be able to draw conclusions of a general nature about the subject of the sort that could excite interest or curiosity at a social gathering. But if the reading has a more serious purpose, touching on deeper, more intimate matters, then the information collected so far must remain part of the very important preliminaries on which one builds the structure of the complete interpretation.

As a rule our reading up to this point can be conducted in silence. When interpreting palm lines we require a certain amount of absorption, not only to apply the rudiments that have been learned but to achieve the degree of concentration needed for quick perception, rapid synthesis, and clarity of thought, all indispensible for gathering the widest range of information. We are probing details that are at times at odds with each other but which must be interpolated together in order to achieve the most balanced, harmonious, comprehensive picture possible. The initial phase of the reading needs to be exceptionally clear and methodical so that at the right moment one can easily retrace corrective elements that tell precisely how to understand the information supplied through gradual examination.

However elementary a hand may appear, it is still the mirror of a personality. Despite few lines on a palm, a sign that is modest in appearance but fundamental in its significance may be extraordinarily important, even profound, in connection with the overall interpretation. We must therefore not let ourselves be misled by appearances, but rather attribute to each element all the shades of meaning that palmistry allows.

Our investigations up to this point, only a small part of the definitive reading, are mainly theoretical, primarily informing us of the capabilities and potential of the subject. They do not account for all the variants imposed by circumstances on a person who lives within a community and is a member of a family. From here on we must look to determine the relationships between the subject and his environment.

In my experience an excellent knowledge of the subject's health is highly important in establishing the reasons for certain behaviour or understanding decisions made. One must accurately identify past and present illnesses that have left a clear sign or altered in temporary or permanent fashion certain aspects of character—perhaps that even conditioned the subject's way of life.

A thorough knowledge of the type of illnesses the subject has had and when they occurred is fundamental to an overall assessment. Dating these illnesses is very useful because we often meet people who, due to a poor memory or misguided feelings of shyness, refuse to confirm certain facts that are clearly written on their palm. They may be trying to hide these symptoms even from themselves, or worse they may attribute them to others, along with the blame for some injury they have suffered. For example, experience has shown how much damage is commonly caused by a nervous disorder in puberty or a glandular malfunction during the formative years of psychological development. The subject may be so profoundly affected that it proves difficult to recognize in the adult the promising young person of only a few years earlier. Thus we can clearly see, and with a touch of regret, the difference between what is and what might have been had some timely intervention occurred.

At this stage in the reading it is appropriate to pass from a silent dialogue of impressions to one of actual words with the subject. The most reliable answers to our questions will inevitably come from the hand and not the subject, but it is very important just the same to hear what sense the subject has of himself. He—all of us, for that matter—has a mistaken image of himself in that he is able to judge only on the basis of his own temperament, which cannot be objective, and to express judgments that cannot take into account the imponderable future, which is clearly indicated in the lines of the hands.

The next area of inquiry essential for building a picture of the subject's personality involves finding out how he relates to his

Opposite, The Fortune Teller *by Valentin de Boulogne (1591–1623).*

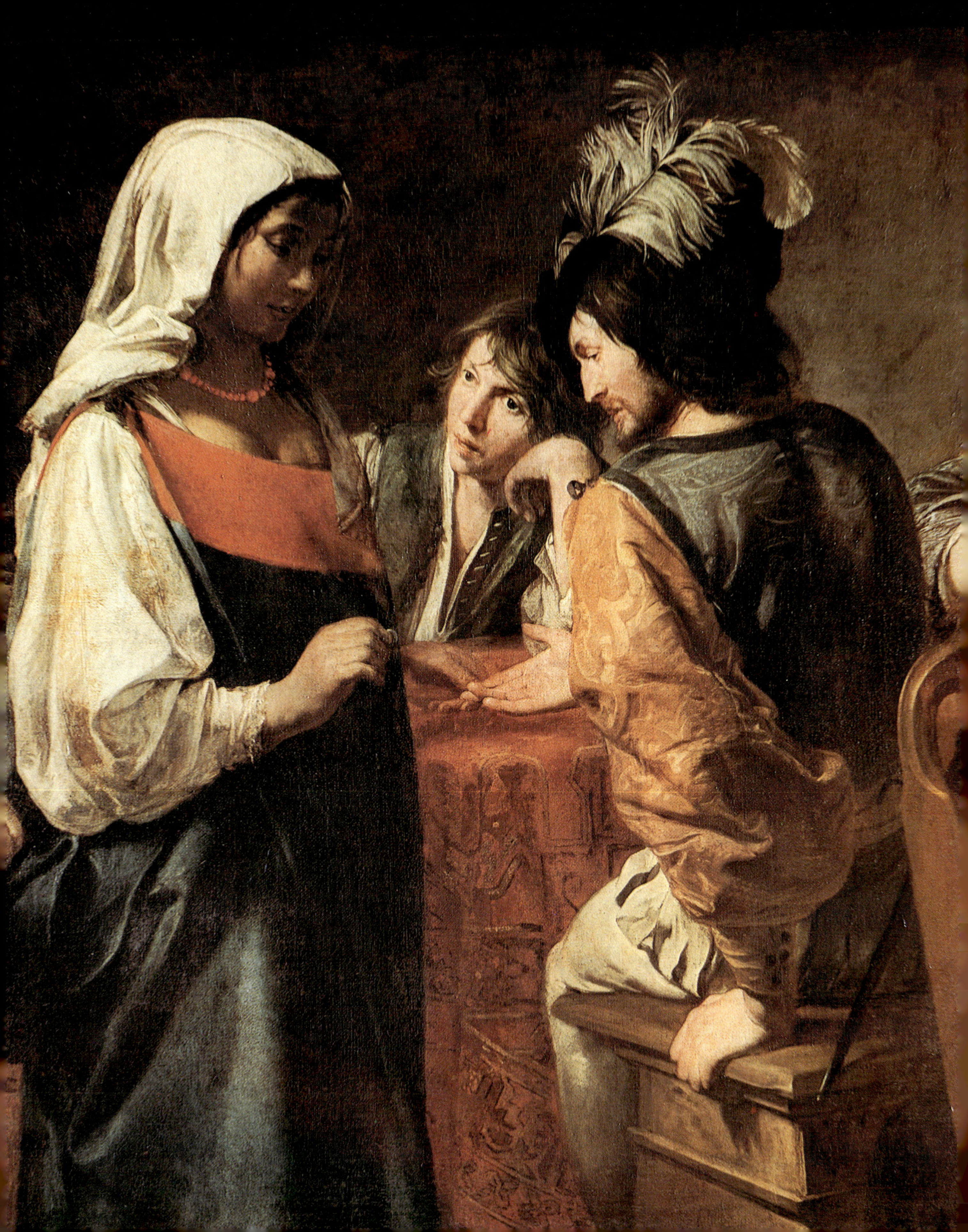

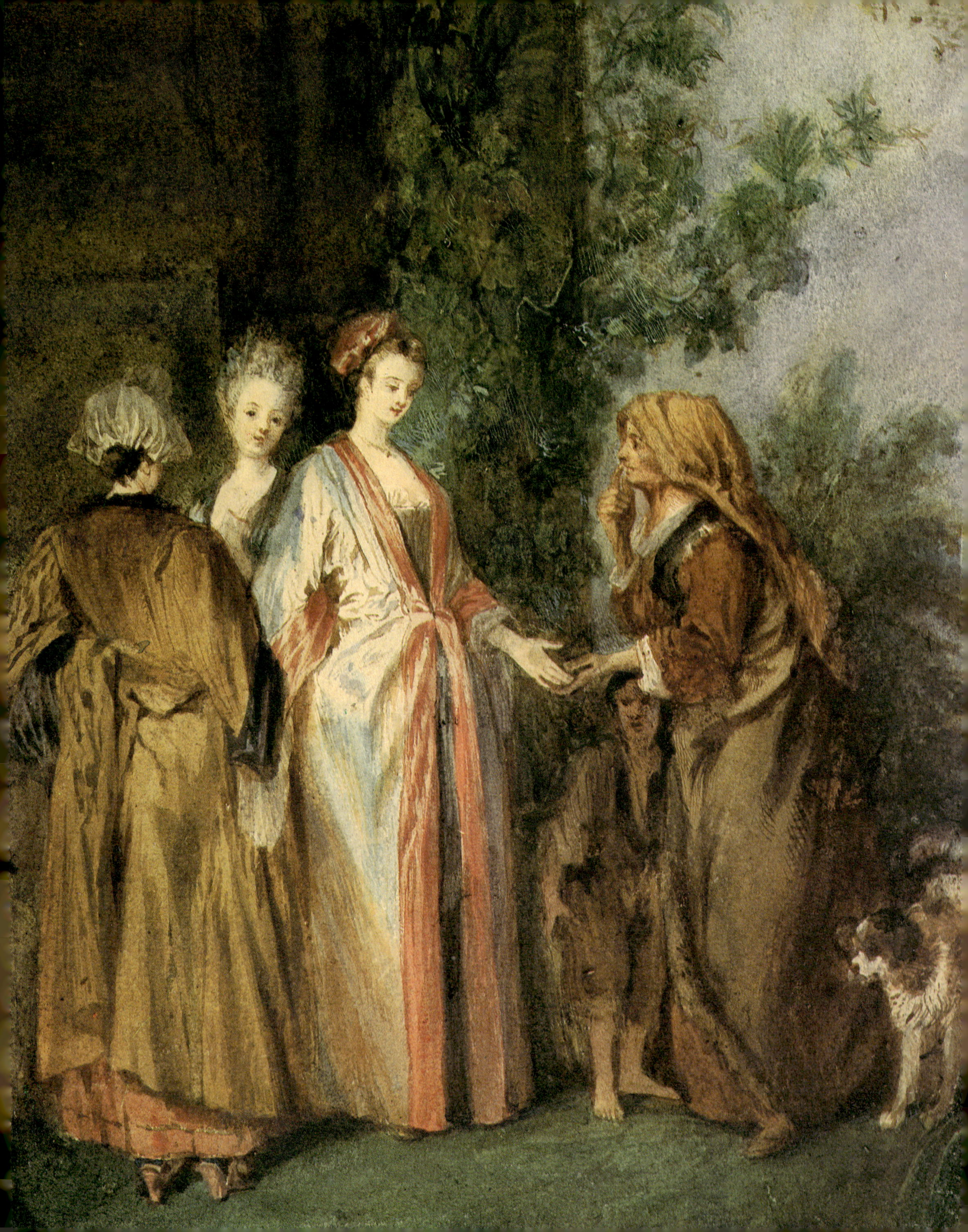

work and work environment. How and why did he make certain choices? How much of it was deliberately choice and how much was due to chance? Most important, especially today now that women are seeking work, not only as a means of supporting themselves rather than depending on a father or husband, but perhaps above all as a means of expressing their own personalities. Obviously the more harmoniously a subject relates to his work and his surroundings, the more balanced a relationship he will have with all the other aspects of daily life: his family, his love life, and his friends.

We are not so much concerned with the financial rewards of the subject's work as with the spiritual satisfaction he derives. And we cannot simply look at jobs that are particularly remunerative, those which are specialized and require special talents. We must extend our evaluation to whatever modest jobs give the people who do them a feeling of belonging and being productive, while working alongside individuals who may not necessarily be friends but for whom feelings of admiration and mutual respect have developed. The human contact involved is difficult to define but represents a test of our ability to establish relationships with people with whom we find ourselves, not by choice but by chance, in a type of enforced cohabitation for many hours on end. In certain respects the relationship resembles that of siblings in a family.

The family is one of the basic factors of our inquiry: those who have followed us this far will have noticed how often we speak of family and the determinant influence it almost always has on the subject's development, especially if he does not have a very strong personality.

In recent years attention has been given to investigating the experiences of children who, owing to various misfortunes in life, have had to spend their formative years in an environment different from that of the typical family, with strangers and without affection. This often happens with children of separated couples who spend their childhood with untrained people or under the inattentive guidance of one or the other parent.

By strange coincidence, these cases do not differ much from those of children brought up with an excess of affection. Fondling, excessive attention, and indulgence can cause similar harm to the weak personality confirming the great advantage of an ordinary upbringing within a family with relatively strict disciplinary standards (in the light of current practices).

Another important point is the relationship of the subject to school. What did he study? Did he complete his studies? Or why did he stop them? Perhaps he is self-taught. This information emerges very clearly from the palm and can tell us a lot about the reasons that led the subject to certain choices: genuine interest in a branch of learning or the prospect of a promising and remunerative career. If necessary, we can also learn why his studies were interrupted: whether he made the choice or whether there were reasons beyond his control, say an illness or financial reverses in the family.

Regarding illness, here is an interesting sideline. I have often observed that when studies have been interrupted owing to a sudden memory failure that prevents the subject from retaining what he has learned, this lapse (mainly temporary and almost exclusively striking young people who are still developing) is indicated on the hand by a small island on the head line, located in an area the dating system places between eighteen to twenty. It is the result of too rapid or troubled a development, causing or caused by a slight hormonal malfunction. Suitable and timely remedies can easily put everything right and avoid any interruption in studies, with all the unpleasant consequences that can bring.

In the group of problems concerning studies, career, and relations with one's surroundings, will and ambition play a leading role. As we know, the former can be identified on the thumb: the first two phalanges and their relationship to each other allow us to determine with near precision what kind of willpower the subject has. When these abstract values are expressed in terms of personality, they have different colours and shading for each person. The aim of our study is to discover the exact nature of the subject's will.

A Prediction of the Future *(water colour by Nathaniel Bacon)*.

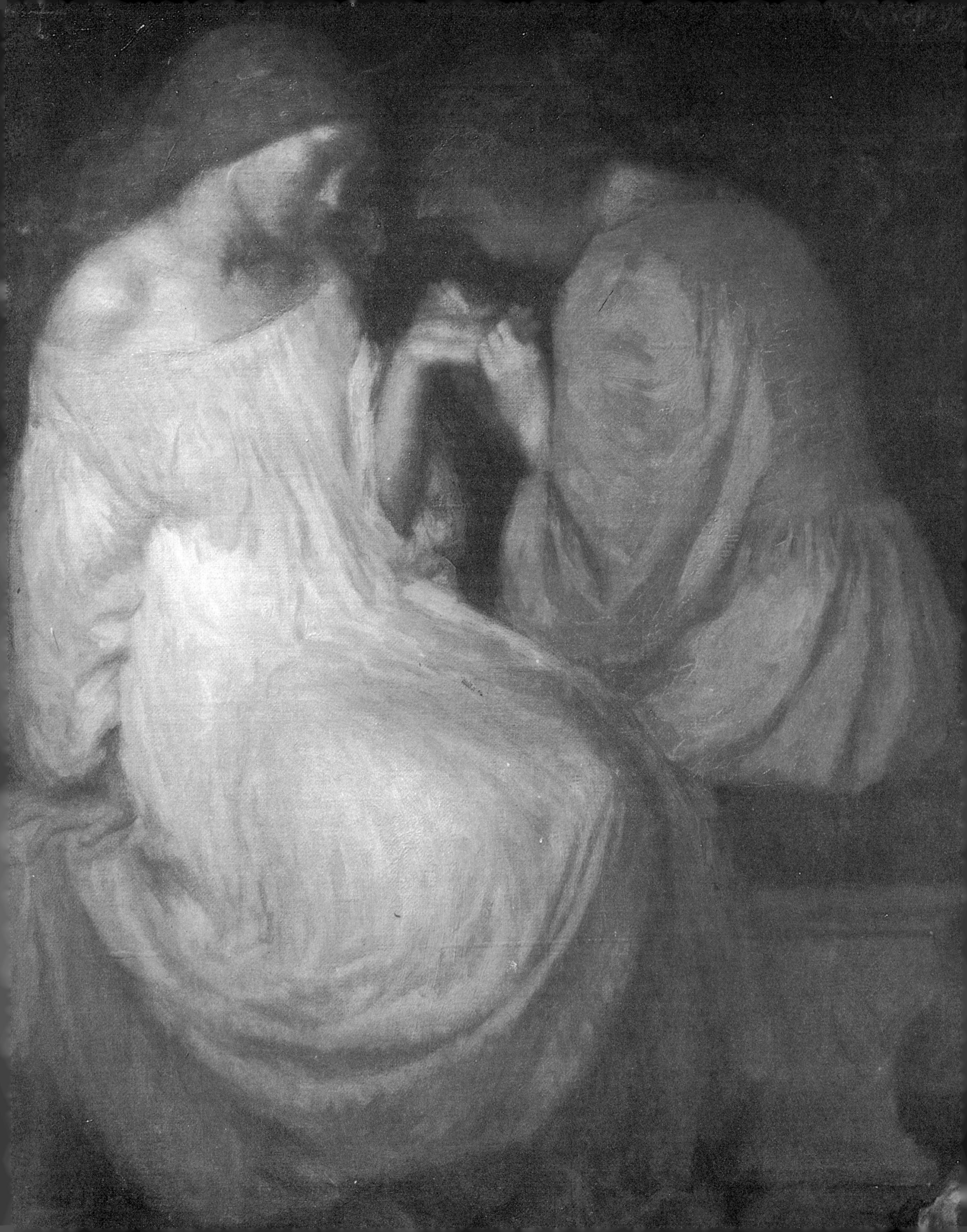

Above, In the Lines of the Hand *by Henriette Siret (Paris).*

Opposite, Reading the Future *by Sir Robert Anning Bell (1853–1933) (Imperial Palace, Tokyo).*

It is obvious that willpower alone cannot induce someone to take up difficult studies or an important career. The will must be fired by ambition, the strongest incentive to achieving success. Discovering ambition on the palm of a hand is easy; it is less easy to establish what form it takes in the subject. However, this too can be done with a fair degree of accuracy.

One can (and sometimes must) distinguish clearly between ambition and vanity. They may be confused in the mind of the subject but not on the hand. The palm defines both with maximum clarity. Vanity—which often drives a person toward goals that cannot be achieved or cannot be maintained if by chance they are achieved—does not provide in sufficient measure the necessary element for any important achievement: intelligence, a third basic factor in our list. A careful study of the head line (in accordance with the advice in the section on the head line) together with the other considerations that our investigations have supplied thus far will establish the precise relationship between the factors of will, ambition, and intelligence. From that will be evident the most rational way to achieve objectives, which are easiest to achieve, and the best method for holding on to them once they have been achieved.

To be able to express ourselves responsibly and knowledgeably on a subject of such importance we must also take into account another aspect of the subject's personality. In addition to the obstacles that life, circumstances, and enemies can throw in one's path when starting up the ladder of success, there are those obstacles that come from the subject himself as an outgrowth of his own particular nature—notably his sensuality.

And at this point in our reading, the subject's sensuality becomes relevant, including the way he relates to it. To what degree does he dominate it or it dominate him? This question should be considered as thoroughly as possible, for it lies at the center of many other issues, in particular career and success. This line of inquiry may place the palmist in an area that the subject finds difficult to understand or articulate (especially if, as frequently happens, the subject is not disposed to making things easy). Each person's sexual makeup—a primary element in sensuality—presents anomalies that are fairly evident. They are not always due to external pressures and can often be caused by disturbances in the hormonal system, such as changes that occur during menopause. In cases of this sort the subject's will, ambition, and basic intelligence are no longer in control of the situation, which will inevitably get completely out of control. The palmist will not find it difficult to learn all this from the subject's hand, provided he focuses on the mount of Venus, which will be fairly firm only in the area where with the dating system we located symptoms of the menopause (male or female).

Experience teaches us that it is possible to calculate in many individuals and in every circumstance the direct or indirect influences that sensuality can exert on behaviour and on choice. (The examples we have discussed, although common, should be considered special.) In general, within the limited band of so-called "normal" people the relevant behaviour will be constant for a long period of time and rather predictable in certain respects, varying in degree from person to person. We can see, then, the importance of having as precise a picture as possible of this area and the benefits of keeping it in mind throughout the reading. It will very often help to explain certain behaviour for which the subject himself is sometimes unable to give a credible explanation.

We now can begin to put the finishing touches on the framework we have constructed thus far. To do so we must penetrate the subject's psychology even further in order to evaluate less obvious but no less important aspects. Traumas that the subject has suffered or will suffer in the course of his life are to be found in this area. Discovering them is not always easy, but they can supply vital information.

Traumas can be either physical or psychological, depending on the cause. The former are due to accidents, serious illness, or operations; the latter are the result of disappointments of various kinds, serious misfortunes in work, or serious financial crises. If the trauma belongs to the first category, it should be located on the life, head, heart, or Mercury line, according to the organ involved. For an emotional trauma we look only at the head and heart lines. Depending on the seriousness of the trauma, the subject will to some extent have to change his usual behaviour for a fairly long period. During the course of this person's lifetime he will experience a change because of serious upsets that affect his whole personality. It is unlikely a trauma will have favourable consequences except in very exceptional circumstances, which will be revealed by a scrupulous reading of the palm lines.

So far, our field of inquiry has been limited to the principal lines of the palm, comparing what is seen on the right palm with that on the left and continually weighing new findings against data already accumulated, so that our interpretation is modified to the extent required. We have obtained a sufficiently detailed picture of the subject's personality and potential and seen what part of these traits he has succeeded in expressing. The picture is nearly complete; it provides a precise enough idea of both the subject's past and future. But it does not sufficiently take into account the present, that brief span of time during which events concerning the subject occur and these events are often behind his coming to the palmist in an attempt to gain insight about himself and some complicated situation he is involved in.

It is at this stage that one can intervene with useful suggestions—supplied by the hand itself for someone who knows how to interpret it—that help reduce the subject's problems to the limited but precious area of free will. To this end we must now direct our inquiry to the capillary lines, about which we have so far said little and about which there is generally little to say for the very reason that their presence depends on more immediate, everyday events. Indeed,

A Noblewoman Having Her Palm Read (*eighteenth-century engraving, Bibliothèque Nationale, Paris*).

Se Vend Paris Chez F. Guerard rue St. Jacques.   avec privilege du Roy.

Dame de qualité faisant dire Sa bonne Avanture

De ces deux femmes occuppée, Car l'une cherche à estre trompée
Les Soins sont bien different. Et l'autre ne cherche que l'argent.

The famous palmist Albane de Siva practising her art.

they appear and disappear relatively easily and change colour and size depending on what caused them. They are so fine that a strong magnifying glass is necessary to see them properly.

As we have pointed out, capillary lines are to be found in those areas of the hand and on main or secondary lines concerned with the event in question. The reading and interpretation of the capillary lines follows precise and established rules, but because they are impermanent and inconstant, an accurate reading may require considerable experience on the part of the palmist. Personal sensitivity is not always able to help. It is experience that enables us well in advance to deduce from the capillary lines how a situation of interest will develop. Then we can take whatever initiative circumstance suggests.

The opportunity to make use of capillary lines depends very much on the subject's sensitivity. The more emotional the subject is, the more easily capillary lines form and change. With calmer, less vibrant subjects this type of investigation is more difficult because the number of capillaries is noticeably reduced. These usually are people who have a clear view of things and know how to lead independent lives. Here again we have evidence of how much a well-balanced sense of judgment governs the mysterious formation of lines on the palm. Someone who is torn by uncertainty created by his own nervous disposition has more lines, and that allows us to pinpoint certain problems and suggest solutions.

Now the picture is complete, but before we leave this subject, one last piece of advice: take another general look at the hand, as though to experience once again that initial sensation, that sum of emotions we can now reevaluate in the light of acquired knowledge. In rare instances this last examination will prompt modification or correction of some of the advice already given. It almost always helps the palmist confirm observations already made.

Four examples of palm reading

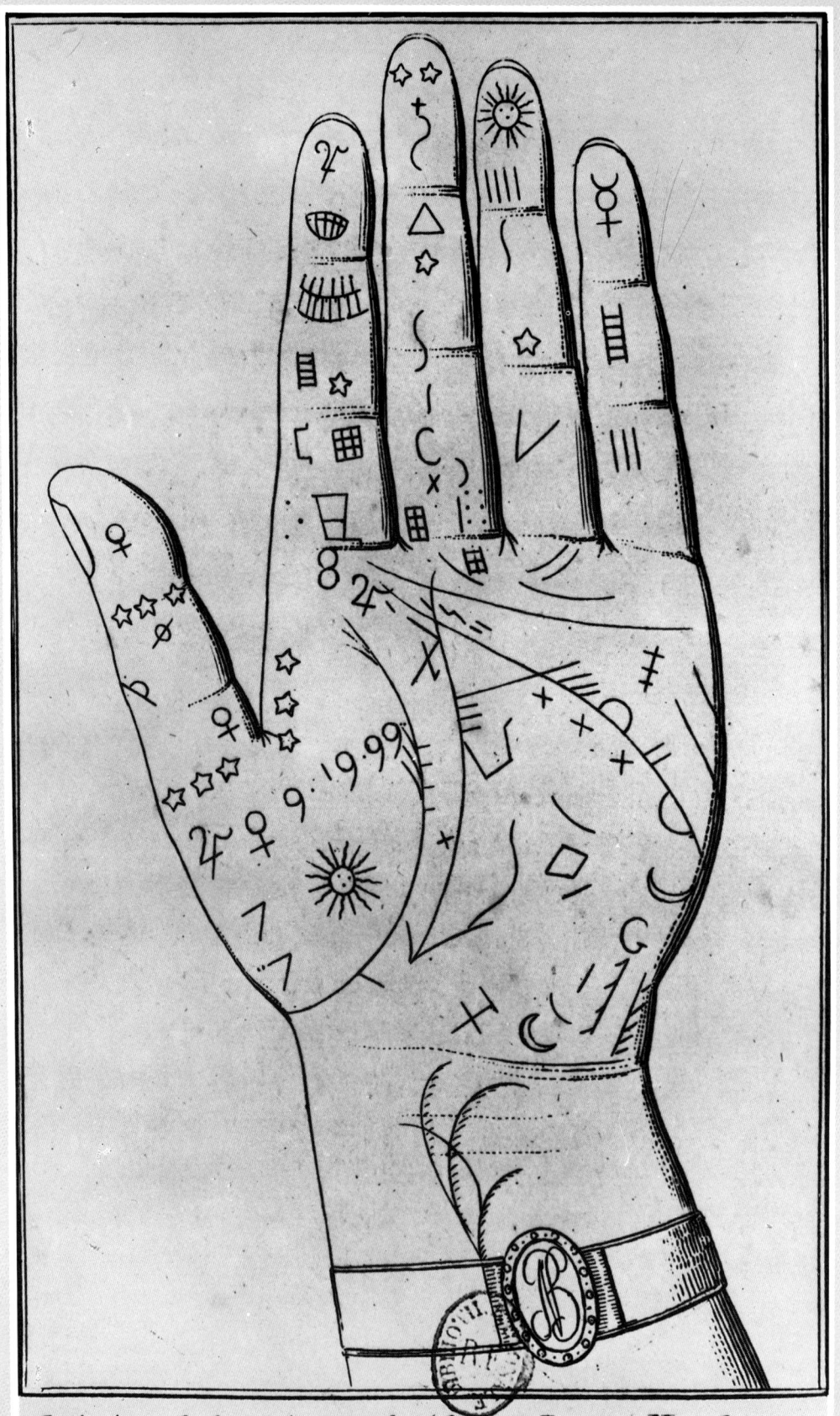

Intérieur de la main gauche (de l'ex Empr.) Napoléon - Buonaparte.

A sixty-two-year-old man

We have chosen as one of our examples of palm reading a lawyer of sixty-two, married, with one son.

We begin by looking at both hands, the backs as well as the palms. We make our first observations: The hands can be classified as the conic type—they are slightly wider near the wrist than at the top where the fingers begin. Our first comment is that the subject has a well-developed sense of reality. He lives each day fully and accepts its negative side; he is well able to look after himself in both professional and social circles.

The summit of the back of the hand is in a low position, towards the mount of the Moon, and this confirms a first impression that the subject's vital energy is mainly physical. The arc where the fingers join the palm is the type we call *uneven*, but the finger of Jupiter is inserted on the same level as that of Saturn so that the two corresponding mounts face each other. This means there are sometimes conflicts between the subject's work and his personality; the latter is not always disposed to tolerate the demands of the former.

The hand as a whole does not appear to be very flexible. This may be due in part to the subject's age, but we can see from the many small indications that this was never a particularly flexible hand. We can conclude that the subject is able to adapt to life's ups and downs, but not without some effort; this assessment is supported by other data emerging from our investigation.

The *fingers* are definitely *long* and firm. This indicates the subject's ability to appreciate the small, simple joys of life, the everyday pleasures he considers worth fighting for. This is how he realizes his spiritual aspirations.

Knots can be seen here and there on the fingers. They are for the most part caused by arthritis, except for one located on the index finger between the first and second phalanges. That knot denotes a rather penetrating, critical turn of mind, sometimes directed toward the subject himself. Starting from this observation and taking into account the overall view, we can say that he has deeply rooted ideas and is prepared to accept new concepts or innovations only after much thought.

Still looking at the general appearance of the palm, we see that the colour is rather dark but still within the normal limits. The skin is thick and consistent but very delicate on the surface. It is springy and pleasant to the touch with a pliancy suggesting a

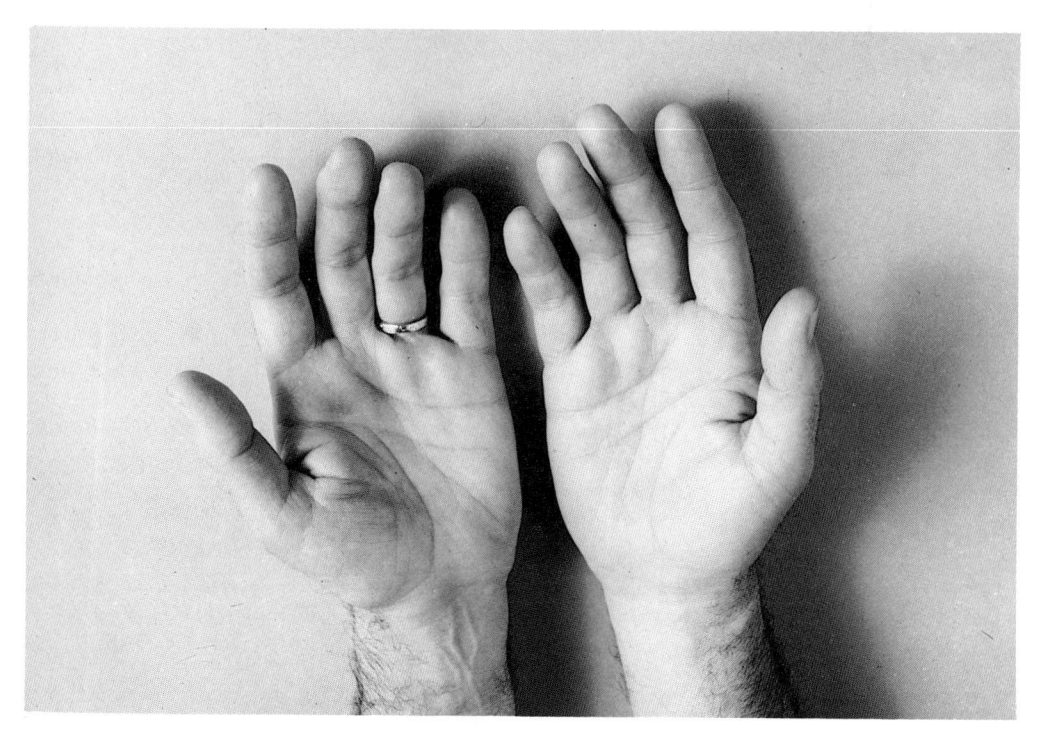

Opposite, the palm of Napoleon Bonaparte's left hand with the signs drawn by the court fortune teller Marie-Anne le Normand; published by Normand in her Souvenirs prophétiques *(Bibliothèque Nationale, Paris). Right, the hands of our sixty-two-year-old male subject.*

well-defined personality as well as a definite willingness to understand the situations and problems of others. In addition we find a good deal of insight into such problems.

The palm as a whole presents a rather confused appearance because of the many lines. They form a complicated network that can nevertheless be deciphered. A palmist well prepared to undertake this reading will not feel in any way confused or overwhelmed. But all this adds an element of complexity to the subject's personality, which it is wise to bear in mind because it will express itself very frequently in both physical and psychic manifestations. This complexity will never reach a pathological level, but the contrasts and contradictions it produces in the temperament and personality of the subject will crop up rather often.

The *fingers of Jupiter, Saturn, and Apollo* tend to have square tips, a further confirmation of the practical sense of the subject, who begins to assume the appearance of a man who respects order, discipline, and conventions. This acceptance is probably seeming rather than real, but the result is the same because the subject's practical realism make him appreciate what is useful. Moreover, the subject is well organized and approaches his work methodically.

The *firmness of the mounts of Mars*, active and passive, tells us that in his time the subject has given proof of his physical courage and demonstrated a considerable spirit of sacrifice. The nails of these three fingers come very close to being square and this detail, seen in comparison with the two mounts of Mars, reveals the subject's lack of imagination and distrust of anything that is not solid and practical.

The *tips of the little finger and thumb*, as we can see, are the *conic type*. Thus the little finger confirms some of the contradictions noted up to this point: the subject is a refined person who loves the comfortable life. He is highly sensitive in artistic matters, though he does not admit to this easily, fearing perhaps other people's scorn. The reason for the subject's unprotesting acceptance of the rules of daily life lies in the shape of the first phalange of the little finger—he accepts for convenience's sake, recognizing practical value while at the same time despising its aridity. In addition, the way in which the little finger adheres to the ring finger denotes an unusually alert intuitive sense, which the subject uses with much restraint. Confirmation of this emerges at various other stages in our reading.

With regard to the thumb, notably the conic termination of the first phalange, we can say that the subject is not known for his willpower, which appears rather uneven. We note that the angle formed by the thumb and index finger when extended at its widest is practically ninety degrees, which means the subject has good self-control even if he is not always able to put up a strong resistance to the desires evident in the other fingers and their respective mounts.

The length of the thumb is slightly shorter than average and this too serves to indicate the absence of strong willpower, especially in conjunction with the conic-shaped first phalange. In compensation, however, the second phalange of the thumb is a little longer than the first, which tells us of the subject's capacity for reflection and hence exerting, in however limited a way, his willpower. We note the presence of a *knot at the level of the nail* indicating a certain stubbornness that in some ways and in certain circumstances compensates for the subject's lack of willpower.

The *nails* are mainly square. Their colour is pink, which means the subject does not have a nervous disposition and is not prone to irritability. He can contain his anger for some time before it explodes. The nails are also convex, which leads us to suspect a tendency to bronchial problems.

The *mounts* of the palm are clearly defined, particularly the mount of Jupiter. Its summit faces downward toward the mount of Saturn.

The subject is attracted by risky situations, even at work, to the extent that he does not realize the dangers and forgets his responsibilities to his family. We can see in this area of the mount of Jupiter some special signs with an irregular appearance: rising from the center of the mount, they turn toward the side of the hand. They could be interpreted as a very incomplete *ring of Solomon*, but it is more likely that they are a grille representing obstacles to the subject's ambitions, which can be achieved only by devoting time, thought, and tenacity to them.

Similar observations can be made regarding the mounts of Saturn and Mercury. The first tells us of the subject's pleasure in spending his own money. This is not prodigality but one of the small enjoyments that characterizes the subject's approach to the pleasure of life. This is accompanied by the knowledge that he is able to obtain more money through his work. Regarding the mount of Mercury, we can say that its position and the presence of some capillary lines (not visible in the photograph) indicate the subject's considerable facility with words and an ability to choose the most convincing argument to suit another's personality.

With this partial portrait of the subject's personality we can now attempt a first balance sheet. This is a man eminently endowed with physical vitality that allows him to be firmly in touch with reality, although he adapts with some difficulty to daily routine. He derives enjoyment from those small pleasures that make life worth living; he obtains these pleasures by accepting, again with difficulty, some compromises. He has a complex personality incorporating some contradictions—e.g., a lack of willpower, which can be compensated for by logic, organization, and sheer stubbornness. He has a good intuitive sense and good self-control. He loves risk when it allows him to distinguish himself.

To this basic outline we shall add what observations emerge from examining the *life line*, which will tell us about the subject's relationship with his parents and his first contacts with the world.

The life line originates together with the head line and this is without doubt a sign of great sensitivity, but also of touchiness, especially with regard to trifles. Faced with important issues, the subject will be able to marshal his forces to make use of them, if favourable, or expose them if they are unfavourable. His considerable qualities, resources, and abilities did not emerge suddenly and effortlessly. Much care and attention were needed because he required—and still does to a certain degree—the approval and acceptance of the people around him in order to show himself to his best advantage.

The life and head lines proceed at length entwined. This signifies that the subject, either for reasons already given or owing to a combination of gratification and laziness, had difficulty for a long time in cutting loose from his parents. Into this whole mix of factors comes the difficult period of his studies. He completed them and that signifies a major event for someone without great willpower, but it involved many difficulties, first in the area of choice, then circumstances. After this phase the life line runs with regularity, describing an arc that reaches the wrinkle under the mount of Venus. The line is cut clearly and deeply; from this we can determine the subject's position in relation to his own family, the one he has formed for himself. As he progressively breaks away from his parents, there is no loosening of the bonds of affection; the break is primarily formative, with the acquisition of new and personal ideas, but the subject still retains an affection for home life, preferring it to anything else. For him the home is fundamental, not a support or a refuge between one problem and another.

The subject has never had a strong desire to travel and the urge to find out about other countries and cultures has tended to diminish over the years.

Some other interesting observations that we can make from the life line come from examining its colour, depth, and pattern. The subject judges objectively both in matters that concern him directly and involving other people's problems, even when these are people who are dear to him and for whom he may have a particular regard. The choices he makes are normally dictated by common sense.

Two incomplete rings of Mars can be seen on the left palm of the mount of Venus in the immediate vicinity of the life line. A comparison with the right-hand palm, where we deal with the realities of life, reveals that these two lines have become one, a very positive sign in terms of health, particularly with respect to an increase in the subject's energy potential. Very probably—and dating will confirm it—this increase in spiritual strength allowed him to leave his parents when he had the energy necessary to face a working life on his own. In principle, however, the break was decided some time before it actually happened, as is shown on the hand by a line that detaches itself from the life line where it is still connected to the head line, only to return lower down, virtually forming a vast island with precisely the same meaning.

The life line can also reveal interesting information about one's professional life. We can see clearly in the photograph of the left hand two lines that both rise from the life line and run in the direction of the mount of Saturn. The first is unbroken and represents the principal occupation of the subject over a period of many years, which he will continue to pursue until retirement. The second line, a little lower down, is not continuous and should be interpreted as a secondary activity. It interests the subject not so much from an economic point of view, even though it does yield some income as and principally from the spiritual satisfaction that it gives. In other words, the evidence is of a kind of hobby but conducted on a professional level to which the subject devotes whatever time is left after his work and family obligations.

Now let us look at the head line, which as we saw originated from the life line. We shall therefore confine ourselves to the section of the line that is independent. On the left hand it is exceptionally long, well drawn, normal in colour, and reaching as far as the passive mount of Mars. After a brief uncertain start the head line proceeds in a clear-cut manner straight across almost the whole palm. This denotes a very acute intelligence capable of great concentration, even the profound. A closer examination reveals a good measure of constancy, expressed through the need to complete things once they have been undertaken, and not to leave anything pending. This tendency is so deeply ingrained that the reverse also holds true: the subject will not undertake a project that he believes he does not understand or could not complete. This does not contradict the lack of willpower mentioned previously.

It is interesting to compare the two palms. We see that on the left hand the head line curves slightly toward the heart line. The head line becomes deeper, the colour slightly darker. In the last section, just under the passive mount of Mars, it tends to turn upward toward the mount of Mercury. This discrepancy signifies that in everyday matters the original line and the intelligence that it expresses have been obliged to follow a siding, to sacrifice some of the possibilities of expression inherent in this very acute intelligence. Initially this restriction was rather onerous, but over the years it took on a positive aspect: the original clarity of ideas has been slightly obscured by a renunciation of certain cerebral aspects to accommodate a less penetrating approach but one more in tune with the affections and daily necessities. It is interesting to observe how much influence the subject's choices in life have had on the complex question of his spirituality—how much more sensitive they have made him in his ability to respond to his surroundings. This is an unusual angle in that the reverse is much more common: one becomes more egotistic.

All this has inevitably been somewhat distracting for the subject. It has, although only minimally, drawn him away from the goals of his youth—those which he has not yet achieved and toward which he is still drawn but with a different sense of commitment and coming from a different perspective.

The head line also gives us the following useful information: the subject tends not to talk about financial interests with family and friends. He has always managed to solve these problems by himself, only rarely seeking the limited satisfaction that can come from unburdening himself, preferring the satisfaction of knowing he has done everything possible for the family's well-being.

We shall now return to the left hand to study the heart line. After some initial hesitation it unwinds in a clean, decisive manner and ends near the summit of the mount of Jupiter. This reveals some interesting aspects of the subject's capacity for affection. Apart from the depth of his feelings in a romantic context, he has a very strong sense of friendship and a certain loyalty toward his colleagues at work. In every kind of loving relationship the subject is able to give something; people think well of him even when the opportunities for meeting and socializing have ended.

Nevertheless the subject does not like to display his feelings and when obliged to do so he finds it difficult, even embarrassing to overcome his natural modesty. For this reason people who do not know him well tend to find him rather cold and arid. In the same manner and for the same reasons he hides his jealousy and never lets it dominate him. When he knows for certain that his partner has been unfaithful, his jealousy ceases immediately and is replaced by a sudden indifference. This same state of mind is created, with perhaps some variation, in his relations with friends or so-called friends.

The heart line here displays numerous branches worth taking into consideration. The most interesting is the one located on the last section of the line, practically creating a fork, sending out a branch in the direction of the meeting point between the fingers of Jupiter and Saturn. This indicates a marriage of love, as confirmed by special signs on the mount of Jupiter not clearly visible in the photograph. There are other descending branches which join the heart line to the head line, the meaning of which is clear: these indicate love affairs at different levels, telling us that for the subject a physical relationship alone is not enough. An emotional involvement is always necessary, though the extent and nuances of such an involvement will vary.

Among the lines that arise from the area of the heart line that the dating system assigns to the subject's youth, there is one that speaks of a profound disappointment occurring when he fell in love for the first time. Fortunately the disappointment was caused by only a temporary aberration in his partner's behaviour. It did not compromise his feelings, so he was able to get over the shock fairly easily without it leaving any lasting scars. This episode was in fact followed by others and the results were quite different, leaving happy memories amounting to positive experiences. There is another line from a more mature period denoting passionate love opposed by circumstances. And another interesting indication emerges from an examination of these lines. For a good part of the subject's life we see the presence of a sentiment that is closer to affectionate friendship than a passionate, romantic love affair. This has not weakened with the passing of time but acquired an ever greater spiritual quality.

Let us turn again to the left hand. We see another palm line that has not yet been examined, the fate line. It is very well defined and drawn with an assurance not commonly seen. What is more surprising is that in comparing the two palms, we find the fate line on the right palm drawn with even greater clarity. The very fact of its being there and in such an unusual form reveals certain characteristics peculiar to the subject. He deserves recognition for having discovered in himself qualities that his choice of studies and career did not require. Not only did he discover these qualities but he nurtured them patiently, while not losing sight of the daily demands of life and responsibilities toward the family and at the same time widening his sphere of action professionally as much as circumstances allowed.

On the left palm, the fate line rises from the depths of the mount of the Moon and cuts very decisively across the palm, crossing the head line and ending on the mount of Saturn just beyond the heart line. One of its branches shoots across to the meeting point between the fingers of Saturn and Apollo. This course is full of implications, rendered even more complex by the presence of branches in the plain of Mars and in the mount of the Moon.

The interpretation of all this in more understandable terms is that at a particular moment in the life of the subject, which can be determined with the dating system, he felt caged in by his parents' house and he had to escape or leave to try his wings. The slow, difficult maturing process was now complete, as were his studies. The time to make this break, never the most favourable, posed objective difficulties that should not be underestimated. Having reached this awareness and evaluated the importance of the step he intended to take, the subject had only to wait for the opportunity and the circumstances to justify his decision, represented in this particular case by a romantic encounter. Incidentally, there are no signs of opposition by the family to the main career chosen by the subject, but there probably would have been if a different profession had been chosen, less in tune with family tradition.

The end of the fate line in the mount of Saturn confirms what has already emerged from our investigations: the desire to pursue as quickly as possible a brilliant career has not prevented the subject from keeping time free for his interests in other aspects of life, not just for his other activity but for family affections and pleasurable and cheering encounters with friends. The understandable desire to follow his own road successfully has not let him forget the importance of the relationships we have enumerated above in maintaining a normal psychological balance.

The branching of the fate line toward the mount of Apollo clearly says that the interests of the subject and the nature of his second activity must be artistic. The fate line reveals as much imagination and generosity as are needed to aspire legitimately to a career in that field. There is also the combination of patience, tenacity, and balance that has allowed the subject to keep his precious interests alive over the years and to add to those with experience.

The dark coloration and depth of the fate fate line on the right hand can give us the measure of the subject's success in life, and from what we can observe from the photograph it is possible to say that he has achieved his aims to the full. The slight differences between the fate lines of the two hands allow us to establish, judging by the right hand, that adjustments had to be made regarding the original ambitions of the subject. Not only were small compromises made—inevitable in any career—but particularly in the subject's estimation of himself. We can say that his greatest asset is that he judges himself objectively at all times. He has done so throughout his life, accepting his qualities and defects and intelligently making positive use of them when choices were called for and implemented.

It would be a mistake, which a careful reading of this hand precludes, to underestimate the contribution that fate has made in terms of opportunities and encounters at favourable moments. But one should emphasize that the subject has known how to take advantage of these with tact, discretion, a sense of timing, and a great spirit of sacrifice.

From the reading it can be seen that the subject has reached a satisfying goal in his career and that henceforth he will have more freedom to devote himself to his other activity, judging by the signs indicating goals that will yet be achieved. A careful examination of the mount of Jupiter allows us to establish that this activity will be of a literary nature or in any event to do with the world of letters. A suggestion is appropriate here: during this period of his life the subject is relying a little too heavily on a group of so-called friends who could do him some harm; their actions could interrupt the normal development of his artistic activity. It is advisable to act with the greatest caution, since the subject is steadfast by temperament but not known for his willpower. For this kind of personality, getting into a contest of wills can be very difficult. Better not to run the risk but diplomatically avoid these risky people. This kind of avoidance is entirely a matter of free will and it is worth exercising that to conserve at least in part the results of so many years of patient sacrifice.

A further examination of the left hand shows a series of lines that appear not to be connected but in fact represent one of the many aspects that the *line of Mercury* can assume. Here we see that it moves from the life line and runs toward the mount of Mercury across the mount of the Moon, indicating that the subject receives very clear messages from his unconscious. This means he has remarkable intuition, which has been a great help in making decisions and solving the most complicated problems.

This aspect of the line of Mercury also indicates, at least at the time of the reading, a somewhat delicate state of health. There is no particular disorder, but rather a general lack of defense organisms and hence a special susceptibility to bronchial problems and the flu.

A thirty-year-old woman

The next hand we are going to examine belongs to a woman who is thirty years old, married with no children, and who works in an office. Both hands are the "mixed type," displaying characteristics of both square and conic hands. Our subject has a strong sense of responsibility, a sincere nature, and a lively personality.

The hands are large but proportionate to the overall size of the woman. This signifies that she is basically well balanced and a person of strong moral courage. In observing the creative curve of the hand we see that the summit is placed fairly high, slightly below the passive mount of Mars. This is another positive quality. It indicates a harmonious combination of physical strength and moral courage, signifying the ability to begin again from scratch, if necessary, with determination and rational thinking. That is expressed very precisely by the conic tendency of the palm, which tells us about the subject's sense of realism.

Looking at the left hand we see that the *arc*, where the fingers are attached to the palm, is of the *uneven* type. In particular we see that the attachment of the finger of Mercury is perceptibly lower than that of the other fingers. The meaning is very precise: an independent mind, often unwittingly independent, manifesting itself through a need to contradict or act on one's own. This results in erratic behaviour, often with excessively strong reactions to situations, justified only partly by the subject's shyness. The subject needs time to get a clear idea of situations and a long period of reflection before she can exercise the necessary objectivity in her judgements. She can do that, but it takes some effort. This type of behaviour does not earn her the sympathy of people on a first meeting, but her uncommon gifts of generosity, goodness, intelligence, and understanding are there to be discovered.

The long, regular *fingers* indicate a restrained spirituality. She has decidedly high ideals and is inclined to indulge in fantasies about the future. However, these have their origins in a potentially artistic nature, and the possibility of realizing them is very real. If we look at the head line, which runs straight with a slight inclination toward the passive mount of Mars, we discover a strong practical sense and hence an inner urge to put plans into action.

The first joint of the middle finger curves slightly toward the ring finger. It confirms that the subject will probably change her present activity in an artistic sense. From

The hands of our thirty-year-old female subject.

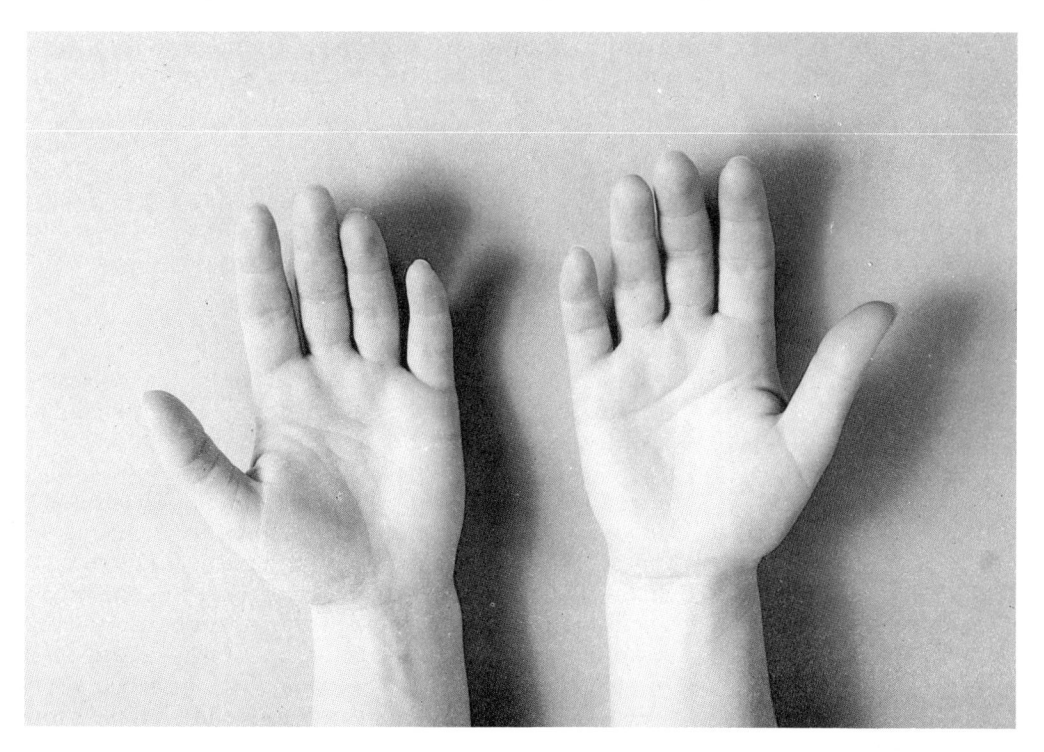

another angle this curving of the finger of Saturn signifies a predisposition to intestinal upsets, which will improve as the subject realizes her dreams, the upsets being due in part to nerves.

The skin is soft, compact, and springy, typical of persons who have considerable sensitivity, although we note signs on the palm of domestic work which confirm a need for order and harmony, and not only in the spiritual sense.

The nails are hazelnut-shaped, which tells us that the subject is logical, always needs to achieve concrete results, and never leaves things unfinished. We cannot tell what colour the nails are because they are varnished, but we can conclude from the hardness and convexity of each that the subject has a tendency to bronchial complaints.

The *palm* is pink and marked with many *lines*. In fact, besides the principal lines of life, head, heart, and fate, there are also (but only on the right palm) the lines of Mercury and Apollo.

With this general picture of our subject we now come to the crux of the reading. If we look at the first section of the life line, there is clear evidence of a very serious trauma. It has profoundly changed the subject's life and personality. By using the dating system, we can place this trauma around the age of eighteen to twenty. It affected the subject's development and health as she experienced the events that caused it. The trauma was a family matter. It brought about changes in the subject's habits and surroundings, causing her to change her educational plans. This seriously affected her ambitions, as is clearly indicated by a deep valley on the side of the mount of Jupiter toward the outer edge of the left hand. This complex situation naturally created great difficulties for the subject in adjusting to life. A stress-related illness was overcome through willpower and bringing into play personal traits we noted previously. Few tangible signs remain of this serious trauma and even the memory of it has faded somewhat, as confirmed by comparing palms. The right palm shows almost no trace of what we have described or of the signs denoting the trauma.

Under the pressure of events she was forced to grow up quickly. In order to accept the new reality without resentment or hate she had to draw on all of her qualities of goodness and comprehension, which, helped by her practical, realistic outlook, caused her to develop a profound humanity, certainly greater than what she would have achieved had the events in life been different.

The interruption in studies and the need to act in haste led to a lower-level scholastic choice than before. The decision, however great a shock, did not prevent her from completing the courses and putting them to use at the earliest opportunity.

During this same period there is clear evidence of the emergence of artistic tendencies, which in terms of sensitivity she can use presently in a much more limited way, benefiting others more than herself. To judge from the shape of the mount of Apollo and the presence of the Sun line on the right palm, it is possible that in the near future she could carry out some artistic work now and again for a modest salary along with her regular job. To succeed, however, she must devote a little more time to herself and not be too generous with friends and especially family.

The heart line on both hands is long and curved and ends with a branch directed toward the meeting point of the fingers of Saturn and Jupiter. The meaning is clear: despite her intelligence, she is more inclined to follow the impulses of her heart than the advice of her head.

Undoubtedly it is her ability to be more available to others than to herself that has allowed her to overcome the serious trauma of her earlier years so successfully, contributing greatly to the formation of those personality traits that characterize her today. Moreover this kind of generosity extends to the sexual sphere as well. The upper part of the mount of Venus is flatter than the lower part. This means that she cannot find contentment without a strong romantic element in a relationship. The finger of Mercury, which tends to separate itself from the other fingers, tells us clearly that the choice in this area will be difficult. There is also another interpretation to the mount of Venus: the possibility of ovarian complications before the menopause.

Opposite, the hands of the sixty-two-year-old man and of the thirty-year-old woman.

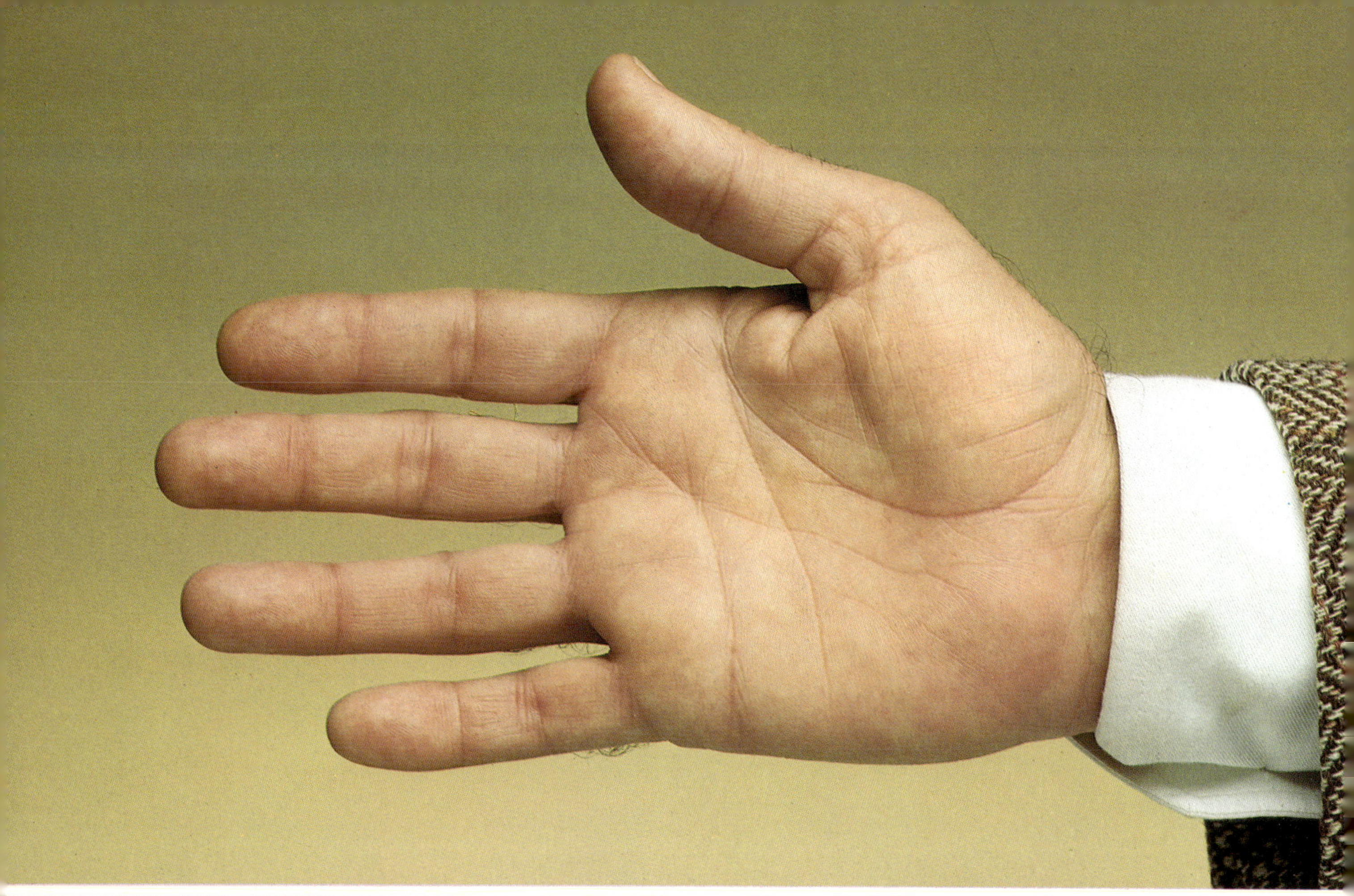

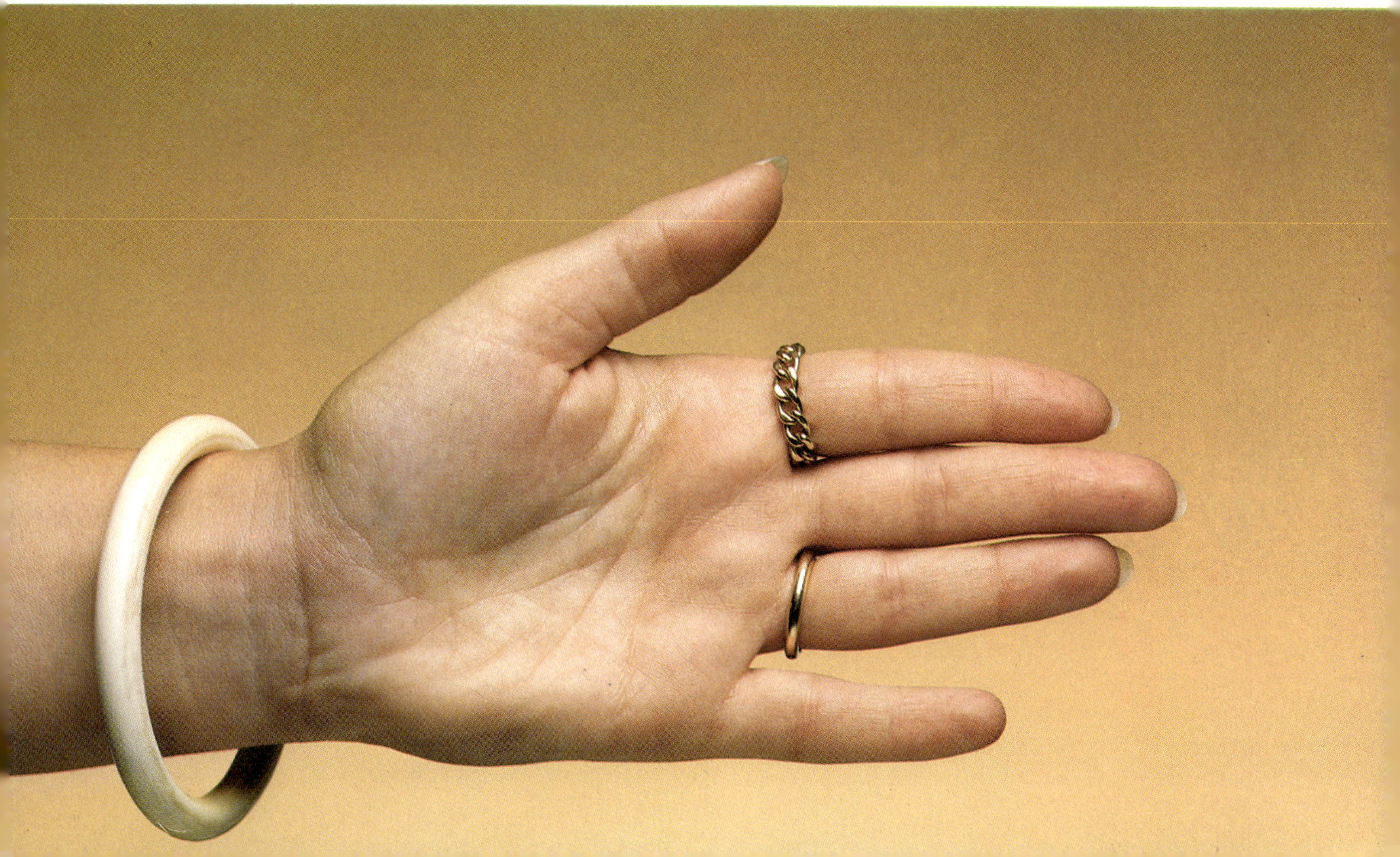

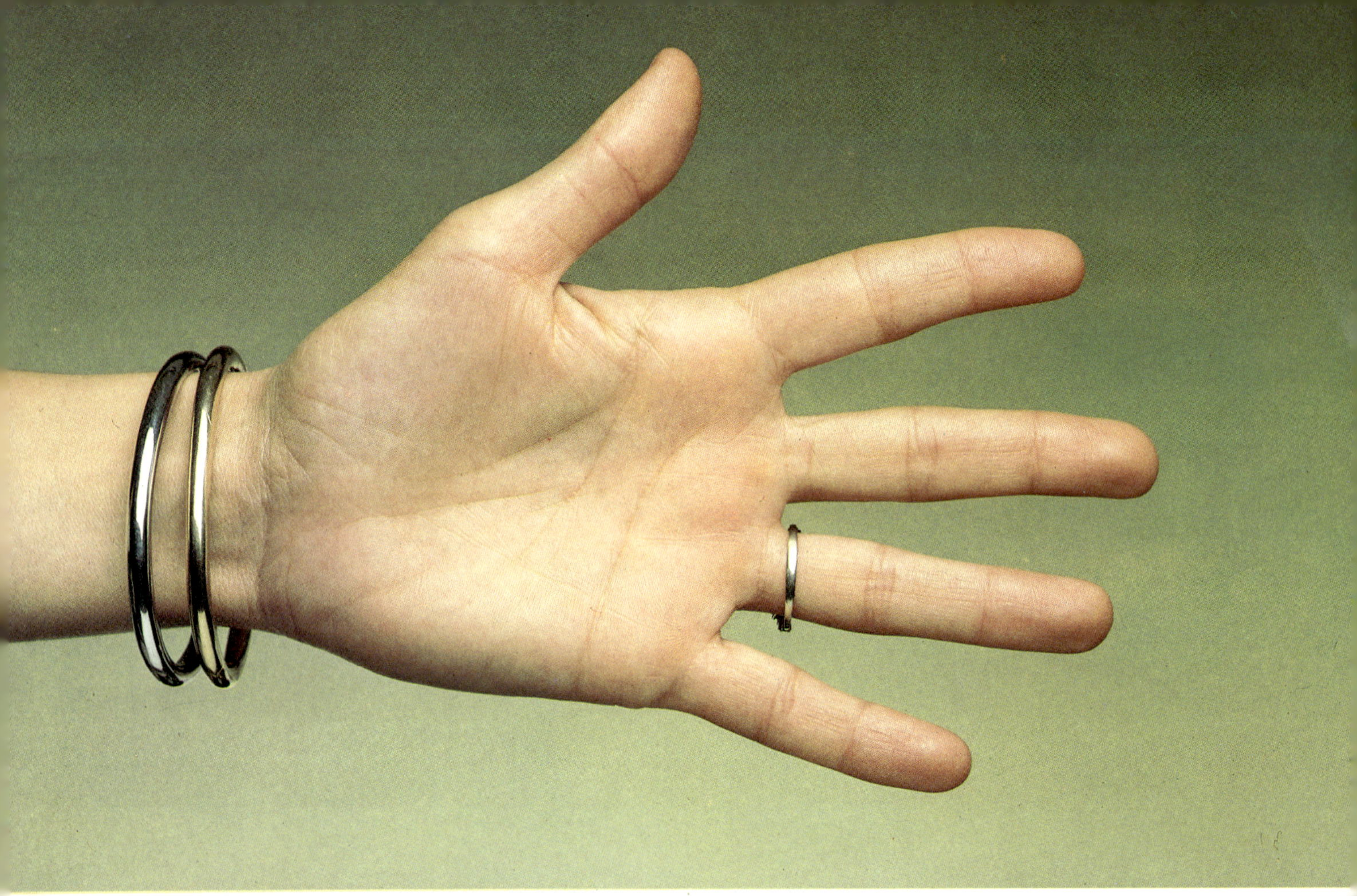

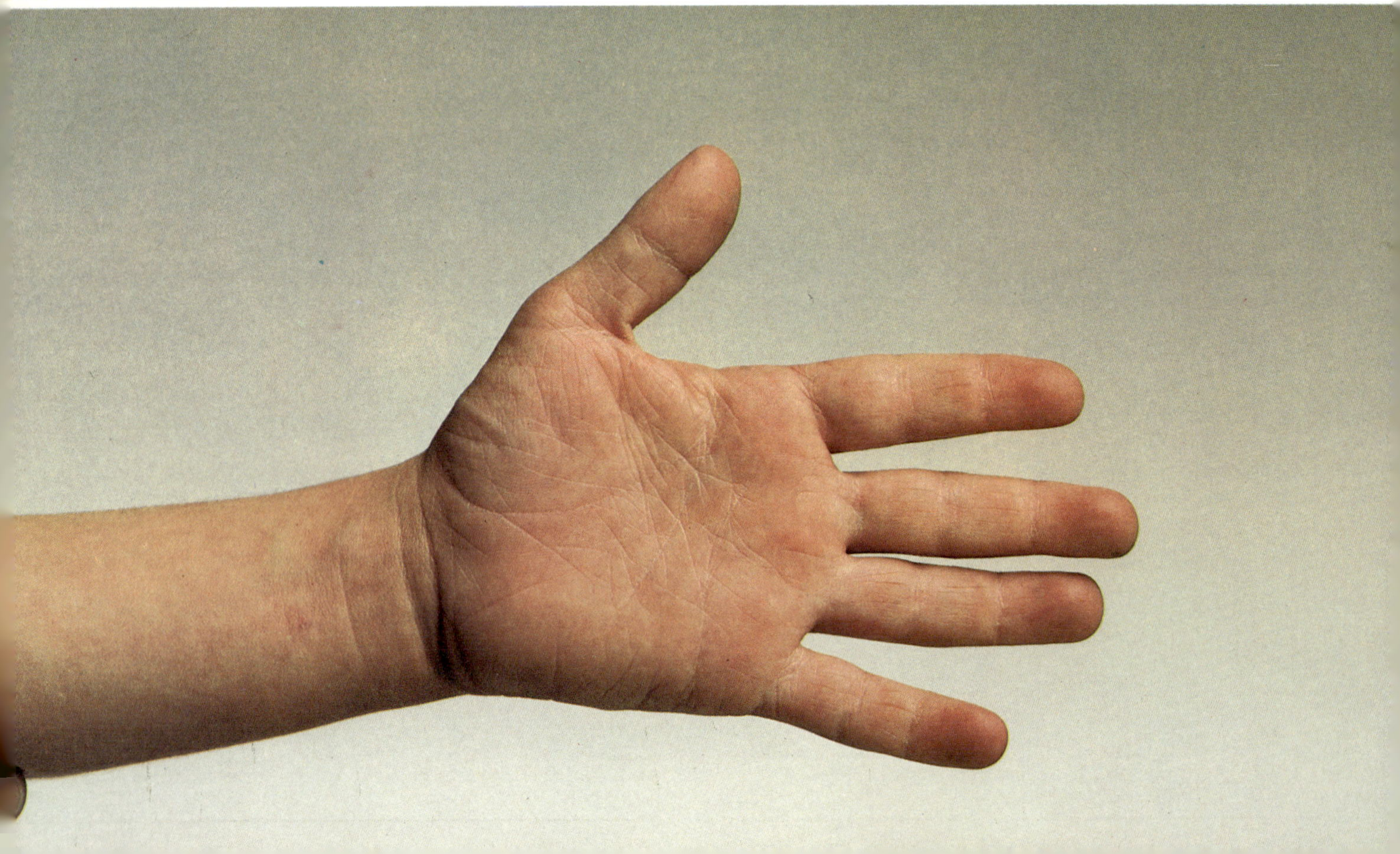

A thirty-four-year-old woman

This hand was chosen because it has two remarkably interesting features on which we shall focus our attention. Here again we shall not undertake a systematic examination of the different parts of the hand in the prescribed order, as nothing new will be added to the reader's knowledge. We shall confine ourselves to those few elements that allow us to draw a fairly complete picture of the subject's personality, so as to provide a background for two features we particularly want to consider.

If we look at the structure of the hand, we can say that this is a very practical-minded person, able to translate ideas—sometimes even fantasies—into concrete terms. The shape of the thumb, with respect to the relationship between the first two phalanges and the length and curvature of the first phalange, confirms our initial observations, to which we can add intelligence and strength of character. The little finger, which is very long compared to the other fingers and very pointed, informs us of the subject's high level of intuition. We note the presence of the *drop of water* on the tip of this finger: the subject has a highly developed tactile sense.

The palm lines on both hands are numerous without being chaotic, and they are deeply etched. Its is obvious they have always been heavily marked, but especially now because of temporary nervous fatigue, which affects the colour. We can confirm this phenomenon by tactile examination. The hand appears generally quite firm but a little soft in the area of the plain of Mars. On the basis of all these observations we can say that the subject suffers from a disorder affecting the liver and stomach. As a rule these organs are healthy but they function erratically. At the time of the reading the subject's psychological state is for the most part depressed.

The head line on the left hand curves decidedly toward the mount of the Moon but without actually reaching it. This denotes a highly inventive imagination but with the danger of sometimes indulging in sterile digressions when common sense fails to exert itself. The blurred ending of the head line tells us that the subject still regrets her conscious decision to give up her career, and that is the reason for her dispirited state, which is sometimes pronounced, as at the time of this reading. A comparison of the two palms will confirm this suspicion. The right hand shows much more clearly the importance of the decision taken by the subject when faced with the

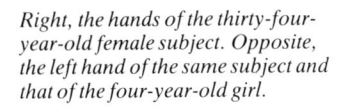

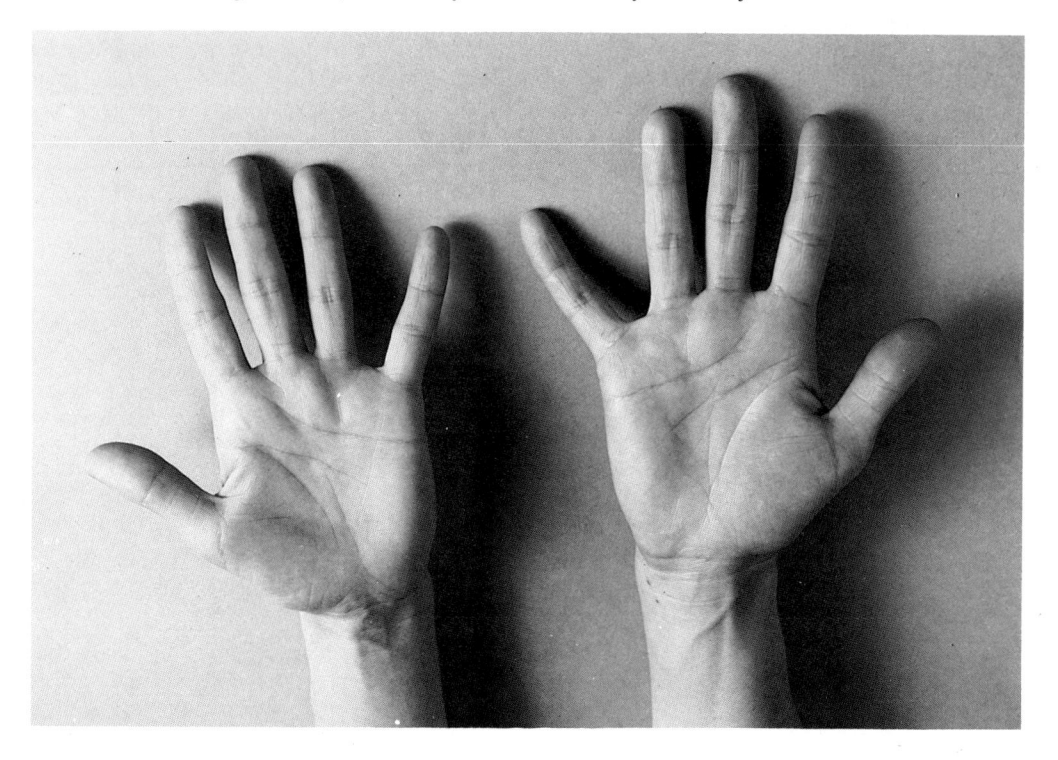

Right, the hands of the thirty-four-year-old female subject. Opposite, the left hand of the same subject and that of the four-year-old girl.

necessity of making a choice between devoting herself exclusively to her work and deriving considerable satisfaction therefrom, financial included (as is clearly indicated on the left hand), or turning to the type of life in which love and care of the family come first. The subject opted for the second, knowing full well that she would be denied a kind of satisfaction that would be extremely gratifying. We see on the right hand, as a result—or in anticipation of this—a break in the head line where it meets the fate line, which resumes with a branch in the direction of the mount of Saturn.

Another consequence of this choice has been the creation of problems and nuisances of both an emotional and family nature. This is accurately reported by the heart line. It is very long and on the left hand runs toward the summit of the mount of Jupiter, forecasting the satisfactions from work that the subject knowingly gave up in favour of the joys of marriage and motherhood, which we see on the heart line on the right hand. There the line tends to end at the meeting point between the fingers of Jupiter and Saturn.

All this signifies that the important decision the subject made has given a new direction to her ambitions. She has taken on the very dangerous task of projecting them onto her daughter, who is the focal point of all her new interests. The daughter's upbringing is a source of friction within the marital relationship, which after some initial ups and downs has become very stable. The daughter's upbringing presents a serious problem for the subject. We can see from a sign on the mount of Mercury that the daughter has a very strong, aggressive personality combined with a superior intelligence, along with a good deal of stubbornness and possessiveness. Owing to the child's very strong character it is difficult to determine from this line alone whether it is a boy or girl due to these very evident, masculine traits.

Bringing up a child who has this kind of temperament inevitably presents serious problems, as the fate line indicates. The subject will have her work cut out for her to achieve her aims. She must not let herself be distracted even for a moment, nor show any weakness so as not to lose in an instant what she has worked so hard to build up.

The task of directing her daughter toward her own goals will absorb the major part of her energies for many years and will also put at risk her relationship with her husband. It would be advisable for the subject not to invest all of her potential in this arduous task. She should keep alive other interests—in work and in her marriage—otherwise she may find that once she has achieved her goals and her daughter has begun her own life, as is only natural, she will find herself alone, lacking scope in her work and a companion in her personal life.

A four-year-old girl

One cannot help wondering, when about to read the hand of a child, how it is that a newborn child's hands are already clearly marked with the principal lines that will remain there for life. The reason is that the palm lines are not the result of hand movements (as many mistakenly believe) but derive from other causes, as yet without a scientific explanation. These have always excited the curiosity of everyone who has ever practised palmistry. The deep-seated desire to know one's true nature has resulted over the centuries in the advancement of the most unlikely theories, some of which we have referred to elsewhere in this book.

Palm lines are like the graph recorded on an electrocardiogram or a seismogram. They indicate in readable terms a number of phenomena that take place within the person's body and psyche, allowing someone who knows how to interpret them to gauge their essential nature as well as follow their continuous and progressive evolution under the impact of the forces that operate on the subject, internally and externally.

Consequently they could serve to establish the hereditary electromagnetic forces acting on the subject in concert with the astral influences present at the time of conception and birth, according to astrological theory. Or they could be the equivalent of the biochemical formula for the combination of essential mineral salts present in the subject when he was born, representing a unique type of balance that indicates the sum of each person's psychophysical qualities.

Seen another way, reading a hand properly is a little like a radiograph of both the body and the mind. Just as the doctor, in interpreting an X ray, can learn what has caused a change in the patient's equilibrium, the palmist can discover from what is expressed by the lines the nature of the psychic or physical disturbances that have altered the subject's equilibrium. By taking the palmist's advice, as we have said before, it is possible to modify in part the consequences of certain mistakes or certain experiences. This area for maneuver, narrow but sufficient to reduce the seriousness of certain situations or to intercept the start of certain illnesses, is called free will. That contrasts with the concept of fate or destiny, which does not allow anyone to escape its inexorable laws. As far back as antiquity destiny has been represented as blind and thus making no distinctions. That is not to say this representation is valid simply because it is old. There are countervailing

The hands of the four-year-old girl.

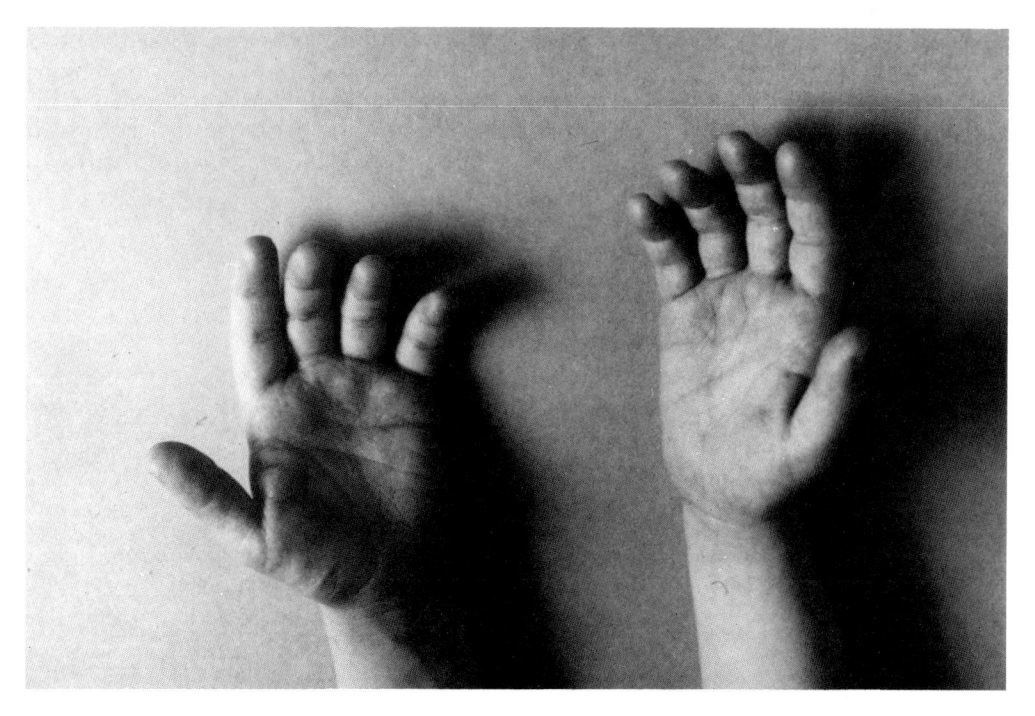

traditions. The Catholic religion grants salvation through an act of will or free choice which no one imposes or can impose. In the sacrament of the confession, when confession is heard by a priest aware of the importance of the task he is carrying out, the possibility of relieving the worries of the confessor is implicit, not only through the remission of sins but via guidance and enlightened advice on the difficult choices to be made in this increasingly difficult world.

Palmistry does not claim to be able to do the same, but by explaining honestly the less comprehensible aspects of certain situations it allows those who are in need to assess situations with greater objectivity and thus make more positive choices in their own interests. This is the case with parents when their child begins to ask its first questions and develop a curiosity. How do you reply to a child's questions? It is the first instructional experience for the parent, whom we cannot reproach if he unwittingly gets off on the wrong foot. To be able to reply one has to know a little about the person asking the question. And who can honestly say that he knows his own four-year-old child even a little?

In dealing with these subjects one needs to put aside absolute values: this is good, this is bad, this is right or wrong. One would be underestimating the problem to take a light-hearted approach to a subject so fraught with difficulties and subtleties. By knowing his child as well as he possibly can, a parent is able to adapt his answers in a way best suited to the child, and the answers given will probably vary a great deal, in form if not substance, from those given to another child of the same age but of a different temperament. It is not appropriate at this crucial phase in the child's education to direct his thinking into precise channels. It is more helpful to explain a subject as clearly as possible so that an informed choice subsequently can be made. Hence it is very important to know the child's level of comprehension, intelligence, and character type.

We want to show with the following example how much can be learned from a careful reading of a child's hand, in this case a four-year-old girl both of whose parents work.

Given the age of the subject, the shape of the hand provides less reliable information because it can change appreciably with growth.

The shape of the palm is (and will remain) decidedly square, which tells us that now and in the future the subject is and will be a very practical person and can assume responsibilities appropriate to her age. The nails are hazelnut-shaped which is evidence of her innate egoism. She tries to obtain the most with the least effort and frequently succeeds. The skin, a fine pink colour, is delicate but fairly thick which leads us to believe the child is mature for her years. As an observation at the time at which the reading took place, we note that the finger of Jupiter, rather large and energetic, is almost as long as the ring finger (or finger of Apollo), indicating considerable pride and egocentrism, the desire to dominate, and ambitious goals. The first consequence of all this is that the subject will tend over the years to increase her high opinion of herself, the consequences of which are well known.

The little finger, or finger of Mercury, has a peculiar characteristic: the first and second phalanges tend to move away from the neighbouring finger of Apollo. The significance is positive with regard to the child's conduct. She has considerable powers of observation that allow her to grasp what goes on at home and perceive even the smallest subtleties—very little escapes her attention. From the physical point of view, however, the above-mentioned characteristic signifies delicate nerves, little resistance, and a tendency to small crises of impatience and irritation. This is nothing to worry about, but it ought to be monitored constantly.

Other important information is provided by the shape and position of the thumb, which is placed very low in relation to the mount of Jupiter, thus producing a very personal view of things. Sooner or later in life the subject will feel the need to talk to other people about this particular way of feeling. The thumb is also long, large, and strong, and this means a complex personality in which the tendency to impose her own point of view predominates. It is clear that the child knows (or will know very soon) what she wants and how to get it.

Looking at the outer edge of the hand, we see that the *summit* is placed very high, above the passive mount of Mars; hence the subject's energy is mainly of a psychic rather than physical nature.

The *fingers* are long in relation to the palm and almost all are the *square* type, indicating the subject is prey to disappointments. Any change in plans that the child has arranged or any delay in keeping a promise made her is sufficient reason to make her feel cheated out of something. It is a temporary state of mind, but one the child will not fail to take advantage of in her own way.

On examining the palm, we immediately see that the mount of Venus is large and prominent. Naturally it is not possible to draw definitive conclusions about a hand that is not fully formed, but the sexual component will always have considerable importance for the subject and consequently some of her choices and preferences will be, and in part already are, unconsciously prompted by the mount of Venus. It is important to keep this in mind.

The mount of Jupiter is very developed, the summit being located at the center. There is an ambitious streak in the child and woman-to-be that drives her to come first in everything, even in things to which she attaches little importance. Ambition of this kind, pursued as an end in itself, sometimes smacks of exhibitionism. It is an understandable attitude at this age, but there is no certainty that it is just a passing phase. Indeed, certain factors suggest that it is a permanent trait in the subject's character.

A rapid glance at the mounts of Saturn and Apollo, which concern matters outside our particular investigation, advise us that the child's genuine artistic gifts will make sense for her only if translated into practical terms—they indicate a specific ability in certain forms of art, not a general artistic tendency.

Proceeding toward the mount of Mercury, we note that the subject is quite fond of money. It would be premature and excessive to talk about avarice, but the tendency to consider money as a basis for security can be seen clearly. It is possible that this indication is the result of discussions the child has heard in the family.

The head line begins together with the life line and for a short stretch the two lines intertwine. It is on this initial track that the events with which we are concerned occur. But we can also foresee that the child's psychological detachment from her family's influence will occur at a fairly early age, within a few years. Her actual departure from the family will take place at a later date and only if certain favourable circumstances develop at certain times. In the area of logic, she expects her wishes to be satisfied as soon as possible or she explodes in a violent fit of anger or, as we have seen, withdraws into herself for long periods of unhappiness. She adopts this attitude mainly when she realizes that her wish has not been satisfied and she has not been given the consideration she believes she deserves.

Looking at the hand as a whole, we can consider the child rather lucky and predict that she will more often than not get what she wants. It will be better not to overdo things or be too permissive. Things should be doled out to her bit by bit.

We can see a line on the child's palm that will have great importance for the future, and in certain respects may also determine some of her present behaviour. We are referring to the Sun line, or line of Apollo, which originates at the lower curve of the life line, crosses the plain of Mars and runs to the mount of Apollo (which, as we have observed, is directed partly toward the mount of Saturn). It is an interesting and uncommon line, occurring on only about twenty per cent of hands. People with this line have a good chance of a successful artistic career. In this particular case it is not yet possible to determine into which area of art the child can direct her energies, because there are too many different tendencies and she is still too young. Art will certainly be one of the easiest and most suitable areas of achievement for her.

In conclusion we can say that we have examined the hand of a problem subject, in that her character is not to be underestimated but must be guided towards self-discipline. Given her impulsiveness, she may frequently and in varied circumstances find herself on the point of making a mistake. Her life could easily be either very interesting or very sad; she will have only herself to blame if she does not make the most of it.

The biggest problem currently is the need to keep her busy with something that interests her and helps her to develop her artistic tendencies, but in such a way that it does not become a constraint, for then she would immediately set herself stubbornly against it with serious consequences to herself.

**A testimony
Bibliography
Index**

A testimony

Between October 1952 and February 1955 a series of twenty experiments in palmistry were undertaken by this writer on behalf of and under the supervision of the Italian Society for Parapsychology. The results were assembled by Dr. P. Cassoli and Dr. E. Marabini and reported in a paper at the Third National Congress of Parapsychology held in Rome in May of 1956. The report was subsequently published in *Minerva Medica* (N.46, 16 June 1957) under the title, "Three Years of Experiments in 'Palm Reading' with the palmist Maria Gardini from Bologna." It was concerned primarily with methodological problems and we can easily assess its interest from the introduction, which we reproduce here.

In 1950 we had the opportunity of meeting Miss Maria Gardini. Famous as a clairvoyant, she was just beginning to make her way among a small group of interested people, students, and those inclined to accept the reality of so-called parapsychological phenomena. We willingly offered to have our palms read by Maria Gardini and sent various relatives and friends to her as well.

However much she was absorbed in occult practices during that period, it soon became apparent that we were dealing with a truly estimable person. Added to this was the happy coincidence that Maria Gardini was particularly intelligent and keen to broaden and improve her own abilities.

An understanding soon grew up between us and we immediately sought to resolve the first query that arose, which was: "Apart from our subjective impressions, apart from any natural scruples (until then only superficially considered), did Maria Gardini really succeed in acquiring knowledge about the person being examined?"

We then thought of conducting a series of experiments on a large scale and over a long period of time, beginning with the kind of experiment that most closely resembles the method by which the phenomena presented by her had been verified. A positive response to our query would open the way to an even more penetrating investigation into the qualities and complete personality of the subject.

The present undertaking, therefore, aims only to reply to the above-mentioned query. In subsequent undertakings we shall study the paranormal potential of the subject by means of different methodologies and tests, such as ESP with Zener cards, the Stuart test modified by Marabini, an examination of hand prints, telepathic experiments with drawings, and so on. Lastly, everything will be placed in proper order with a thorough parapsychological and clinical case history, by objective examination, by laboratory examinations, and by an exhaustive psychological profile of the subject. At the end of this complete and complex study we hope to prove two assumptions: (1) that the subject, having been carefully examined by the most reputable parapsychological tests, has demonstrated that she has ESP; (2) that she has shown that she acquires through palm reading a knowledge of the past, present, and future life of a person under examination who was heretofore unknown to her. If these two assumptions can be proven, we believe we can then claim to have made a new contribution to resolving another age-old problem—whether palmistry, as with dowsing and the like, is a means of expressing the faculty of ESP, or whether the lines on the palm, correctly interpreted, actually correspond to real situations and events in the life of that individual?

The first series of experiments carried out with our subject, Maria Gardini, would perhaps have enriched only the archives of the Center for Parapsychological Studies, though they represented three complete years of meticulous work, had not another extremely important fact convinced us of the usefulness of publishing these experiments in their entirety. We refer here to the current trend among the most respected people in our field to view all natural phenomenology in an objective light.

We like to recall in this regard that in October 1953 we published a work emphasizing the need for adopting the American methods of investigation, which are mainly quantitative, as well as for experiments using qualitative methodology, as these bring us closer to the field of natural phenomenology.

With a renewal of interest in parapsychological manifestations, we are once again faced with the problem of method—finding a method that allows us to observe and study manifestations which by their very nature appear continually to escape objective experimental research.

The intention of many palmists today is to resolve once and for all the question of method. We too shall make our small contribution to this research with a footnote to the records of these experiments; a methodological contribution deriving from an impartial and extensive analysis of all the so-called "weak points" presented by our experiments—experiments which, we need hardly say, have been the most popular and considered satisfactory in metapsychic circles.

The experiments—twenty in all—were held between October 1952 and February 1955. This length of time was necessary to satisfy the first requirement of the experiments: making certain that the persons presented to Maria Gardini were complete strangers. This meant that the selection of people had to be made very carefully. Once we had satisfied this requirement with our preliminary inquiries, we took the subject (S) to the house of Maria Gardini in the evening after dinner. We decided to eliminate all formalities and introductions and S was instructed not to engage in the usual preliminary conversation. Furthermore, on those rare occasions when it was necessary, we cut short any involuntary attempt by S to take part in our conversations. This we did regardless of the subject's personality or position.

The experiment was conducted as follows: Maria Gardini carried out a study on S by means of a dowser's pendulum—S standing up while she "explored" in detail all the areas of the body from head to toe, front and back. We allowed her to carry out this experiment each time as it seemed to create a kind of "psychic relationship" or to establish contact or an understanding between her and S.

When this study was completed, she proceeded to read S's palm. The pendulum experiment took ten minutes; the palm reading required from a minimum of twenty minutes to a maximum of forty-five. While the palm was being read, S could only answer "yes" or "no" to Maria Gardini's statements when that was absolutely necessary.

At the end of this experiment, she repeated, in the presence of S, the affirmative statements made during the examination. At the last stage, each statement (or response) made by Maria Gardini was read again to S in its elementary form. S had to tell us whether in his opinion the statements could be considered exact or not exact, or if he did not have information in this regard, was to provide detailed elucidations.

We then proceeded to evaluate the information we received with the strictest objectivity, providing (if needed) medical examinations, laboratory tests, or psychological investigations, which helped us to express a definitive opinion. We thought it appropriate to express these evaluations in the following way: *yes* = Gardini's statement is correct; *no* = Gardini's statement is not correct; *future* = statement refers to events that have not yet happened; *doubt* = it is not possible to give an answer to Gardini's statement as the elements necessary to form an opinion are lacking. This would be the case when the statement was either too vague or S did not know how to reply.

When we reached this point in the experiment, we regarded it as finished. Each session lasted from a minimum of two hours to a maximum of three hours and thirty minutes.

As noted, we divided the opinions about the single statements into four categories: The total number of statements made by Maria Gardini was 506. For each experiment she made a minimum of fourteen statements and a maximum of 38, with an average of 25 statements for each subject.

Our results were:

367 *yes*   72·52%
 24 *no*   4·74%
 93 *future* 18·4%
 22 *doubt* 4·34%

Bibliography

Achillini, Alessandro. De subjecto chiromantiae et physiognomiae. *Bologna 1503.*
Aristotle. De historia animalium.
Beamish, Richard. The Psychonomy of the Hand. *London 1865.*
Bell, Charles. The Hand—Its Mechanism and Vital Endowment as Living Design. *London 1833.*
Belot, Jean-Baptiste. Instructions pour apprendre les sciences de chiromancie et physiognomie. *Rouen 1647.*
Benham, William G. The Laws of Scientific Hand Reading. *London 1922.*
Bulwer, John. Philocophus, or the Deafe and Dumbe Man's Friends. *London 1660.*
Carus, Carl Gustav. Über Grund und Bedeutung der verschiedenen Formen der Hand. *1848.*
Cerasari, Patrizio Tricasso da. Epitoma chyromantica. *Paris 1560.*
Cerasari, Patrizio Tricasso da. Esposizione del libro "Chyromazie" da Bart. Coclés. *Venice 1531.*
Cheiro (Louis Hamon). Cheiro's Language of the Hand. *London 1894.*
Coclés, Bartolomeus (Andrea Corvo). Chiromantia—opus rarissima de eadem chiromantiae. *1515.*
Craig, A.R. The Book of the Hand. *1867.*
Cureau de la Chambre. L'art de connaître les hommes. *Paris 1659.*
D'Arpentigny, Casimir-Stanislas. La chirognomie. *1839.*
Desbarolles, Adrien-Adolphe. Les mystères de la main. *Paris 1859.*
Desbarolles, Adrien-Adolphe. Révélations complètes. *Paris 1879.*
Fabricius, Johann Albert. Gedanken von der Erkenntnis der Gemüther. *Jena 1735.*
Gettings, Fred. The Book of the Hand. *London 1965.*
Goclenio, Rudolph. Chiromantische Anmerkungen. *Hamburg 1692.*
Goclenio, Rudolph. Aphorisma chiromantica. *Nuremberg 1592.*
Hasius, Johannes. Praefatio laudatoria in artem chiromanticum. *1519.*
Heron-Allen. A Manual of Cheiroscopy. *1885.*
Hoeping. Chiromantia harmonica. *1681.*
Hortlich, Johann. Die Kunst Chiromantie. *1475.*
Hyll, Thomas. A Brief Hand Most Pleasant Epitomye of the Whole Art of Physiognomie. *London 1556.*
Indagine, Johann. The Book of Palmistry and Physiognomy. *London 1651.*
Indagine, Johann. Introductiones apotelesmaticae. *1522.*
Ingeber, Johann. Chiromantia, metoposcopia et physiognomia. *Frankfurt 1724.*
Jaquin, Noel. The Human Hand—The Living Symbol. *London 1956.*
Lavater, Johann Kaspar. Physiognomische Fragmente zur Beförderung der Menschenkenntnis und Menschenliebe. *Zurich 1775-1778.*
Lutz, Ludwig Heinrich. La Chiromancie médicinale. *Paris 1650.*
Meissner, Georg von. Beiträge zur Anatomie und Physiologie der Hand. *Leipzig 1853.*
Moreau, Adèle. L'Avenir dévoilé—Chiromancie nouvelle. *Paris 1869.*
Muchery, Georges. Traité complet de chiromancie déductive et expérimentale. *Paris 1958.*
Nostradamus. Centuries astrologicae. *1550-1556.*
Pompeius, Nicholas. Praecepta chiromantica. *Hamburg 1682.*
Ronphile. Chyromantie naturelle. *Lyon 1653.*
Rothman, Johannes. Chiromantiae theorica practica. *1595.*
Saint-Germain, Conte de. Practical Palmistry. *Chicago 1897.*
Saunders, Richard. Physiognomie and Chiromancie, Metoposcopie. *London 1653.*
Saunders, Richard. Palmistry: the Secret Thereof Disclosed. *London 1664.*
Spier, Julius. The Hands of Children. *1944.*
Taisniers, Johannes. Opus mathematicum. *Cologne 1562.*
Zeitlingen, Joannes Praetorius of. Cheiroscopia et metoposcopia. *Jena 1659.*
Zeitlingen, Joannes Praetorius of. Ludicrum chiromanticum. *Jena 1661.*

Index

(Numbers in italic refer to illustrations)

active mount of Mars, *see* mount of Mars
Alexander the Great 7
Alfieri, Victor *19*
Apollo line, *see* line of the Sun
arc *29*
    case histories *135*, *141*
    perfect *29*
    Roman *29*, 30
    straight *29*, 30
    uneven *29*, 30, *135*, *141*
Aristotle 7, 13
Art de la Chiromancie, L' (Coclés) *14*
astrology
    and palmistry 16, 24, 27, 28, 33

Bacon, Nathanial *127*
Beauharnais, Josephine 7
Bell, Sir Robert Anning *129*
Belot, Jean-Baptiste *79*
Benham, William 33
Boulogne, Valentin de *124*
breaks
    on line of Mercury 110, *110*
Bruegel, Peter *16*
Bulwer, John *42*

capillary lines 23, 117-19
    case histories 137
    danger of illness 119
    free will and 117, 130, 132
    obstacles in love 119
    obstacles at work 117-19
Caravaggio *34*
Carus, Carl Gustav 26
    hand types 26, *27*, *29*
Cassoli, Dr. P. 153
celibacy ring 116, *117*
Cerasari, Tricasso de 123
chains
    on heart lines 87, *87*
China 13, 45
chirognomy 26, 123
    definition of 11, 20, 23, 24
chirology 11, 20
chiromancy 11, 20, 23
Chiromantia, opus rarissima de aedem chiromantiae (Coclés) 14
Chiromantiae (Rothmann) *16*
Chiromantie medicinal (Lutz) 16
chirosophy 13
Coclés, Bartolomeus (Andrea Corvo) 14, *14*
Crivelli, Carlo *54*
cross (special sign) 61, *62*
    mount of Apollo 67, *67*
    mount of Jupiter 66
    mount of the Moon 72, *72*
    mount of Saturn 66, *67*
    on heart line 87, *87*
    on life line 80, *80*
    on line of Mercury 110, *110*
curve of creativity 28, 30
    summit of 28, *29*, 30

dactyliomancy 23
D'Arpentigny, Count Casimir 19, 24, 26

dating system
    amended oriental method 63, *63*
    Anglo-Saxon method 63
    French method 63-4, *63*
    oriental method 61, 63, *63*
Desbarolles, Adrien-Adolphe 19, 45, 63, 75
destiny
    palmistry and 11, 147
Diamont, Salamon 28
Doré, Gustave *123*
"drop of water" *41*, 42, 145
Dürer, Albrecht *57*

Egypt 7
Epytoma chyromantico (Cerasari) 123
ESP (extra-sensory perception)
    palmistry and 153-4

Fabre, François Xavier Pascal *19*
family
    and palmistry 127
family ring 116, *117*
fate line 75, *75*, 99-104
    attributes 99-100
    beginning of 100-101, *101-2*
    branches from 102-3, *103*
    case histories 139-40, 146
    endings of 101-2, *102*
    islands and breaks on 103-4, *104*
    perfect 100, *100*
finger of Apollo, *see* ring finger
finger of Jupiter, *see* index finger
finger of Mercury, *see* little finger
finger of Saturn, *see* middle finger
fingers 23, 26, 29, *see also* fingernails, fingerprints, fingertips, thumb
    case histories 135-6, 141-2, 149
    flexibility 33-4, *34*
    index 33, *33*, 45, 46, 51
    knotty *39*, 40, 135
    length 34, 39, *39*
    little 33, *33*, 53-4, *53-4*
    middle 33, *33*, 51-2
    represent spiritual world 33
    ring 33, *33*, 34, 52-3, *52*
    smooth 39, *39*
fingers, shape of
    crooked 39, *39*
    long and slender 34, *39*
    long and thick 34, *39*
    short and fat 34, *39*
    short and thin 34, 39, *39*
    straight 39, *39*
fingernails 23, 54-8
    case histories 136, 142, 148
    colour 57, 91
    half moons 58
    profile 58
    shape 55, 57, *58*, 91, 136, 142, 148
    size 54-5, *58*
    spots on 58
    vertical ridges on 58
fingerprints 23
fingertips
    conic 40-41, *41*, 136
    "drop of water" *41*, 42
    mixed *41*, 42
    pointed 39-40, *39*, *41*
    spatulate 39, *39*, *41*, 41-2

square 39, *39*, 41, *41*, 136
fissure of Roland 23
fourth finger, *see* ring finger
free will
    palmistry and 11, 117, 130, 132, 140, 147

Galen 13, 27,
George III, King 7
Greece 13
grille (special sign) 61, *62*
    mount of Jupiter 66
    mount of the Moon 70, *72,*
    mount of Venus *69,* 70
    on head line 98, *98*
    on heart line 87, *87*
    on life line 79, *79*
Grünewald, Mattias *34*

Hamlet (Shakespeare) 7
hand *see also* fingers, lines, mounts, thumb *etc*
    colour 24-5
    consistency 25, 123, 145
    different types 23-30
    left hand 23, 24, 30
    measurements 26
    rationabilis area 25-6
    right hand 23, 24, 30
    sensibilis area 26
    shape 24, *25, 28,* 29-30, 46, 135, 141
    suppleness 25
    "three worlds of" 25-6, *26*
    vegetabilis area 26
hand, shape of
    conic 24, *25, 28,* 30, 135, 141
    elementary 24, *25*
    knotty (philosophic) 24, *25*
    mixed 24, *25*
    narrow *28,* 29
    outer edge, *see* curve of creativity
    psychic 24, *25*
    spatulate 24, *25, 28,* 29-30
    square 24, *25, 28,* 29, 141
    wide *28,* 29, 46
hand, type of
    elementary 27-8, *27*
    motoric *27,* 28
    psychic *27,* 28-9
    sensitive *27,* 28
handshake 25
head line 14, 75, *75,* 87-99
    beginning of 88-92, *88, 91-2*
    branches from 96, *98*
    case histories 138, 141, 145-6, 149
    course of 92, *92,* 93-5, *94*
    double 94-5, *95*
    endings 95-6, *95-6, 98*
    fate line and 103-4, *104*
    intellectual ability and 93-5, 129
    length of 93
    merges with heart line 98-9
    perfect 88, *88*
    special signs 98, *98*
    type and nature of 92-3, *93*
health
    and palmistry 11, 124
heart line 14, 75, *75,* 82-7
    beginning of 82-3
    branches from 84-5, *84-5,* 86
    case histories 138-9, 142, 146

colour 86
course of 83, *83*
depth 86
endings 83-4, *84*
fate line and 104, *104*
marriage line and 111
merges with head line 98-9
perfect *82*
special signs 86-7, *87*
width 86, *86*
Henry VIII, King 7
Heron-Allen 7
Hippocrates 13
Hortlich, Johann *13,* 14

illness, *see* health
index finger (finger of Jupiter) 33, *33,* 51, *51-2*
    attributes 51
    case histories 148
    knots 51
    length 51, *52*
    relationship with thumb *45,* 46, 51, *52*
    termination 51
India 13, 45
Ingres, Daniel Tenois *119*
island (special sign) 61, *62*
    on fate line 103, *104*
    on head line 98, *98*
    on heart line 86-7, *87*
    on life line 77, *77,* 79, *79*
    line of Mercury 109-10, *110*
    line of the Sun 105, *106*
    on marriage line 111, *112*
    mount of Apollo 67, *67*
    on ring of Venus *116,* 116
Italian Society for Parapsycology 153

Jocho (Japanese sculptor) *51*
Josephus 7
Julius Caesar 7
Jung, Carl 8
Jupiter (planet) 28

knots (finger) *39,* 69
    common sense 40, *40*
    orderly 40, *40*
    philosophical 40, *40*
Kunst Chiromantie, Die (Hortlich) *13,* 14

Largillière, Nicolas de *11*
Lavater, Johann Kaspar 19, *19*
life line 14, 75, 75-82
    branches 80, *80*
    case histories 137-8, 142
    course of 77, 79-80, *79-80*
    end 76-7, *76*
    perfect 76
    special signs 80, 82
    starting point 76, *76*
line of children 75, 112-14
    different types of 112-14, *113-14*
line of fate, *see* fate line
line of the head, *see* head line
line of life, *see* life line
line of marriage 75, 110-12
    beginning of 111
    branches on 112, *112*
    details of 110, *111*
    special signs 111-12

line of Mercury (health) 75, *75*, 105-10
    appearance 109, *109*
    case histories 140
    special signs 109-10, *110*
line of the Sun (Apollo) 75, *75*, 104-5, *105-6*, 149
line of widow(er) hood 75, 114, *114-15*
lines, *see* fate line, head line, heart line *etc*
lines, secondary, *see* secondary lines
little finger (finger of Mercury) 33, *33*, 53-4, *53-4*
    attributes 53-4
    case histories 148
    cretinism and 54
    knots 69
    length 54, *54*
    separation 53-4, *54*
Lucius Silla 7
Ludicrum chiro chiromanticum 13
Lutz, Ludwig Heinrich 16

Manual of Cheirosophy, A (Heron-Allen) 7
Marabini, Dr. E. 153
Mercury (planet) 28
Mercury ring, *see* celibacy ring
Michelangelo *48, 109*
middle finger 33, *33*, 51-2, *51*
    attributes 51-2
    relationship with ring finger 52-3, *53*
mount of Apollo *64*, 66-7
    case history 149
    special signs 67, *67*
mount of Jupiter *64*, 66, 136
    case histories 140, 149
    special signs *64*, 66
    summits *64*, 66
mount of Mars
    active *64*, *67*, 69, 136
    passive *64*, *67*, 69, 136
mount of Mercury *64*, 69
    case histories 137, 149
    special signs *67*, 69
    summits *67*, 69
mount of the Moon *64*, 70, 72, *72*,
    special signs 70, *72*, 72
mount of Saturn *64*, 66
    case histories 137, 149
    special signs 66, *67*
    summits 66, *67*
mount of Venus *64*, 69-70, *69*
    case histories 142, 149
    family ring *69*, 70
    line of Mars *69*, 70
    special signs *69*, 70
mounts, *see* mount of Apollo, mount of Jupiter *etc*
Mystères de la Main, Les (Desbarolles) 19, 75

Napoleon Bonaparte 7, *135*
Newton, Sir Isaac 45
)rmand, Marie-Anne le 7, *135*
Nostrodamus 14

palm, *see also* hand, lines, mounts *etc*
    case histories 142, 148
    dating system 61-4
    flat with few lines 61, *62*
    orderly, well-drawn lines 61, *62*
    special signs 61
    structure of 29-30
    very complicated lines 61, *62*
palmistry, history of 13-20

palms, reading
    case histories 135-50
    general observations 123-32
Papus 63
Paracelsus 16
passive mount of Mars, *see* mount of Mars
Physiognomie and Chiromancie (Saunders) 7, 16, *16*
Physiognomische Fragmente (Lavater) *19*
physiognomy 24
Pignori *69*
plain of Mars 72
plain of Neptune 72, *72*
plait 106
Plato 13, 24
prediction
    palmistry and 11, 13

Raphael *34*
rationabilis area 25-6, *26*
ring finger (finger of Apollo) 33-4, *33*, 52-3, *52*, 120
    attributes 52
    heart and the 53
    length 53
    relationship with middle finger 52-3, *53*
ring of Mars 117, *117*, 137
ring of Saturn 66, *67*, 116, *116*
ring of Solomon 66, *115*, 116, 137
ring of Venus 67, *67*, 116-17, *116*
rings (jewellery) 120
Rothmann, Johann 16

Saturn (planet) 27
Saunders, Richard 7, 16, *16*
secondary lines
    line of marriage 75, 110-12
    line of Mercury 75, *75*, 105-10
    line of widow(er)hood 75, 114, *114-15*
    lines indicating children 75, 112-14
    sun line 75, *75*, 104-5, *105-6*
    wrist wrinkles 75, *75*, 114-15, *115*
self-knowledge
    palmistry and 11
sensibilis area 26, *26*
sensuality 129-30
short line (special sign) 61, *62*
    head line and 98, *98*
    heart line and 86, *87*
    on life line 79, *79*
    on line of Mercury 110, *110*
    on marriage line 111
    mount of Mercury and *67*, 69
Siret, Henriette *129*
skin
    case histories 135-6, 142, 148
    colour 24, 123, 135
    quality 24, 135-6
spots
    on fingernails 58
    on head line 98, *98*
    on heart line 86, *87*
    on life line 79, *79*
    on line of Mercury 110, *110*
square (special sign) 61, *62*
    line of the Sun 105, *106*
    mount of Jupiter 66
star (special sign) 61, *62*
    on heart line 87, *87*
    on life line 80, *80*
    on line of Mercury 110, *110*

mount of Apollo 67, *67*
mount of Jupiter 66
Suetonius 7
superstition
  palmistry and 13

thumb 33, 45-8
  angle of insertion in palm *45-6*, 46
  behaviour of 48
  case histories 145, 148
  flexibility of 46, *46*, 124
  joints 48
  length 46, *47*, 136
  phalanges of 45, *45*, 47, *47*, 48, *48*
  relationship with index finger *45*, 46, 51, *52*
  tip 47-8
  willpower and 127, 136
thumb, tip of
  bulbous 48, *48*
  conic 47-8, *48*
  pointed 47, *48*
  slender 47, *48*
  spatulate 48, *48*
  square 48, *48*

Van Eyck, Jan *91*
Vasishtha (Vedic text) 13
vegetabilis area 26, *26*
Venus (planet) 29

widow(er)'s line 75, 114, *114-15*
wrist wrinkles 75, *75*, 114-15, *115*

Picture sources

Archives Snark, Paris: pages 14, 16 right, 43, 44, 68, 128, 134.
Biblioteca Trivulziana, Milan: pages 32, 74.
Centro Documentazione Mondadori: pages 12, 13, 15, 16 left, 17, 19, 36 bottom left, 42, 60 (Lotti), 71, 78, 89 (Del Grande).
Foto Dani, Milan: pages 2, 38.
Photographie Bulloz, Paris: pages 10, 118, 122, 126.
Photographie Giraudon, Paris: pages 18, 36 bottom right, 125.
Museo de Arte de Cataluña, Barcelona: page 36 top right.
The National Gallery, London: pages 55, 90.
Lionel Pasquon: pages 34, 35, 135, 141, 143, 144, 145, 147.
Roger-Viollet, Paris: pages 20, 22, 65, 81, 129, 131, 132.
Sammlung Thyssen-Bornemisza, Lugano: page 56.
Scala, Florence: pages 37, 49, 108.
Shogakukan Ltd., Tokyo: pages 50, 107.